Research perspectives in education

Research perspectives in education

Edited by

William Taylor

Professor of Education
and Director of the School of Education
University of Bristol

Routledge & Kegan Paul
London

First published 1973
by Routledge & Kegan Paul Ltd
Broadway House, 68–74 Carter Lane,
London EC4V 5EL

Printed in Great Britain by
Alden & Mowbray Ltd
at the Alden Press, Oxford

ISBN 0 7100 7600 2

Contents

Contributors

Noel Entwistle, Professor of Education, University of Lancaster

Howard Glennerster, Lecturer in Social Administration, London School of Economics and Political Science, University of London

Kjell Härnqvist, Professor of Educational Psychology, University of Göteburg

Eric Hoyle, Professor of Education, University of Bristol

Frank Musgrove, Sarah Fielden Professor of Education, University of Manchester

John Nisbet, Professor of Education, University of Aberdeen

Richard S. Peters, Professor of the Philosophy of Education, University of London Institute of Education

Brian Simon, Professor of Education, University of Leicester

Donald F. Swift, Professor of the Sociology of Education, The Open University

William Taylor, Professor of Education and Director of the School of Education, University of Bristol

John P. White, Senior Lecturer in the Philosophy of Education, University of London Institute of Education

Introduction

The purpose of this book is to say something about the conceptual foundations and the organization and management of the activity known as educational research, and to suggest some of the questions that need to be considered when the future of this activity is discussed. Most existing books about educational research deal with its techniques, and are focused mainly upon empirical psychological studies. It is argued here that research in education needs to be much more broadly conceived, especially if it is to influence educational policy-making and educational action.

The book originates in interests developed in the course of work as Research Adviser to the Department of Education and Science 1968 to 1973, Chairman of the Educational Research Committee of the Council of Europe from 1969 to 1971 and Chairman of the Research Committee of the Universities Council for the Education of Teachers since 1971. In these roles I have become aware of the extensive monitoring of educational research and development activities that has been undertaken in other countries, especially in the United States, and of the paucity of similar material in this country. To match the analyses that have been undertaken elsewhere would be a significant research undertaking in its own right, for which this book cannot be regarded as an adequate substitute. For example, there is little here about the nature and possibilities of such recent developments as 'action research' in education, and only brief references to the work of some of the independent foundations that support educational research, and of bodies such as the Scottish Council for Research in Education. But the book's inadequacies may at least help to point up our lack of systematic information about how research and development in education is initiated, supported and conducted, and to suggest ways in which a better level of co-ordination might be achieved.

The nine papers that make up the book are ordered in three parts. Part one has to do with resources, organization and staffing. My own paper in this section was written specially for this volume. That by Professor Härnqvist was originally given at the London Colloquium of Directors of European Educational Research Agencies, which I directed in November 1971.

Part two comprises five papers dealing with the contributions that philosophers, psychologists, historians and sociologists make to educational research. That by Professor Peters and Mr White was prepared for a Schools Council Seminar, and subsequently published in *Educational Philosophy and Theory*, volume 1, no. 2. The papers by Professors Nisbet and Entwistle, and by Professor Simon were specially commissioned and have not been published elsewhere. This volume has been a long time in the making, and both these sections were originally drafted in 1969. Professor Musgrove's contribution is an amended and updated version of a paper prepared for a Schools Council seminar, but not previously published, and that by Professor Swift was written for this volume.

The two papers in Part three relate educational research to our knowledge about education and to the formulation and execution of educational policy. My own paper was written for this book; some sections of it were included in an address to the 25th annual meeting of the National Foundation for Educational Research, subsequently published as 'Retrospect and prospect in educational research' (*Educational Research*, 15:1, November 1972). The contribution by Professor Hoyle and Mr Glennerster has appeared in the *Journal of Social Policy*, vols 2 and 3.

I am grateful to the authors and editors concerned for their permission to reprint material that has already appeared in journal form.

William Taylor
Bristol

Part one

Resources, organization and staffing

1 The organization of educational research in the United Kingdom

William Taylor

Conditions for effective research

If research is to be effective in advancing our knowledge and understanding of the educational process, and in helping policy makers, administrators, teachers, and pupils, to achieve their objectives, three interrelated conditions must be met—adequate resources, appropriate structures, and a sympathetic political, social and educational climate. Despite major advances in the past decade, our present arrangements leave much to be desired in respect of important elements of these three conditions. We are at present digesting the effect of what was, given the small base from which we began, a massive increase in resources for educational research and development in the sixties. We need now to give careful attention to the resources, the structures and the climates that may enable the impetus of the recent past to bear fruit in the seventies and eighties.

Resources are inevitably, but not exclusively, a problem of money. The active research worker always needs money. Sometimes he is led to claim that his activities will help to save it. Take the following quotation as an example:[1]

> In the present ferment of opinion as to national education, the work of a well equipped educational intelligence office might do much to provide unity of educational effort, understanding of the needs of different types of schools and a clearness of educational aims. In the past, much public money has been wasted through failure to make a careful study of educational methods and problems before embarking on schemes entailing large expenditure. It is probable that great savings would be effected by the supply of timely information on many educational subjects for

> the consideration of those locally interested in the supply and management of schools. The aim of the writers of such reports should be to give practical help to educational workers, without being narrowly statistical or doctrinaire . . . It should be their aim to disentangle what is valuable from what is obsolete or antiquated in our English educational traditions, and to preserve all that is good in our present educational arrangements. . . .

Here are many of the elements of the contemporary researchers' claim—a stress upon the importance of information, a hope that research might help to avoid waste of money, the importance of being of practical help to the educationist, the dangers of the 'narrowly statistical' and the doctrinaire, the emphasis on innovation within a stable institutional structure. Yet this is not a contemporary statement. It was made in the year 1903, seventy years ago, in a departmental minute from Michael Sadler, Director of the Office of Special Enquiries and Reports, to the President of the Board of Education. The way in which we distribute money symbolizes the importance that, as individuals and as a society, we attach to different kinds of activities. In authorizing the establishment of the Office of Special Enquiries and Reports in 1894, the Treasury permitted an annual expenditure not exceeding £2,400. Sadler, in an exchange of minutes with Morant, prior to his resignation of the directorship, claimed that the expenditure of his branch had never run above £1,700. Not so, replied Morant. There was a hidden element:[2]

> There is an item of cost as to which you appear to have been wholly misinformed. The volumes of special reports which you describe as 'practically self supporting' are really published at a considerable loss. The expenditure on these volumes has in seven years amounted to nearly £3,700; the amounts realised are barely £1,400. You must therefore add to the cost of your office the sum of £2,300 distributed over the period of the publication of these reports.

But there was more to it than money. Sadler protested the need for independence:[3]

> In order that the scientific work of educational enquiry may be searching and fruitful, it must be intellectually independent. Those engaged in it must be free to state what they believe to be

> true, apart from preconsiderations as to what may at the time be thought administratively convenient . . . .

But in 1903 such a claim for independence, which today is such an important element in the work of bodies such as the National Foundation for Educational Research and the Schools Council, could not be conceded. Morant made the position abundantly clear:[4]

> The President is fully sensible of the value not only of the reports, but of the enquiries made, the information supplied, and the library work done by you and your staff; but it cannot be too clearly impressed upon you that the work of the Office of Special Enquiries and Reports is done and must continue to be done, for the benefit of the Board, at the instance of the Board, and under the direction of the Board.

We have come a long way in the seventy years that have passed since these minutes were written. We now have a better understanding of how official interest in, and responsibility for, educational activities, reflected in the spending of public money in support of research, can be reconciled with the essential independence of the research worker. The limits and points of contact of both public interest and professional independence none the less require to be kept continually under review.

We have also come a long way in the last seventy years in the amount of money spent on educational research. The Treasury's £2,400 of 1894, even at today's prices, would hardly support many of the hundreds of research and development projects that are at present being undertaken. The best estimates currently available are that we spend about 3½ million pounds annually on all the activities that come under the heading of research and development in education. By transatlantic standards, actual or projected, the sums involved are small. In money terms, American expenditure is vastly greater. *Per capita*, and after making allowance for different price levels, their present outlay on education R and D (which they regard as inadequate) is about four or five times our own. Taking public and private sources together, the financial resources we devote to R and D amount to some 0·16 per cent of our educational budget.

But comparisons between countries are perhaps less useful than comparisons over time. Our current expenditure is very large in comparison with what we were doing ten years ago, and it has imposed strains—on the attitudes of teachers who have had little opportunity to become familiar with research during their training, on the small number of well qualified educationists and social scientists with the knowledge, experience and the interest to be good practitioners of research, on the university departments of education, often the poor relations in their own university family, on the means for the diffusion and dissemination of research findings and development materials, and on those who administer and distribute the research funds.

Over the last ten years most of the new money provided for educational research and development has gone into specific enquiries of limited duration, usually lasting three to five years, sometimes less, employing a director and a couple of research assistants, and costing between twenty and fifty thousand pounds. But too little money has been devoted to building up the other kinds of resource on which the success of such projects depends—especially research facilities and trained manpower. In 1971 the Council for Scientific Policy issued a report of a working group under the chairmanship of Sir Harry Massie on the support of scientific research in universities.[5] The document is particularly concerned with the dual support system, whereby university research is funded partly through UGC allocations and partly by means of research council grants for specific projects. The working party argues that the ability of universities and research organizations to sustain a high level of project based research activity is dependent upon the existence of an adequate 'research floor'. This basic floor of support includes the provision of supporting staff, such as technicians and secretaries, library and computing facilities, a proportion of regular staff time that can be devoted to research, and 'sufficient freely disposable funds to ensure that relatively inexpensive research can be initiated by academic staff and carried to a stage at which, if appropriate, Research Council support can be sought'.[6] Such provision is reflected in published returns of departmental expenditure. The working party calculated that, including salaries other than those of the teaching and research staff themselves, the average departmental expenditure per full-time member of staff in science faculties was £1,574, in medicine, dentistry and health £1,618 and in engineering and technology £1,845. Similar calculations for education yield a figure of £389—or about a quarter of that for medical, scientific and technological subjects. This suggests that the research floor for education is not adequate to support the large number of individual projects that have in recent years been placed upon it. It is significant that the small number of universities that received specially earmarked UGC grants in the sixties to stimulate educational research activity are those that today undertake more than their share of contract research work, train larger numbers of research workers, and produce some of the more noteworthy research reports and findings.

If the funds currently devoted to the support of research projects are to be well spent, and a climate created in which requests for additional project money receive sympathetic attention, then the research floor needs strengthening. It is not only the overall magnitude of the sums available in support of educational research that matter, but the way in which they are distributed between different functions. Too high a proportion of free funds at the disposal of the academics and professionals may generate complacency and too many way-out studies; too high a proportion spent on specific short-term projects inhibits long-range planning and encourages the erection of rickety multi-project structures, inadequately supervised by absentee landlords. A proper balance needs to be kept between the two kinds of support if research workers are to be productive and research reports fruitful. The current imbalance means that we are getting less than full value from the money that we are spending.

Research manpower is another aspect of resources for research that needs attention. The late Dr Stephen Wiseman in his statements as Director of the NFER repeatedly drew attention to the shortage of properly trained and qualified research workers in education. At the end of 1970 the Social Science Research Council conducted a survey of enrolments of students for postgraduate courses in the social sciences in 1968 and 1970. Education recorded a 58 per cent increase in enrolments in the two years, exceeded among the twelve areas into which the SSRC divides its work only by management. But if the education figures are broken down according to the type of study programme followed, a different picture emerges. The proportion of full-time students starting on higher degrees by means of taught courses increased from 146 to 265, a growth of 82 per cent. But the proportion of full-time *research* students in education rose only from 105 to 131, an increase of only 25 per cent. Given that only just over a fifth of all these full-time students were supported by means of SSRC postgraduate studentships, it seems likely that the majority were experienced full-time teachers.[7]

There is a widespread opinion that the successful educational researcher needs substantial teaching experience if he is to understand the kinds of things that he will see going on in schools and be acceptable to the teachers and heads on whose co-operation the success of this research depends. The pattern of postgraduate qualifications in education that has developed during the past twenty-five years is, with notable exceptions, closely geared to the needs of the mature candidate with teaching experience. Unfortunately, such evidence as is available on this issue suggests that productivity in research is negatively correlated both with length of teaching experience and with general qualifications in the field of education. The research in this field is almost wholly American and the productivity criteria employed are somewhat crude, but there is virtual unanimity that:[8]

> Potential researchers need to be identified, selected and encouraged while they are young; that persons engaged in educational research should have a strong background in the liberal arts, rather than extensive courses in education; and that their grounding in the behavioural sciences should be strengthened as they study the philosophy and science of education.

Many first-class research workers have come, and will continue to come, from the ranks of experienced teachers, and some classroom experience must remain a *desiderata*. But it is important, if the quality of educational research is to be enhanced, that a larger proportion of young graduates, with sound knowledge and understanding of one or more of the social sciences, together with appropriate research skills, be recruited to educational research. In so far as a larger proportion of such work is now undertaken in teams, it is easier to provide an appropriate mix of age, qualifications and experience. But if genuine breakthroughs in our knowledge of the dynamics and correlates of children's learning are to be achieved, then we cannot rely entirely upon the existing pool of experienced teachers as a source of future educational researchers.

Adequate resources of money and manpower constitute only one of the necessary conditions for successful educational research. Unless there exist appropriate structures within which these resources may be deployed, we are likely to be disappointed with the outcomes of the work that is undertaken. Such structures are of four kinds.

First, there needs to be machinery by means of which the interested parties may formulate their ideas about the direction in which educational research should be proceeding, determine their priorities for future work, and stimulate and inform the activities of the funding agencies, the independent research organizations and the universities. To some extent this function is fulfilled through the many conferences and gatherings that discuss educational issues, and by means of the educational press. There would be nothing worse than integrating the efforts of the funding bodies in such a way that a refusal of grant from one meant a refusal from all. There are few fields of academic activity in which a measure of pluralism is more important. None the less, if priorities and areas of neglect are to be identified, and an effective lobby for the maintenance of a high level of educational research activity created, there needs to exist more effective machinery than at present for discussing and reconciling priorities, needs and resources.

Second, appropriate structures are needed for funding and monitoring educational research and development. The past decade has seen a rapid increase in the amount of research support provided by the Department of Education and Science. It has seen the creation of the Social Science Research Council, and the emergence of the Schools Council. But development work, rather than basic research, accounts for a large part of the increased level of activity. Difficult as it is, such development work often seems to have a clearer pay-off than basic research.

The relationship of research and development in education is complex. There are those who see development as parasitic upon more fundamental kinds of understanding, and observe with anxiety that, both here and in the United States, a large volume of development activity is currently dependent upon a rather limited and only slowly growing body of host ideas and findings. Others see no sharp distinction between R and D; applied, policy-oriented and action research can sometimes contribute directly to our basic knowledge about the social and psychological worlds of teaching and learning. Whatever the conceptual, conventional and managerial distinctions between different kinds of research and development activity, it seems clear that some kind of balance has to be kept if the work done is to provide real increments to knowledge and is to influence educational policies and practice. The attractive practicality of development work, in comparison with the doubtful promise of more theoretical studies, is dangerous if it results in the neglect of the theoretical foundations on which all educational efforts must rest.

Third, there need to exist appropriate structures within which the actual research work can be carried on, and within which suitable employment and career possibilities for research workers exist. The importance of an adequate research floor within such organizations on the basis of which short and medium term contract and commissioned work can profitably be undertaken has already been mentioned. There are numerous questions to be answered about the optimal internal structure of research organizations, the possibilities of designating 'centres of excellence' that will concentrate upon particular areas and types of research, and the necessity of ensuring that those concerned with educational research have opportunities for establishing and maintaining contact with teachers, students and researchers in other related social science fields.

Fourth, we need means whereby information about on-going research, and the findings of completed research, may be made available to other workers, and to policy-makers, administrators and teachers for whom it is intended. Once again, despite, or perhaps as a result of, the very rapid growth of research activity in the sixties, the scale of our project activities has overtaken the means available for the dissemination of information and results. There are a number of bright spots, such as the National Foundation's popular series of research reports, the Schools Council's willingness to add dissemination years to the life of some of their major projects, and the clear and helpful character of the research abstracts published in the annual reports of the Social Science Research Council. But these do not add up to a coherent system of information and dissemination. There are still huge gaps, not only in the teacher's knowledge of research findings that might be useful to him, but also in the means that researchers have available for finding out about what is going on elsewhere in their own field of interest. Any hopeful prospect for educational research requires that information, dissemination and abstracting services be still further improved. In the meantime, without any vast additional expenditure, there would be a considerable gain from such simple devices as each of the funding bodies deciding to adopt a common format in reporting the current and completed projects within its programme.

Another condition for effective educational research is the existence of a climate of political, social and educational ideas sympathetic to research pursuits, and in which research is seen by policy-makers, administrators, heads and classroom teachers as capable of making a real contribution to the rationality of decision making. Such a climate has been slow to develop in the United Kingdom.

Early developments

The first two elements in the study of education to receive systematic attention in this country, and to generate something that justified the term research, were history and comparative studies, and psychology. The Scottish universities were among the earliest to establish chairs of education (Edinburgh and St Andrews, 1876) and incumbents such as Meikeljohn and Laurie did much to establish the outlines of the study of education and to stress the importance of its scientific basis. But the opportunities to develop such a science were few. Meikeljohn complained in 1884 'There is in the three kingdoms no man who gives the whole of his time to observing and thinking about the educational processes which are going on in schools every day'[9] and Laurie indicated the paucity of material on which the educationist had to draw:[10]

> It will be granted that the uncorrelated phenomena of consciousness, which empirical psychology offers us, cannot in itself yield a theory of knowledge, much less a philosophy of life. There must be some principle, idea (call it what you will) which correlates and unifies. And until that principle emerges out of the laboratory (if that is to be its birth place) we may be allowed our own thoughts as to its probable whereabouts . . . In any case a writer on the theory of education is really writing at once a theory of life and a treatise *de emendatione intellectus*, and he cannot dispense with a rational and rationalised scheme of mind, be it right or wrong. He will be thankful for all that physiology and physics can give him, but meanwhile, and until better advised, he must follow his own course.

Within a few years the vice-president of the Committee of Council on Education, Mr Acland, was minuting to the Treasury in the following terms:[11]

> There are a large number of matters affecting education as to which the department lives merely from hand to mouth, failing to record the knowledge it obtains for future use and unable to obtain information as to what is being done elsewhere, whether at home or abroad, in an efficient manner. There is now much

waste of power through this deficiency, and the appointment of an officer with a limited amount of help, whose duty it shall be to collect and supply information, and to make occasional reports on special matters under the direction of his chiefs, has become essential if the education department, including the science and art department, whose field of work is now so large, is to do its work efficiently.

From the virtual demise of the Office of Special Enquiries and Reports in 1903 (although it continued in existence until 1936) up to the end of the second world war, the volume of educational research undertaken in this country was small, and the funds available for its support very limited. The three-year projects that have become such a familiar feature of the research scene today hardly existed. But some of the work that *was* done was very influential on both policy and practice. Educational psychology dominated the scene. On the one side the work of men such as Cyril Burt and Godfrey Thompson and P. B. Ballard fostered an interest in the new science of mental testing, whilst on the other a concern with principles of child development was stimulated in diverse ways by the activities of the Froebel society, the New Education Fellowship, Susan Isaacs at the London Day Training College (later the London University Institute of Education) and the psychoanalysts. At times, both here and in the United States, the psychologists came close to making claims that their concerns and research interests constituted the sole basis of educational practice—no more and no less. For example, the American psychometrician E. L. Thorndyke had as early as 1910 shown a fine confidence in the possibilities of his subject:[12]

> Psychology shares with anatomy, physiology, sociology, anthropology, history and the other sciences that concern changes in man's bodily or mental nature the work of providing thinkers and workers in the field of education with knowledge of the material with which they work. Just as the science and art of agriculture depends upon chemistry and botany, so the art of education depends upon physiology and psychology.
>
> A complete science of psychology would tell every fact about everyone's intellect and character and behaviour, would tell the cause of every change in human nature, would tell the result which every educational force—every act of every person that changed any other or the agent himself—would have. It would

> aid us to use human beings for the world's welfare with the same surety of result that we now have when we use falling bodies or chemical elements. In proportion as we get such a science we shall become masters of our own souls as we now are masters of heat and light.

Although few of those concerned with studies and research in education in this country during the first four decades of the century would have gone as far as that, there were many who agreed with Thorndyke in his assertion that 'to an understanding of the material of education, psychology is the chief contributor'. And indeed, in so far as the evidence of empirical work during this period was concerned, so it was. There were virtually no competitors for the *British Journal of Educational Psychology*, founded in 1931. Individual academics and research students continued to undertake historical studies, and there was the beginning of the tradition of sociological investigation of social class and educational opportunity that was to reach its fullest flowering in the fifties, but it was the psychologists who made the running.[13]

During the second world war discussions took place about the possibilities of a more systematic approach to educational research during the period of educational expansion that was expected to begin after hostilities ended. In 1943, the same year in which R. A. Butler's 'Green Paper' setting out the broad lines of such expansion was circulated, a number of teachers' associations came together with the Carnegie foundation and the Leverhulme trust to follow up the immediately pre-war initiative of Sir Fred Clarke and Sir Philip Hartog, in establishing a foundation for educational research at the University of London Institute of Education. The foundation became the National Foundation for Educational Research in 1947, financial support initially being provided mainly by means of a payment by local education authorities of one farthing per head of their school population.

Given the climate out of which the idea for the foundation had emerged and the kinds of problems that national and local authorities faced in establishing and administering the new policy of 'secondary education for all', it was inevitable that the diagnosis of individual abilities and aptitudes, and the selection of children for different types of school, featured prominently among the foundation's early concerns. The foundation also became one of the chief

sources of standardized tests and other instruments used by the authorities to aid their selection and allocation procedures. But it was also from the NFER that later came some of the most influential studies critical of these selection procedures, and which confirmed findings that were beginning to emerge from independent sociological enquiries and surveys such as the Central Advisory Council's *Early Leaving*.[14]

Right through the fifties, the NFER continued to be an important focus of research undertaken in education. But the volume of such work being done in universities and elsewhere was increasing, as were the number of advanced students doing research in fulfilment of the requirements of Master's and Doctor's degrees in education. The lists of theses compiled by the late Mrs Blackwell, and continued by the register of current researches maintained by the NFER, document the growth that took place between 1950 and the early sixties. In comparison with the rates of increase in available funds and numbers of projects that characterized the latter part of the decade, the speed of this growth was rather slow. But there was a growing conviction among educationists, politicians and administrators that more research was needed, and it was this that laid the foundations of development in the sixties. The strictures concerning the lack of research activity contained in the report of the Central Advisory Council's *Fifteen to Eighteen*[15] led to the setting up of a working party in the then Ministry of Education, which in 1961 recommended that the Ministry should itself take the initiative in promoting interest in a larger volume of educational research.

Statutory provision for such support already existed in Grant Regulation no. 4 of the 1944 Education Act. Later in 1961 Research and Intelligence Branch was established and soon afterwards the Ministry also set up a curriculum study group, the forerunner of the present Schools Council for Curriculum and Examinations. Pressure was growing for the establishment of a research council for education, on similar lines to those which existed for medicine and agriculture. The Conference of Directors of Institutes of Education and of Heads of University Departments of Education (CID and CHUDE) were prominent in their support for such a body and put their case directly to the Ministers concerned. But there were also those who felt that research in education should not be divorced from social science research in general, the future of which was currently under review by an official committee under the chairmanship of

Lord Heyworth. The matter was remitted to the Heyworth Committee, which recommended that an educational research board should be one of the constituent parts of the new SSRC.

Meanwhile, the role of the independent foundations in supporting educational research had been growing. The advancement of education was one of the major interests of the Nuffield foundation, established in 1943 on the basis of a benefaction from the late Lord Nuffield of £10m shares in Morris Motors. By the mid-sixties about a quarter of the foundation's annual income was being spent on education, mainly on curriculum development. Gulbenkian, Leverhulme and several other smaller foundations were also financing educational research. A number of universities benefited from earmarked grants from the University Grants Committee to stimulate research in the institutes and departments of education, and the numbers of students undertaking independent research for higher degrees continued to increase.

Thus by 1965 the main elements in the provision for education research that we have today had been laid down. The nature of this provision must now be examined a little more closely.

Sources of support

Now that the resources available to support educational research are, at least in comparison with a decade ago, so substantial, and the agencies which disburse and make use of them are such a prominent part of the educational scene, it is easy for an examination of existing research activity to become little more than a description of the structure and activities of the Schools Council, the NFER, the SSRC and the rest. But the title 'educational research' cannot be limited only to projects and programmes of the kind supported by the various funding agencies. There are substantial numbers of individuals and groups in universities, colleges and elsewhere engaged in 'sustained, systematic enquiry' without any kind of foundation support for their endeavours. Work of this kind is capable of having an important effect on the agendas and attitudes that characterize our educational discussions, and of influencing the determination and execution of the policies to which these discussions give rise. The amount of money available in support of a project has little relation to its ultimate impact on either thinking or practice. But although expenditure and impact may be poorly correlated, it is clear that without the availability of resources on a large scale, many kinds

Table 1.1: Research spending

Source	*Year*	*Projects, programmes & research support*	*Administration & dissemination etc.*	*Note*
Department of Education and Science (including NCET)	1970/71	501,000		1
Social Science Research Council				
(a) Research grants	1970/71	209,000		2
(b) Studentships	1970/71	81,000		3
Educational projects supported by other research councils	—	50,000		4
Schools Council	1970/71	750,000		5
Nuffield foundation	1970	188,000		6
Leverhulme, Gulbenkian & other independent foundations		250,000		7
University Grants Committee				
(a) 10% of education staff time	1970	595,000		8
(b) Research support	1970	128,000		9
Local Authorities				
(a) Grant to NFER	1970/71	130,000		10
(b) Own research		50,000		11
(c) Secondment of teachers to research based advanced study programmes	1970	300,000		12
Total		3,232,000	500,000	13
		£3,732,000 approx.		

Notes on sources

1 Project expenditure—Department of Education and Science, *Education and Science in 1970*, London, HMSO, 1971, Para. 50, p. 76.

2 *Social Science Research Council Annual Report 1970/71*, London, HMSO, 1971, p. 13.

3 Calculated from *SSRC* Report. Studentships in Education account for 4·53 per cent of the total, and the figure given represents this percentage of the overall awards expenditure of £1·77m.

4 For example, the Medical Research Council has supported a unit at the London School of Economics that has produced a number of important books on educational issues, and there are other research council supported studies that are to a greater or lesser extent concerned with education. The figure shown is little more than a guess.
5 *Schools Council Report 1970/71*, London, Evans/Methuen Educational, 1971, p. 21.
6 Information supplied by Nuffield foundation.
7 Based upon the most recent annual reports of a number of the major foundations.
8 There are approximately 850 UGC funded education staff, and it has been rather arbitrarily assumed that they each spend an average of 20 per cent of their time on research and development activities. On the basis of an average salary of £3,500 per annum, the resulting figure is as shown.
9 This represents 20 per cent (see 8 above) of departmental expenditure (other than the salaries of teaching and research staff), and is calculated from figures in Statistics of Education, Volume 6, *Universities*, Table 46, p. 112, 1970.
10 *NFER 25th Annual Report 1970/71*, Income and Expenditure Account, p. 30.
11 Several local authorities engage in 'in-house' research, notably the ILEA, which has its own Research Unit.
12 *Statistics of Education*, Volume 6, 1970, shows 287 full time and 1083 part time Research route students. It has been assumed that about half the full time group are teachers on secondment. The figure shown is thus 150 multiplied by £2,000, taken as the average salary of the teachers concerned.
13 The total of Administrative expenditure, etc., is based upon figures supplied by some of the bodies listed and estimated for others.

---

of needed educational research and development would be totally impracticable. In the past there have been many potentially important researches which have failed to come to fruition because of the lack of such resources. A description of the work of the major research agencies does not in itself constitute an adequate account of the nature and scope of educational research that is undertaken in the United Kingdom.

It is not possible, on the basis of existing data, to calculate with any accuracy the total resources committed in support of educational research and development. In the first place, it is difficult to draw sharp dividing lines between, on the one hand, research in education, and on the other, research in subject fields which has implications for education. Furthermore, while details of the expenditure of the major funding agencies on projects and programmes are readily obtained, any total based on these figures (as some of the existing estimates seem to have been) will seriously underestimate the overall commitment. This must include not only the money spent on particular projects, but also a proportion of the time of those full-time university, college and school staff who supervise, carry out and assist project work and individual research studies, and the administrative expenses of the bodies that make funds available. The National Foundation for Educational Research has recently undertaken a survey of research resources, the report of which is not available at the time of writing. Together with the results of the survey of how university teachers use their time, this study should permit much more accurate estimates than are included in this chapter. But crude approximations may be better than no approximations at all, and Table 1.1 shows some of the main features of research spending in the most recent years for which figures are available. Some of the entries are little more than informed guesses; notes on how each of the figures has been calculated are given after the Table.

The sponsorship of research

In this section we shall be concerned with the principal agencies that provide resources for research—the Department of Education and Science, the Social Science Research Council, the Schools Council, the NFER, and the independent foundations. It is a convenient over-simplification to suggest that the first three of these are concerned with policy-oriented, fundamental and development work respectively. This pattern has emerged and been made explicit only very recently, although it has been reflected for some time in the grant awarding policies of the bodies concerned. It may be useful to say something about each of them in turn.

THE DEPARTMENT OF EDUCATION AND SCIENCE

Reference has already been made to the circumstances that led up to the Ministry of Education's decision in 1961 to provide support for educational research. Until that time the provisions of Paragraph 100(i) (b) of the 1944 Act and Grant Regulation 4 had only been used in respect of an annual grant to the National Foundation for Educational Research, paid each year since 1946. Initially, the Ministry acted like most other grant awarding bodies in responding to initiatives from outside rather than commissioning work of direct relevance to its own problem solving and decision making. Thus the first lists of Ministry (later Department of Education and Science) grants included support for such fundamental work as that of Bernstein on language development; curriculum studies, both with a view to producing new programmes and evaluating some of the work that had already been undertaken with help from independent foundations; educational measurement, such as the production of a new British Intelligence Scale; and a very varied programme of other work in such fields as examinations, teacher training, and educational technology. At first, the sums involved were small; only some £20,000 was spent in 1962/63. But they grew rapidly, and by 1969/70 had reached close on half a million pounds. In 1966 the short lived Research and Intelligence Branch became Planning Branch, which assumed responsibility for the Department of Education and Science's (as it had by then become) research programme. By that time the decision had been taken to establish the Social Science Research Council, with a specific remit to concern itself with educational research. The small curriculum study group in the former Ministry had, together with the former Secondary Schools Examination Council, become the Schools Council for Curriculum and Examinations. The contribution of the independent foundations to educational research was growing, and the UGC had taken steps to encourage more attention to the subject in universities. Thus the context in which the Department had taken its original initiative to stimulate research had changed, and a process of rethinking the Department's role in respect of research began. There was no immediate public announcement, but individuals and groups that solicited funds from the DES in support of what seemed to be fundamental or curriculum work were encouraged to take their requests to the SSRC or the Schools Council. An outline of the Department's new policy of commissioning research relevant to its needs was given in statements to the Standing Conference for Studies in Education at the end of 1968, and in the DES submission to the SSRC Annual Conference in Bristol in July 1969, but it was not until the end of the following year that a clear public declaration was made. In her speech to the Annual Meeting of the NFER in December 1970, the Secretary of State for Education, Mrs Margaret Thatcher, explained that, in the light of the changes in the pattern of research support that had emerged by the late sixties:[16]

> There was clearly only one direction that the Department's research policy could sensibly take. It had to move from a basis of patronage—the rather passive support of ideas which were essentially other people's, related to problems which were often of other people's choosing—to a basis of 'commission'. This meant the active initiation of work by the Department on problems of its own choosing, within a procedure and timetable which were relevant to its needs. Above all it meant focusing much more on issues which offered a real possibility of yielding useable conclusions.

The theme for her speech was the need for a new partnership in educational research between officials and research workers. The former must 'think hard about the problems that are likely to face them . . . [and] expose these problems, and their own thoughts about them, to people whose background and approach will . . . lead to awkward questions.' They must 'take an active interest, perhaps even an active part, in the work as it develops'. On the other side, the new approach 'does not allow him the liberty which many research workers rightly feel they must have, to define the problems as he sees it and approach the problem by his own route, in his own time'. Instead, it 'presses upon him perspectives and constraints which not all will be able to accept', but in return offers 'the expectation that his work will contribute to the formation of national policy'.

In order to implement its new research policy, the Department made a number of changes during 1970 in its procedures for commissioning new work. More responsibility was given to individual branches in defining their research needs. Instead of always commissioning research from outside bodies, such as the NFER or a university, it was agreed that research funds might be used to engage temporary research officers and others who would undertake the research within the Department itself. Block allocations from the research funds were made to some branches in order to give them greater freedom of operation in commissioning. An official in each branch was designated branch research officer, and regular meetings of such officers instituted. Early in 1971 Planning Branch ceased to exist, and was replaced by a Departmental Planning organization serving the needs of the new Policy Review groups.

It is as yet too early to say if the 'new partnership' foreshadowed in Mrs Thatcher's speech will become a reality, and if it will have the desired outcome in terms of a greater volume of timely, policy-relevant research. As was implicitly acknowledged, the role imperatives of civil servants and of university research workers by no means always ensure a common outlook on the purpose and prospects of research. It will take time for the kinds of orientations that the new approach requires to develop.

THE SOCIAL SCIENCE RESEARCH COUNCIL

The SSRC was established in 1965, following the report of the Heyworth Committee on the future of Social Science Research in Britain, and began work at the beginning of 1966. Reference has been made in a preceding section of this chapter to the debate that went on in the early sixties concerning the possibilities of establishing a separate Educational Research Council. When education was included within the functions of the SSRC, the committee that was set up to deal with it alongside those for economics, geography, management, political science, psychology, sociology and the rest, was designated, in recognition of the case that had been made for separate treatment, as the Educational Research *Board.* Its first chairman was Lord James of Rusholme, Vice-Chancellor of the University of York and a former High Master of Manchester Grammar School. In a statement in the SSRC *Newsletter* early in 1968, Lord James examined some of the difficulties that arose from the fact that the Board was not the only body interested in and responsible for, supporting educational research. He suggested that the particular contributions of the Board might best be made in the fields of inter-disciplinary research ('researches . . . which are not purely "educational", but overlap with sociology . . . psychology . . . with economics and other disciplines'), in questions of a broadly philosophical character which fall outside the normal interests of the DES or the Schools Council ('e.g., what are the criteria which enable us to judge a school as "good"?') and those which call for long term research by a 'continuing team on some specialist field, not covered by existing resources'. Lord James also felt that the Board might help to bridge the gap between the research workers and the classroom teacher by encouraging the participation of teachers and administrators in research, stimulating research in colleges of education, and establishing a scheme for Senior Research Fellowships, which would provide grants large enough to make it possible for serving teachers to undertake periods of full-time research.

This last point emphasizes one of the difficulties that arise in finding enough people with the right kinds of training and experience to undertake educational research. Rather few students in the social sciences develop during their undergraduate years the kind of interest in education which leads them to apply for a studentship in a University School of Education. Lack of contact with and information about the work of such institutions, plus the somewhat negative image that they possess among the student community (strongly coloured by their role in providing one year postgraduate courses of professional training for intending teachers) are partly responsible for this lack of interest. But at the same time many of those within the educational community feel that in order that the educational researcher should be able to understand the kinds of things that he sees going on in schools, and be acceptable to the teachers on whose cooperation the success of his research depends, he must himself be a trained teacher and have some direct experience of work in the classroom. Furthermore, the pattern of postgraduate qualifications in education that has developed during the past twenty-five years is closely geared to the needs of the mature candidate with teaching experience. It is factors such as these that have resulted in the number of SSRC postgraduate studentships in education constituting only a small proportion of the total of such studentships, in many recent graduates undertaking research on educational issues within departments of sociology and psychology rather than education and in the fact that most of those pursuing individual researches for higher degrees on a full-time basis are experienced teachers on local authority secondment.

Some of the reasons for the relatively higher rate of rejection of applications in the social as compared with the natural sciences were discussed in the SSRC annual report for 1969.[17] The uncertainty of criteria for judging a proposed piece of research; the difficulties of empirical testing of hypotheses and of replication; the difficulty of formulating convincing cases for the support of essentially 'open-ended' studies; the lack of centres in which groups of like-minded individuals can provide continuing support for work of particular kinds; all these were cited as among the factors which cause the ratio of administrative input to approved grants to be worse in the social sciences than elsewhere. Equally, these arguments are applicable to education. It may also be the case that the reconciliation of the interests of the various specialisms within the community of educational 'professionals' is a more difficult task than in some other fields, even other social science fields. There is probably less agreement among these specialisms about the nature of what can be called the existing paradigms of knowledge, or about what ideas are 'in good currency', than in most areas of social science research. For, as Burns has argued (see p. 204) the specialisms themselves help to define what are to be regarded as important problems and issues worthy of research; these do not simply emerge from the common everyday experience of those engaged in educational practice.

One further point needs to be made about the grants awarded by the SSRC for research in education. A substantial proportion, both in terms of number of grants and volume of money, goes to departments of sociology, psychology and social sciences other than education. In 1969 only 31·8 per cent of the number of grants, and 20·8 per cent of the money made available for support of work in education went to departments, institutes and schools of education. It has not been possible to investigate whether these proportions reflect the pattern of applications made for SSRC support, or whether a larger number of the applications from departments of education fail to come up to the necessary standard, and are thus not recommended for grant.

During the period from June 1969 to March 1971 the SSRC received requests to support 115 programmes and projects in the field of education, and made 52 awards (45 per cent).[18] Only eight of the 115 applications were for sums in excess of £50,000. Seventy requests were made for amounts between £4,000 and £50,000, and a further 37 for amounts of less than £4,000. This last group of applications was dealt with by means of 'Chairman's powers' procedure, and is not discussed in detail by the members of the Educational Research Board. During the period under review, these 'Chairman's powers' applications had a success rate of 81·1 per cent, against only 25·7 per cent for the range of projects in the £4,000 to £50,000 category. The then Chairman of the ERB has commented:[19]

> We are not aware of any relaxation of standards in evaluating Chairman's Powers applications; in general these do seem of a higher quality than the more expensive projects, many of which are small things writ large.

After two years of operation, the ERB began looking at its own procedures and took the first steps towards developing a policy for research support. In a statement to the SSRC Conference in mid-

1969 the Chairman of the Board voiced anxiety about the supply of suitably qualified research workers, and expressed the hope that there might be a move towards establishing a larger number of research groups and programmes which might help to ensure continuity of research effort and provide opportunities for the training of young researchers.[20] Among the fields in which such programmes might be established, teacher training and utilization, nursery and pre-school education, minority education, and the evaluation of educational innovations have all received mention in recent years.[21]

A Chairman's paper on the policy of the ERB, published in 1972, argued that the SSRC had a major role to play in sponsoring basic educational research, and that for this reason:[22]

> the ERB has come to favour a policy of centralisation in research awards. That is, given the necessity to choose, we would prefer to support *programmes* in priority areas, and to award *small grants* for other research topics, rather than to fund a large number of short term medium cost projects (current mean cost £11,611).

On the other hand, it was admitted that it had proved difficult to stimulate large scale programme research, due perhaps to shortages of senior and well qualified research workers, the absence of an adequate career structure, and to the fact that 'SSRC may be typed, in the minds of academics, as an organisation which funds worthy projects in the middle ranges of funding'.[23]

When the SSRC was established, many people hoped that the ERB would serve as a means of formulating educational research policy and identifying research needs on a broad front. In practice, this has not happened. The two main activities of the ERB, both important and of great value to the development of research activity, have been to act as a responsive agency in the provision of grant support for short-term research projects of a mainly fundamental or 'curiosity oriented' nature and to distribute postgraduate studentships among the departments, institutes and schools of education.

The scale of the first of these activities places the SSRC in a junior role amongst the other funding agencies in the educational research and development field. The fact that most higher degree work and personal research in education is undertaken by experienced teachers and lecturers on secondment, and that there are not enough established research posts to which holders of SSRC studentships can proceed, has limited the impact of the second main activity. The chairmen, secretariat and members of the ERB have had a heavy volume of work in processing the large number of applications for research support that are received and there has been little opportunity for the consideration of long-term policy and for developing active links with other funding agencies. The relationship of the ERB to the SSRC seems to be exactly that of other subject committees.

The importance of appropriate links between research in education and in the social sciences is clearly of the first importance. The SSRC has provided support for types of work that might otherwise have been neglected, has helped to create a positive research climate and has developed information services of a kind that are a model for developments elsewhere. But the scale and nature of its present activities in the field of education are not such as to ensure that it can play the major role that the advocates of an independent Educational Research Council had seen as necessary.

THE SCHOOLS COUNCIL

Mention has already been made of the establishment in 1962 within the then Ministry of Education of a Curriculum Study Group. The initiative for such a group owed a good deal to the late Derek Morrell, then an Assistant Secretary in the Ministry, and to a recognition on the part of a number of educationists that something positive was needed to ensure that the content of what was taught in schools was both up to date and matched the needs of the pupils. Interest in curriculum development reflected the operation of three significant factors. First, the growth in the volume and complexity of human knowledge, and the problem of selecting appropriate and relevant materials from the vast range available. Second, growth in our knowledge of how children learn, and of the social influences on learning; the 1959 Report of the Central Advisory Council, *Fifteen to Eighteen*, had emphasized and given statistical confirmation to the importance of such influences. Third, a recognition that the types of knowledge and the styles and modes of learning that might serve a production-line society could be a handicap in the face of the demands of a newer technology, and that changes were needed.

In 1958 UNESCO published a report on Curriculum revision and research in twenty countries.[24] The entry for England and Wales provides some interesting comparisons with the present ferment:

Although for over 50 years there has been no directive to

teachers from the central or local government about their curriculum or syllabuses, except concerning religious instruction, the curriculum is basically the same in all primary schools, and syllabuses have sufficient in common for teachers and children to be able to move from school to school without undue confusion. Parents expect a definite ground to be covered in their children's education, and a head would omit any part of it only with good reason. If Her Majesty's Inspector found part of the curriculum neglected or an ill balance in the treatment of it, he would certainly enquire into the cause. Thus, although the teachers are 'free' in the sense that they are not directed, tradition and public expectation maintain a common curriculum, which only gradually changes . . . The whole traditional growing structure has been kept steady, and to some extent directed by successive issues of the 'Handbook of suggestions for the consideration of teachers' published by the Ministry of Education at intervals since 1905. The last edition was in 1937. There has also been a long line of Ministry pamphlets on various aspects of the curriculum . . .

But the curriculum is always under fire. Every teachers' course and conference, every educational paper, examines or criticises the curriculum, in part or as a whole, and, being free from directives, the schools can respond as best they can, holding firm to what experience has proved to be good, and adapting new ideas to local circumstances and needs . . .

Teachers are helped towards getting a sense of the level of performance they can expect from children of varying ability, partly from their own training and experience, partly by guidance from the head, partly by consultation with local authority inspectors or organisers and Her Majesty's Inspectors in school or at courses. Children's work may be shown and discussed. Teachers move from one school to another during their career and may also visit other schools. The news of good work being done in a school soon spreads. Progress thus comes from recognising and developing what is proved good in practice, though the inspiration for it may have come from theory or report . . .

That passage admirably sums up the manner in which curriculum change had been conceived in this country up to less than fifteen years ago. But the informal consensus on aims and the reliance on HMI, local advisers, and Ministry pamphlets and courses, which was adequate at a time when educational growth and change were relatively slow, needed the addition of something more systematic if it was to survive the more rapid shifts in knowledge and opinion that characterized the sixties.

The setting up of the curriculum study group gave rise to a good deal of controversy, mainly centred on the fears that central government might come to have too great an influence on the content and organization of teaching. The traditional freedom of the teacher to determine his own syllabuses and methods was stressed and the disadvantages of centralized European models underlined. The effect of all the argument and anxiety that the setting up of the curriculum study group produced was to create a much greater interest in the need for and problems of curriculum reform. (It has since been suggested that far from trying to assume central control, this was the Ministry's intention all along!) A conference in July 1963, under the chairmanship of the Minister, brought together a large number of the interests that had responded to the establishment of the Curriculum Study Group, and a working party was appointed under the chairmanship of Sir John Lockwood to examine what kind of co-operative machinery was needed to stimulate, organize and co-ordinate curriculum change. A further conference in July 1964 accepted the Working Party's recommendation that a Schools Council for the Curriculum and Examinations should be set up, with teachers in the majority, and the Council began its work towards the end of that year.

The organization of the Schools Council, as befits the range of educational interests of which it has to take account, is complex. The Council itself has seventy-three members, including representatives of no fewer than thirty-one separate organizations. The largest single number of representatives (seventeen) is nominated by the National Union of Teachers. Two other bodies—the National Association of Schoolmasters and the Committee of Vice-Chancellors and Principals—have four members each, the rest three, two or one. It is specified in the constitution of the Council that at least a majority of the membership of the Governing Council shall be teachers.

There are thirteen main committees and a large number of subcommittees. The eighteen strong Programme Committee is the central decision making body, and there are three Curriculum Steering Committees, labelled A, B and C, which look after 'all matters relating to the curriculum and examinations' for pupils in the age ranges two to thirteen, eleven to sixteen, and 'fourteen upwards' respectively. Using a long-standing nomenclature the 'First Examinations' committee deals with 'O' level of the General Certificate in Education and CSE, and the 'Second Examinations' Committee with 'A' level. There are also committees dealing with publications, Welsh interests, and finance. Within one of the thirteen categories of committee are the sixteen subject committees, which serve 'as a source of professional information for the Council and as a forum for discussion among those from different areas of education', each committee again having a teacher majority. There are numerous sub-committees at various levels, including, for example, fourteen for 'A' level examinations alone. The staff at the central headquarters of the Council numbers more than one hundred, there are some seven hundred Committee members, and five hundred or so research workers and teachers are engaged in a full-time or part-time capacity on research and development projects sponsored by the Council.

The Schools Council indexes its work under a composite title of 'Enquiries, Research and Development Projects', and, as has already been indicated, it is a matter of some difficulty to identify individual projects as belonging to one or the other of these categories; some belong to all three. The Council has a central research team under the direction of Professor Jack Wrigley, who also acts as an assessor to the Educational Research Board of the SSRC. The team advises on the Council's research needs, helps in designing programmes of work, and identifies existing research which is relevant to new or proposed studies.

From the beginning, the Schools Council has given particular attention to the dissemination of information. Working papers, examinations bulletins, guides, field reports, pamphlet series, and a termly newsletter, *Dialogue*, which is distributed free to every school in the country, are all in addition to the project materials arising from work that the Council has sponsored. These latter are issued by commercial publishers by arrangement with the Council; royalties go to the Council, and not to the members of the development team. In one year (1969/70) there were seventeen new publications and two new editions from the Council itself; one of the new editions, a revised version of *Mathematics in Primary Schools* has already sold nearly a quarter of a million copies.

The sheer range and complexity of all the activities for which the Schools Council is responsible makes it difficult to reach any simple conclusions about its contribution to the total educational research effort. If, as is argued in a later chapter, we look at research findings as only one kind of information that reaches the professional educationist and the teacher, and we define research as 'sustained systematic enquiry', then there is little doubt that the Schools Council's activities do indeed constitute an important increment to knowledge that is 'relevant to initiating people into what is worthwhile' and also to ways in which educational provision might be more 'efficient'. It is probably true—there is no way of telling for certain—that knowledge of, or participation in, work sponsored by the Council has caused some teachers to restructure their images of what it is they are doing in classroom, workshop or laboratory, and that this work has acted as powerfully for them as some striking new set of educational ideas or research findings might act for what we have here called the 'professional'. It is also possible that the results of some of the Council's enquiries, researches and development projects may feed back to the research and development teams, and to the educational community in general, findings which will be of fundamental importance in shaping future thought and practice about particular kinds of teaching and learning. As yet, it is early days. But there is little doubt that this is not the Council's central concern. Its focus of attention is on the practicalities of improving what goes on in classroom and school, and not on the acquisition of fundamental knowledge of learning and social processes. As such—and using the word in its technical rather than pejorative sense—it is to some extent parasitic upon findings and ideas that derive from elsewhere.

Schools Council projects have a variety of locations, such as in the National Foundation for Educational Research, in colleges of education and examining boards, but the majority are university-based. Nearly all the projects in universities are the responsibility of departments, institutes and schools of education, and, with certain exceptions, are directed by members of staff elsewhere categorized as 'school-oriented'. There is sometimes rather little contact between this group of staff and those of their colleagues who identify themselves with particular social science disciplines and who, whether in education or in departments of psychology or sociology, are responsible for most of the research in education that is sponsored by the

SSRC and other bodies. From one point of view this merely reflects the different foci of interest, background and training of staff concerned, the different responsibilities of the funding bodies that support their work, and the necessity of some kind of division of labour among the education 'professionals'. From another, it underlines the difficulty of ensuring that sufficient attention is given to the production of new knowledge about basic educational processes, and of using such knowledge for the improvement of educational provision.

No formal statement about the committee and decision-making structure of a particular funding body can do justice to the process whereby priorities are determined and decision to award grants are taken. The individuals who are concerned with research support constitute their own invisible college within the educational community. They share information about the interests and capacities of particular universities, departments and individuals as a result of the informal contact that takes place between salient individuals through membership of committees, attendance at conferences and meetings, and personal friendship. It is important that an informal system of this kind should exist; it is equally important that it should not become so powerful as to subvert the functions of official committees. Too great a measure of co-ordination between the various funding bodies needs to be avoided; applicants who are refused a grant by one such agency should be free to make other approaches without feeling that their cases are prejudged. There seem no grounds at present for suggesting that the levels of informal contact and co-ordination threaten such dangers; if anything there is too little of this contact at the present time.

The grant-giving body that commissions research in accordance with a specific research or development strategy relies, to an even greater extent than the 'responsive' funding agency, upon informal contact and knowledge of the people and places where the work might be done. Despite the increasingly explicit nature of the funding policies of some bodies, a responsive element remains. The individual who makes an unsolicited approach with worthwhile ideas concerning a possible research or development project, even when this does not correspond with existing strategies or programmes within an agency, is unlikely to receive an outright rebuff. His scheme may be used to persuade a committee or official that this is something to which attention should be given, or modifications may be suggested that bring it within an acceptable area of interest, or his name may be passed on to someone else in another agency that might be willing to provide support.

THE INDEPENDENT FOUNDATIONS

The role of independent foundations in supporting United Kingdom research and development in education has been considerable, not least in stimulating activity of a kind that has later been taken up by official agencies. At the present time the bodies involved in such support include the Nuffield, Leverhulme, Gulbenkian and Rowntree trusts, the Van Leer foundation and the Ford foundation. There are also a large number of smaller foundations and trusts that are active in the field of education—the *Directory of UK Trusts* contains a full list. Research is only one of the kinds of educational activity in which most of these bodies involve themselves; support for educational experiments, capital grants for buildings, books and other resources, the endowment of lectureships and chairs, and travel grants make up the bulk of some trusts' expenditure. During the past twenty-five years, it is the Nuffield foundation that has made a larger contribution to the growth of education R and D, and which has had the most explicit policies relating to work of this kind.

From its inception until 1962 the foundation had, in accordance with the article of its trust deed referring to the 'advancement of education', made grants to educational research and development totalling some £300,000. Within four years the *annual* allocation for this work had risen to beyond £700,000. The educational allocation for the year 1964/65 was four times that for the five year period 1954/59.[25] The foundation's annual report for 1962 stated that the trustees had decided that initially work should be concentrated upon the reform of teaching in science, mathematics and languages. A quarter of a million pounds was set aside towards a comprehensive long-term programme of work on school science and mathematics curricula, concentrating on individual programmes in physics, chemistry and biology for 11–15 year-olds, secondary school mathematics, and primary and secondary school science in general. The aim of the programme was stated as being to 'provide a complete range of aids . . . designed by teachers for teachers'.[26] During the following years the range of curriculum projects and associated research supported by the foundation continued to widen, but in 1965/66 the annual report stated:[27]

> . . . no further schemes have been initiated during the period under review, and it is unlikely that any substantial new ventures in curriculum research will be embarked upon in the future.

The reason was the establishment of the Schools Council for Curriculum and Examinations, which, having been associated with the foundation's projects since its inception as the Curriculum Study Group of the Department of Education and Science, would now assume responsibility for the initiation of new work. The foundation's existing commitments to its own and joint projects were to continue until the early seventies, but from 1968 the emphasis of the foundation's educational programme fell increasingly on higher education. The annual report for 1969 set out the criteria employed by the trustees in making grants for university education:[28]

> The first is that each project should give promise of bringing about a more effective use of teaching resources (which are expected to become selectively more scarce under pressure of expansion in the 1970s); the second that the results should be of possible benefit to more than one institution; and the third that what is learned in the course of carrying out the project may also be usefully applied in other areas of university study.

The Nuffield foundation's educational programmes have never reflected any sharp distinction between research and development, and executives of the foundation have argued that fundamental research and discovery are as likely to result from developmental activity as the other way round. The effect on classrooms and schools of the foundation's activity during the past ten years has undoubtedly been very great. As a result of its pump priming efforts in the early sixties, and its continued support for major curriculum projects, the word 'Nuffield' now evokes for many teachers the image of new methods and apparatus in the teaching of science, modern languages and mathematics. But in the words of a report in the 1969 SSRC conference, 'A Foundation's existence is . . . essentially nomadic; when permanent settlers come on the scene, it is time to fold its tents and depart'. Of all the independent foundations, it is Nuffield that has had the closest contact with the other major funding agencies, with NCET, the Schools Council and the DES. These contacts and the fact that, although the foundation acts as a responsive agency in respect of initiatives from the field, it also has a more explicit policy for its educational programmes than some of its counterparts, have given Nuffield a distinct position on the research and development scene. Just as the early interest in school curriculum helped to develop a consciousness of the need for change and reform in content and methods of learning and teaching at primary and secondary level, and contributions towards the establishment of new institutions for these purposes, so the foundation's current concern with higher education can be expected to stimulate developments in an area in which there is at present little provision for the support of projects aimed at the improvement of teaching.

Few of the other independent foundations that have been mentioned have a policy of involvement in educational research and development quite as explicit as that of the Nuffield foundation. In financial terms, however, their contribution to the total research effort is considerable. For example, the Leverhulme foundation has commitments in education in excess of a quarter of a million pounds,[29] the Gulbenkian foundation made new grants in 1970 in education of over £125,000,[30] and the Rowntree trusts, the Wolfson foundation and a number of other United Kingdom and international foundations have in recent years made substantial grants in support of a variety of research and development activities.

THE NATIONAL FOUNDATION FOR EDUCATIONAL RESEARCH

The first steps towards the founding of the National Foundation for Educational Research were taken in the late thirties when Sir Philip Hartog and Sir Fred Clarke, who had been closely associated with the International Examinations Enquiry, obtained an undertaking from the Carnegie Corporation to provide $10,000 in support of educational research, subject to an equal amount being raised in this country.[31] An advisory committee was set up, but due to the war its first meeting was delayed until 1943. Action was then put in hand to create an autonomous national body, and the support of the teachers' associations, the Leverhulme trust, and the local authorities (acting in accordance with a clause in the 1944 Act that empowered the provision of funds for research purposes) made it possible formally to establish the National Foundation in 1947. For the first few years of its life the Foundation's future was made somewhat precarious by lack of financial resources. The annual report for 1951/52 emphasized that effective research required 'some measure of security and continuity . . . concerning the existence of the institution itself' and that 'preoccupation with budgetary issues, severe financial stringency involving the uneconomic use of staff time, a lack of funds to arrange for reasonable salary adjustments in the face of rapidly rising living costs, and an atmosphere of chronic uncertainty regarding the future, are conditions prejudicial to the mental composure required for the long term planning and reflection so essential in research'.[32] As long ago as 1948 there were references in the foundation's reports to the lack of suitably qualified manpower—an issue which has been much to the fore during the recent years—and as Yates[33] has pointed out the shortages were not only of money and manpower. During the early years paper was very difficult to come by—'Never since that period have the research officers had such an unassailable excuse for any failure on their part to provide adequate dissemination of their results'.

By 1953, following agreement to a doubling of the local authority and corporate subscription rates (which caused a withdrawal from membership of a number of local authorities that fortunately proved to be only temporary) the foundation felt able to issue a statement of policy which reflected the way in which it proposed to tackle its three main tasks, defined as:[34]

(a) Independent research appropriate to a central organisation
(b) Provision of practical instruments of educational guidance such as tests for the assessment of abilities and attainments, and for the diagnosis of difficulties in learning
(c) Communication of results through publications, etc., and co-operation and liaison with other organisations concerned with educational research in this country and abroad.

Over the next eight years the size of the foundation's income and the volume of its activities continued to increase, but really rapid growth did not start until the beginning of the sixties. Due to the initiatives of, among others, the then Minister of Education, Sir David Eccles, to the strictures of the Central Advisory Council concerning the lack of national research effort, to the interest of the Committee on Higher Education (Robbins Committee) in commissioning research studies, and to the activities of the Nuffield foundation, a new impetus was given to research and development in education. But in his introduction to the National Foundation's seventeenth annual report in 1963, the Director, Dr W. D. Wall, cautioned against the enthusiasm that was being shown in some quarters for development work:

> Development and experiment without research—which some appear to be advocating—are little more than an elaborated application of intuition . . . Development and experiment should follow and be accompanied by rigorous research activity of many kinds . . . In terms of organisation, quality and quantity of trained staff and resources for analysis, we are at present in the position of a man sweeping a sandy beach with a small vacuum cleaner; what we have is highly efficient, more so than the forty maids with forty mops now proposed, but just not big enough . . .

Subsequent reports of the foundation continued to draw attention to dangers consequent upon the rapid expansion of interest in educational research and development. These were of four kinds. First, there were the amateurs, who flooded the schools with questionnaires of doubtful value and published biased interpretations of their results. Secondly, there were those who promulgated the doctrine that research in education was best carried on by specialists in a variety of social science disciplines, and who sometimes used 'the word "educationalist" as a term of polemical abuse and the tag about war being too serious a matter to be left to the generals'. Thirdly, there were the critics who claimed that the schools had been largely unaffected by such educational research as has so far been undertaken, and who would replace the careful, long term analysis of substantive problems with loosely conceived atheoretical projects that promised a more immediate payoff. Finally, there were the politicians, who urged 'that political or social commitment is desirable and inescapable in research in the social sciences'.

The context within which the foundation was operating by the mid sixties, with the Schools Council and the Social Science Research Council beginning to commission work, the DES research programme undergoing rapid expansion, and the number of staff and students in departments, schools and institutes of education in universities increasing yearly, was very different from that which characterized its early years. The DES and the Schools Council soon began to place research contracts with the foundation, and the size of its annual grant in aid from the Department rose to £10,000. By 1971, when the foundation celebrated its twenty-fifth anniversary, income had risen to nearly half a million pounds (see Table 1.2).

The proportion of the foundation's income obtained from short term research contracts with sponsoring bodies such as the Depart-

Table 1.2: National Foundation for Educational Research

Source of funds (1971)	*Percentage of total*
Subscriptions (local authorities and corporate)	31
DES grant in aid	2
Publications	10
Receipts from tests	7
Research contracts	44
Other income	6

ment of Education and Science and the Schools Council substantially increased during the decade of expansion. In the 1970 financial year, the Department contributed £91,000 and the Schools Council £53,000 in this way. The foundation now undertakes more than twice as much research on such outside funds as it supports from its own resources. Some activities that played only a small part in the early work of the foundation are now important features of its programme; in particular, the range of publications issued under the foundation's imprint has shown very rapid growth. Twenty-two books appeared during 1970, and 90,000 copies of each issue of *Educational Research News* were distributed to schools and colleges. In that year the research programme comprised eighteen projects, and the foundation had a staff of over one hundred and fifty.

Each director of the National Foundation—Sir Peter Innes from 1947 to 1950, Ben Morris from 1950 to 1955, Dr W. D. Wall from 1955 to 1967 and Dr Stephen Wiseman from 1967 until his premature death in 1971—has given a distinctive character to the annual report. Some of Dr Wall's concerns have already been outlined. Although the period of office of his successor was all too short, he took the opportunity provided by the three annual reports for which he was responsible to make a number of significant points about the future development of educational research. The major hindrance to the expansion of educational research—even to its continuance on the present scale—was seen as the shortage of trained, competent and suitably experienced research workers. The universities were criticized for their failure to make such a supply available, and Dr Wiseman placed a different emphasis from that of his predecessor on the types of persons that were needed:[35]

> There is no doubt that a high proportion of researchers must come from the ranks of the teaching profession . . . But I believe we have now reached the stage of development where the main body of workers, trained in the traditional way, could be supplemented by others. I am thinking of young graduates—particularly those with degrees in psychology and sociology—who could go straight on to postgraduate work and to Master's and Doctor's degrees. American experience suggests that this is a most profitable source, and one producing highly effective research workers with a minimum of wastage . . .

To this theme we shall need to return in the chapter that follows.

THE SCOTTISH COUNCIL FOR RESEARCH IN EDUCATION

Founded in 1928, the SCRE was in 1972 supporting some 19 projects involving a total commitment of more than £135,000. The recent policy of the Council has been to concentrate its activities in the four main fields of secondary education, environment, further education and examinations and assessment. The last mentioned is a long standing interest, and over the years the Council has published a long series of reports on problems of testing and selection, including the well known Scottish Mental Survey. Some two-thirds of the Council's income is derived from central government, nearly a fifth from the local authorities, and the remainder from teachers' organizations (4 per cent) foundations (9 per cent) and publications (5 per cent). The self-contained character of Scottish activity in this field is illustrated by the Council's *Annual Report*, which in less than 100 pages provides a full statement from each committee, reports on in-house and sponsored projects, articles by staff members reprinted from the journals, and a list of all the researches in education and educational psychology presented for degrees in Scottish universities in the year concerned. An up to date register of all educational research being undertaken in Scotland is maintained.

THE NORTHERN IRELAND COUNCIL FOR EDUCATIONAL RESEARCH

The NICER is the most recently established (1963) and the smallest of the three 'national' foundations. In 1970 the Council employed a total staff of five, on an annual budget of some £7,000, 85 per cent of which was obtained from education committees in the province.

The Social Science Research Council made a grant of £16,000 to the Council in 1970 to undertake a modified replication of the Schools Council Enquiry No. 1 *Young School Leavers* (1968). The research activities of the Council are carried on by an independent research unit located in Queen's University, Belfast.

EDUCATIONAL RESEARCH IN THE UNIVERSITIES

Most of the funded educational research and development activity in the United Kingdom is undertaken in university schools, departments and institutes of education, and in other departments such as psychology and sociology. A small number of projects is based in colleges of education, polytechnics and colleges of technology, local authorities and independent research agencies (other than the National Foundation). In 1970/71 just under 1,100 college of education, polytechnic and further education lecturers, local authority administrative and advisory staff, school teachers and advanced students were working for research degrees on a full-time (287) or part-time (805) basis, and a proportion of the 1,083 men and women registered for taught courses leading to higher degrees were undertaking minor projects in connection with dissertation requirements. Some research is also done by groups of lecturers and teachers associated with a university department, college or teachers' centre, without outside funds and not leading to named awards.

Thus the range of institutions and individuals who are concerned with research and development in education is very wide—wider still if one adds the teachers who co-operate in the trial and development of teaching materials. In terms of available resources, it is the university education staff who play the major role. In 1969, expenditure from research grants averaged £554 per full-time member of UGC financed education staff of English and Welsh universities. To this must be added a sum of £389 which represents the 'floor of support' provided in the form of the salaries of non teaching and research staff, consumable material and 'other expenses'.[36]

There are considerable differences in the extent to which universities are involved in research. In order to quantify these differences, all the research grants awarded in the period 1965–1970 by the Department of Education and Science, by the Schools Council, the National Council for Educational Technology and the Social Science Research Council were totalled, and the percentage of the money obtained by each university calculated.

As might be expected in view of its overall size, and the size of individual institutions (such as the Institute of Education) within it, the University of London is by far the most important recipient of research funds, receiving 21 per cent of all funds from the sources named in the period surveyed. No other university came close to this figure. Manchester was next with 12 per cent, followed by Oxford with 10, Cambridge with 7, Birmingham and Leeds with 6, Bristol and Brunel with between 4 and 5, Keele and Sussex between 3 and 4, Essex and Lancaster between 2 and 3, and the remaining twenty-one universities with less than 1 per cent apiece.[37]

Given that several institutions shared the half million pounds' worth of projects allocated to the University of London, it is clear that resources are in general spread thinly, rather than, as in some other fields, concentrated on a limited number of 'centres of excellence'. The average size of research grant during the period reviewed was just over £10,000. Since many grants are for periods of two or three years, this means that a large number of projects involved the employment of no more than one or two full-time research officers, plus a limited amount of secretarial support.

Much of the work in connection with funded projects is undertaken by members of university staff who carry a full teaching and administrative load. The number of full-time research staff on permanent appointments is small. The nature of teaching and administrative duties in departments, schools and institutes of education tends to be rather different from that in many other university faculties. Staff/student ratios are among the poorest for any subject; there is a good deal of supervisory work in schools; even if they are not formally members of the area training organization staff, lecturers are heavily involved in committee work in connection with the Certificate and B.Ed. studies of students in the colleges of education associated with the university. None of this makes it easy to initiate new projects or to provide adequate supervision for existing ones.

But there are other ways in which the position of the university teacher of education differs from that of his colleagues in other subjects. In an earlier study I have argued that their basis of recruitment tends to place such staff outside the university career structure which, especially in the arts and social science faculties with which education staff have most professional contact, is typically based upon entry soon after graduation or assimilation from an outside institution of university status. A survey conducted in the mid-sixties showed that education staff were a good deal older when recruited to university work (frequently from schools, or from colleges of education) and they included a larger proportion of women. Their prospects of promotion to senior grades were much poorer. They had a lower proportion of men and women with first class honours degrees than the staff of other faculties, and a smaller percentage of Ph.Ds.[38]

On the basis of the data provided in this survey, it appeared that education staff could be divided into three groups. The first, which included a large proportion of the lecturers responsible for the initial professional training of graduate teachers, retained many of their links with the classroom, tended to identify with the schools and with the teaching of particular subjects, and were not infrequently engaged in the preparation of books for school use and the utilization and development of teaching aids. In more recent years, many lecturers with these interests have become associated with the curriculum development activities of the Schools Council.

A second group were seen to maintain their identification with the subject field in which they originally graduated, to undertake 'hard' research in this field and to publish in the specialized journals.

The third group were characterized as concerning themselves more directly with educational processes and institutions as such. They might or might not possess qualifications in psychology, sociology or philosophy. Frequently they had acquired advanced qualifications and higher degrees in the applications of these disciplines to education, having initially graduated in some other subject.

The data on which these categorizations were based is now some seven years old, but there has been no more recent survey which might indicate changes in the basis of recruitment to education faculties. There are at present a number of developments in prospect which might change the situation. Within the last year or two there has been a very substantial increase in the numbers of graduates who pursue their year of professional training for teaching in a college, rather than a department of education. In some area training organizations, the number of postgraduate students in the colleges now exceeds the size of the university based groups. It has been argued that an opportunity exists for universities to shift the balance of their attention away from initial teacher training towards the pursuit of high level research and studies in education. In fact, some of the departments of education in the new universities—Lancaster is an example—have no students of their own on initial courses, although close contact is maintained with the colleges in which such courses are provided. The idea that university effort in the field of education should be concentrated upon research and advanced work has met with no great enthusiasm among the staff and organizations concerned. It is maintained that to deprive staff of the kinds of direct contact with the work of schools that the supervision of practical teaching affords would have the effect of etherealizing educational studies. In any case, large numbers of such staff were recruited, not for their expertise as educational researchers, but as experienced classroom practitioners. It may be suspected that departments of education are also loathe to give up 'student numbers' as their chief bargaining counter within the university as far as the allocation of staff and resources are concerned.

Within the past decade, just as initial training for graduates has spread more widely among the colleges, so more universities have been introducing undergraduate courses which include an education component, either as part of a four year concurrent degree that includes professional training, or as a subject of study of interest to students who do not intend to enter teaching, as well as to those that do. The content and organization of these courses varies widely, but in many of them education is treated as a social science, and staff are involved as psychologists, sociologists and so on, rather than as practitioners of the teaching art. Efforts have been made in one or two of the new universities to organize educational studies round an 'education centre', with only a very small full-time core staff, but able to draw upon the services of specialists in other departments and schools of the university.

These developments, and other changes consequent upon the James Report and the 1972 White Paper on Higher Education, are all likely to have their effects on the staffing of schools, institutes and departments of education within universities, and on the extent to which these organizations are able to initiate and carry through research projects and programmes. There has in the past been a considerable reluctance on the part of funding bodies to commit themselves to long-term programmes and the establishment of units devoted to different aspects of educational research. Such commitments involve certain obvious risks, including empire building, the irresponsible initiation of 'wild' studies that would never secure support as individually funded projects, and the difficulty, should need arise, of bringing the activity to an end. Yet such units and programmes as do exist, do seem to be both more productive and more influential than the somewhat fragmented scatter of short-term projects that is the norm in some other areas of concern. Part of the reason for this is that a unit, with some free money, some security of tenure for its members, and something by way of a long-term policy, is much more of a political reality than a short-term project sometimes rather precariously associated with a university department or institute of education. As will be argued more fully in the third part of this book, the influence that research has upon policy and upon practice is as much a matter of politics as of science.

It is unlikely that the next few years will see the emergence of any kind of considered policy for the funding of educational research or for the recruitment of educational research workers. In the United Kingdom context it is difficult to see from where the initiative for such a policy might arise, and how, given the pluralism of our funding arrangements, it might be implemented. But however *ad hoc* the nature of our decision-making, it is important that we should be aware of international experience in these matters, particularly in the training of educational researchers, much of the evidence concerning which is very relevant to our own present concerns.

This experience is reviewed by Professor Härnqvist in the chapter that follows.

NOTES

[1] Board of Education, *Papers relating to the resignation of the Director of Special Enquiries and Reports*, Cd 1602, 18 May 1903, London: HMSO.

[2] Ibid.

[3] Ibid.

[4] Ibid.

[5] Council for Scientific Policy, *Report of a Study on the Support of Scientific Research in the Universities*, Cmnd 4798, London: HMSO, 1971.

[6] Ibid.

[7] J. Humphreys, 'Growth in the Social Sciences', *Newsletter Special*, London: SSRC, October 1971.

[8] G. T. Buswell *et al.*, *Training for Educational research*, Berkeley, Calif., 1966, quoted in Härnqvist in his contribution to this volume.

[9] Quoted in J. W. Tibble, *The Study of Education*, London: Routledge & Kegan Paul, 1966.

[10] S. S. Laurie, *Institutes of Education*, Edinburgh, James Thin, 1892, p. 4.

[11] Board of Education, *Papers relating to the resignation of the Director of Special Enquiries and Reports*, Cd 1602, 18 May 1903, London: HMSO, p. 3.

[12] E. L. Thorndyke, 'The contribution of psychology to education', *Journal of Educational Psychology*, vol. 1, 1910, quoted in M. L. Borrowman, *Teacher education in America*, Teachers' College, Columbia, 1965, p. 175.

[13] Willard Brehaut has contributed some valuable points to the history of educational research in Britain in his chapter in J. Butcher (ed.), *Educational Research in Britain III*, London: University of London Press, 1973.

[14] London: HMSO, 1954.

[15] London: HMSO, 1959.

[16] DES Press Notice dated 1 December 1970.

[17] *SSRC Annual Report 1969/70*, p. 38.

[18] J. Tizard, 'The Policy of the Educational Research Board', *SSRC Newsletter 14*, March 1972.

[19] Ibid.

[20] J. Tizard, 'Strategy of the ERB', paper given at SSRC Annual Conference, Bristol, 1969.

[21] *SSRC Annual Report*, 1969, p. 40.

[22] J. Tizard (1972) op. cit.

[23] Ibid.

[24] UNESCO, *Curriculum Revision and Research*, Educational Studies and documents, No. 28. Paris, 1958.

[25] *Annual Report of the Nuffield Foundation*, 1964/5, p. 54.

[26] *Annual Report of the Nuffield Foundation*, 1962, p. 43.

[27] *Annual Report of the Nuffield Foundation*, 1965/6, p. 1.

[28] *Annual Report of the Nuffield Foundation*, 1969, p. 52.

[29] *The Leverhulme Trust Sixth Report*, 1965–7.

[30] Calouste Gulbenkian Foundation, press notice, 1 May 1970.

[31] *NFER Annual Report*, 1947.

[32] *NFER Annual Report*, 1951/2, p. 5.

[33] *The NFER: The First Twenty-five years*, London: The Foundation, 1971.

[34] *NFER Seventh Annual Report*, p. 9.

[35] *Annual Report*, 1967/8, p. 16.

[36] Calculated from Statistics of Education, Volume 6, 1969, *Universities*, Table 42, p. 114, London: HMSO, 1971.

[37] Calculated from DES Research Lists and Annual Reports of the Social Science Research Council.

[38] W. Taylor, *Society and the Education of Teachers*, London: Faber, 1969.

2 The training and career structures of educational researchers

Kjell Härnqvist

Introduction and basic definitions

The rapid expansion of educational research and its orientation towards problems of direct importance for educational policy have brought the questions of research personnel—their recruitment, training and careers—into the foreground among the problems that confront, or ought to confront, research organizations and those bodies responsible for the supply and allocation of resources for research. In some places this expansion might have been more rapid if lack of adequately trained and experienced personnel had not hampered further investment in educational research. In others restrictions imposed by lack of competent personnel do not seem to have been properly observed, with the result that the outcome of research has not reached the level expected, neither in quantity nor quality. Bad research for good money is even more detrimental to the future of educational research than no research at all.

The concept of educational research, as used here, is a broad one, and before discussing its personnel implications it is necessary to outline its scope and main dimensions of diversity.

Following the definitions of a committee of the United States National Academy of Education on 'research for tomorrow's schools' (Cronbach and Suppes, 1969) educational research is seen as all kinds of disciplined inquiry into educational matters. The essence of this concept is best conveyed through a few quotations from the report (pp. 15–18):

> Disciplined inquiry has a quality that distinguishes it from other sources of opinion and belief. The disciplined inquiry is conducted and reported in such a way that the argument can be painstakingly examined . . .

> The report of a disciplined inquiry has a texture that displays the raw materials entering the argument and the logical process by which they were compressed and rearranged to make the conclusion credible . . .
>
> In each such field there has evolved a consistent system of concepts, techniques, and critical questions, together with a prescribed form for presenting completed arguments. Each has a style well suited to investigate a certain range of problems . . .
>
> [But] Disciplined inquiry does not necessarily follow well-established, formal procedures. Some of the most excellent inquiry is free-ranging and speculative in its initial stages . . .
>
> A disciplined inquiry does have an internal consistency that requires colleagues to take the findings seriously, even when they disagree with them . . .
>
> Fundamental to disciplined inquiry is its central attitude, which places a premium on objectivity and evidential test.

Defined in such a way educational research not only comprises empirical inquiry with quantitative techniques but also naturalistic observations, logical and philosophical analyses, and historical studies. It can take place within the conceptual and methodological framework of different academic disciplines such as psychology, sociology, economics, philosophy, and history.

Stressing the concepts and methods of the disciplines and not their institutional place in the academic organization makes it possible to avoid, or at least postpone, the tricky discussion whether education or pedagogy, when organized as a university subject parallel to the traditional disciplines, is a discipline *per se* or just a conglomerate built up from a professional point of departure (cf. Sjöstrand, 1967). In this context it is sufficient to conclude that educational research is a multi-disciplinary and multi-method enterprise. This is also in agreement with the view taken by the Council of Europe in its surveys of educational research in 1968 and 1970.

The discipline-method dimension does not, however, completely describe the diversity of educational research. Variations also exist as regards (among many other things) the aims of research. The distinction most frequently used concerning this aspect is between basic, applied and developmental research. The difficulties met in using these categories are also well-known. A more recent distinction is between 'conclusion-oriented' and 'decision-oriented' research (Cronbach and Suppes, 1969, pp. 19–27). They say (pp. 20–1):

> In a decision-oriented study the investigator is asked to provide information wanted by a decision-maker: a school administrator, a governmental policy-maker, the manager of a project to develop a new biology textbook, or the like . . . The conclusion-oriented study, on the other hand, takes its direction from the investigator's commitments and hunches. The decision-maker can, at most, arouse the investigator's interest in a problem . . . The aim is to conceptualise and understand the chosen phenomenon.

The distinction made here is a distinction in respect of initiatives and basic commitments and not in respect of potentialities for educational improvement. Both conclusion-oriented and decision-oriented research can be of utmost importance for educational policy and practices and should be supported each in its own right, but perhaps with different methods of resource allocation.

Among the decision-oriented studies the Cronbach–Suppes report further distinguishes between (a) operational or institutional research, and (b) product or developmental research. Operational studies are done in order to provide the decision-maker with systematic information, 'not to tell him what to do'. Developmental research should be used not only for evaluation of final products but as a basis for decisions throughout the design and try-out sequence.

This excursion into problems of defining educational research was made in order to establish a background for specifying the requirements concerning research personnel. It is evident that the diversity of research calls for a diversity of personnel. Educational researchers can come from many disciplines and many applications. In addition, there is a need for specialists of various kinds at both professional and technical levels as well as for clerical and other support personnel. Although this paper will primarily deal with educational researchers some comments will be made about the specialists and their training, for instance subject matter experts in product development, design and data analysis specialists. As regards educational researchers, on the other hand, a limitation has to be made within the broader framework in so far as research training will be discussed primarily in a behavioural science perspective. The involvement in educational research of economists, historians, philosophers etc. will be seen mainly as a problem of recruiting persons with such backgrounds for disciplined enquiry into education. This means that the educational research career is seen as having two main inputs: (a) through research training in the behavioural science field, and (b) through recruitment of trained researchers from other fields. The paper is planned according to this division of inputs and the subsequent career. The different parts have been written more as an inventory of problems for further discussion than as a report on the author's own views, even if they inevitably have influenced the selection of items.

Training for behavioural educational research

This part of the chapter will be organized according to a modified instructional technology model, beginning with goals and prerequisites for training, going on to programmes, content and methods, and concluding with evaluation. In addition, the organizational settings in which the training takes place will be discussed. In order to avoid too much dependence on the author's own experience and biases, a search through the relevant literature was undertaken. Most of what has been found are discussions by various authors and committees, mainly in the United States and Scandinavia, but some empirical studies of student input and research output will also be cited.

GOALS

Graduate education in general Explicit goal formulations for research training are rare. In addition to the difficult and forbidding task that making goals explicit seems to present generally in higher education, the sophisticated skills involved in research competence, the small number of students up till now and the highly individualized apprenticeship-type of training usually given at this level (if given at all) explain very well the lack of explicitness. But with increasing numbers and organized courses also at graduate level this lack may be detrimental to the results of training.

This does not mean that the goals have not been discussed. Some issues that are relevant for goal formulation can easily be extracted from these discussions. Since the main instrument for research training in most countries is the programme leading up to a Ph.D. or similar academic degree, it is natural to start with some issues concerning such programmes. Discussion of whether the doctoral programme is a suitable form for training for educational research will be postponed.

When discussing the purposes of graduate education in the United States, Berelson (1960) focuses on two somewhat conflicting aims: training of researchers vs. preparation of college teachers. The Ph.D. programmes had been criticized by some groups for being too specialized and also for failing to prepare adequately for the teacher role. Some graduate schools had tried to broaden the training either within disciplines or through inter-disciplinary programmes. One argument for stressing college teaching was that a majority of the doctoral candidates were supposed to choose the teaching profession (pp. 44 ff). Berelson, however, shows that the trend is changing to a majority staying in research-oriented settings. In his recommendations he maintains that training in research and scholarship should be the primary purpose of doctoral study and that training at this level must be specialized, usually within a sub-area of an established discipline. The graduate school should aim at providing the skilled specialist with a greater depth of knowledge and understanding (pp. 220 ff).

Another focal point in Berelson's discussion is the growing professionalization at doctorate level, i.e. using Ph.D. programmes for increasing and specializing competence in professions (outside research and teaching). This means a trend toward skills and technical expertise at the expense of traditional academic values. At the same time the basic disciplines seem to strengthen their impact on programmes for professional degrees in, for instance, medicine and engineering (pp. 80 ff). Berelson is in favour of these trends (p. 223).

A third major issue regarding graduate education is the purpose of the dissertation. Traditionally the dissertation was supposed to be 'an original and significant contribution to knowledge' (p. 173), bearing witness of the doctor's competence to do independent research. With team research, individual originality has become difficult to evaluate, and the contributions to knowledge have so often been just additions of marginal interest that the fruitfulness of the aim can be questioned. Instead the dissertation is now seen as a training instrument—a start in research and not, as so often has been the case, both the first and the last contribution to knowledge.

Even if Berelson's evaluation refers to the American system of graduate education, the main issues—specialization, professionalization, dissertation as a training instrument—are relevant in most countries. In small countries it is even more likely that a Ph.D. or similar degree must serve many purposes simultaneously and then the goal conflicts are present.

In Sweden the system of research training was reorganized in 1969 after having been discussed by a government committee, *Forskarutredningen*, that published its main report in 1966. In the old system there were two research degrees: in the arts and science faculties *Filosofie licentiat* (*Fil. lic.*) and *Filosofie doktor* (*Fil. dr.*). The first, ideally, took about three years from the first academic degree, the latter an additional period of three years but with very great variations. A new *Fil. dr.* with a four-year programme from the first degree was substituted for these two degrees. The government did not accept the committee's proposal for an intermediate degree after two years, but a two-year professional training for psychologists has been started instead of the *Fil. lic.* that served as a professional degree for this category. So much for the organizational background.

The committee expressed the requirements of research education in the following way (*Forskarutredningen*, 1966, p. 43): (1) The researcher shall receive a broad methodological training and an orientation concerning the research frontier in his discipline. (2) Through his training he shall receive knowledge and skills that enable him to write a 'good' dissertation. The dissertation shall be based on independent research work and have importance for research in the discipline.

The committee, however, was aware of the conflict between the two requirements and aimed at a balance between them. The government bill (*Proposition*, 1969) stressed the training instrument aspect of the dissertation somewhat more than the committee had done and also the need for flexibility of programmes in order to meet the demands of professions other than research.

The Swedish reform is cited as an example of the importance of the goal issues that were highlighted by Berelson. Its on-going implementation in Ph.D. programmes for different disciplines is an illustration of the difficulties in finding consensus in and between disciplines on questions such as specialization, professionalization, and independence. On the whole, however, the trends go in the same direction as Berelson's recommendations and this seems to hold also for reforms at graduate level in other countries.

Goal formulating of the kind discussed so far is not very specific and does not give much guidance concerning the details of the programmes. More specific goals usually have to be inferred from the relative weight of general vs. individual requirements, from the content of the courses and the characteristics of the dissertations. These are likely to vary between disciplines.

Training for educational research The purpose of graduate programmes has been treated so far in general terms. It is now time to see how the main issues of specialization and professionalization manifest themselves within training programmes for educational research. In 1964, the American association Phi Delta Kappa devoted a symposium to 'the training and nurture of educational researchers' (Phi Delta Kappa, 1965). In his contribution to the symposium Krathwohl (pp. 73 ff) described current programmes for educating empirically oriented researchers and methodologists. He tried to fit them into a model that is reproduced in Figure 2.1.

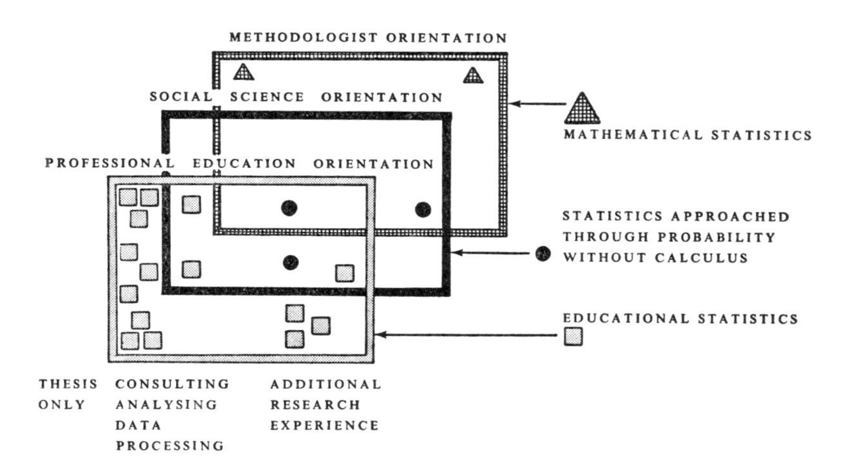

Figure 2.1

The dimensions of this model are (1) sophistication of research methods taught, particularly in statistics and experimental design; (2) concentration of work in education vs. social science disciplines vs. methodology; and (3) own research experience.

These dimensions seem to be correlated, in so far as the methodologist orientation goes together with more sophistication in statistics and experimental design and at least consulting experience in addition to the thesis. The most typical example of such a programme is

Stanley's Wisconsin programme (Stanley, 1967) with a strong emphasis on mathematical statistics. Researchers trained in this methodological specialization are supposed to work as consultants to, or in teams with, persons having field experience. Through this contact they gradually become acquainted with educational practices and problems. An example of institutionalized interaction between design specialists and school personnel is given by Stanley (1964, 1966a) describing the work of the Wisconsin Laboratory of Experimental Design. In the 1966 article he also outlines a training programme for research specialists in school systems whose main responsibilities are operational research (as defined above) and liaison between a school system and a design laboratory.

Combined efforts by methodologists and education-oriented researchers which look excellent for decision-oriented research may not be as well suited for conclusion-oriented studies (as defined above). Here a thorough grounding in a basic discipline seems indispensable, and it is unlikely that the methodologist can pick up enough of this through incidental learning from consulting contacts with discipline-oriented researchers. Nor is it likely that the profession-oriented researcher, usually starting his graduate education on the basis of a course in teacher training, has had enough preparation in basic social sciences to undertake discipline-oriented research except in co-operation with social scientists, who in their turn need just as much the support of field-experienced people for many kinds of problems.

From this might be concluded that all three orientations are needed in educational research, and students and programmes are usually not well-rounded enough to combine all aspects. This would mean that good educational research as a rule must be done by teams representing the three orientations (of which the discipline-based can be sub-divided into psychology, sociology, etc.). This, on the other hand, makes stronger demands on the supply of research personnel than most institutes can meet and, therefore, it is desirable to try to specify the requirements of a programme aimed at training a researcher who can support himself most of the time in all three respects. From Krathwohl's model it follows that the social or behavioural scientist is most likely to hold this place.

One such specification is found in the Cronbach–Suppes report (1969, pp. 212 ff) where recommendations are given for a training programme which include the following (pp. 212–13):

1 full-time study for three consecutive years, preferably at an early age;
2 training as part of a student group individually and collectively dedicated to research careers;
3 participation in research, at a steadily advancing level of responsibility, starting in the first year of graduate school if not earlier;
4 a thorough grounding in at least one academic discipline, together with solid training in whatever technical skills that discipline employs; and
5 study of the educational process and educational institutions, bringing into a single perspective the social goals of education, the bases on which policy decisions are made, the historical development of the curriculum, the nature of the learners, and other factors.

This quotation could just as well have been inserted in the programme, content and methods part of the paper but, as said before, goals often have to be inferred from content. And what is important to notice here is the combination of (4) and (5), but without the requirement for teacher training and teaching experience that usually characterizes profession-oriented programmes like the American Doctor of Education (Ed.D.) to which we are going to return below. Nor are the mathematical aspects of methodology explicitly stressed.

Before going on to more specific levels it might be well to sum up the major goal issues treated so far. In graduate education in general these were specialization, professionalization, and purposes of the dissertation. In research training for education the question discussed in the preceding paragraphs was the balance between methodology, substantive knowledge in a discipline, and substantive knowledge of education as a professional enterprise. In both sections the aims were looked upon primarily within the framework of a doctoral programme.

In 1969 the American Educational Research Association (AERA) appointed a Task Force on Training Research and Research-related Personnel. The group has produced a series of technical reports, many of which are of great relevance for this paper. In this context a report by Glass and Worthen (1970) will be cited at some length. The paper tries to specify essential knowledge and skills for educational research and evaluation. The following list includes skills judged necessary for educational research, primarily of an empirical-behavioural character even although what the authors call 'rational inquiry and methodological research' draw upon most of these skills.

1 Drawing implications from results of prior research
2 Formulating hypotheses or questions to be answered by the research
3 Procuring and managing resources (material and human) necessary to reach the research objective
4 Specifying data or evidence necessary for a rigorous test of the hypothesis
5 Identifying the population to which results should be generalized, and selecting a sample of the population
6 Applying experimental design and recognizing and controlling threats to validity
7 Identifying the classes of variables for measurement
8 Selecting or developing techniques of measurement
9 Assessing the validity of measurement techniques
10 Utilizing appropriate data-gathering methods (tests, interviews, analysis of documents, etc.)
11 Understanding the general role, types, and assumptions of statistical techniques and drawing on such knowledge in using appropriate techniques of data analysis
12 Interpreting and drawing appropriate conclusions from data analysis
13 Reporting research findings and implications.

In a similar way, Glass and Worthen specify ten skills necessary for educational evaluation. Finally, they list essential knowledge about methodology common to educational research and evaluation. The methodology list is divided into five parts, namely

Statistics (10 items)
Experimental design (8 items)
Psychometrics (9 items)
Measurement (8 items)
General considerations in research and evaluation (3 items).

It is beyond the scope of the present study to cite these specifications, however interesting they are. Contrary to what might be suspected from the number of items and the authors' background and reputation, the methodology list does not put any extreme demands on the students' mathematical competence.

Compared to the other statements of goals referred to above, the Glass–Worthen lists are more specific—for example, the methodology section could be directly translated into course content—and they come closer to actual research operations than any of the others. On the other hand, they do not specify theory and concepts in any basic discipline, nor knowledge of educational processes and institutions as, for instance, the Cronbach–Suppes report demands (see above). But it would be wrong to classify all of their categories as methodology (as defined above) since a great number of the operations mentioned are closely tied up with specific substantive knowledge. Rather the specification should be regarded as an operational dimension in an operation × content taxonomy and thus complementary to other approaches.

Another interesting feature of the Glass–Worthen report is that the lists of operations include logistic and administrative functions necessary for research and evaluation (budgeting and managing human and material resources). These are skills that are probably not trained in doctoral programmes but have an important role in all policy-oriented research.

Before concluding the section on goals a few additional points will be made. When discussing the traditional dissertation requirements originality was judged to be a difficult criterion for evaluation. This does not mean, however, that originality and creativity should be excluded from the goals of research training. On the contrary, one goal must be to make the training attractive for creative young people, another to arrange it in such a way that it develops creativity among all its students. These aspects will be treated in the following sections of the paper, but just one further remark on creativity is perhaps called for here. The neat and orderly sequence of operations described by Glass and Worthen gives an idealized picture of research. Great innovations often come in a much more haphazard way (cf. Engel, 1966; Polanyi, 1969), results in 'normal science' also. This makes it necessary to balance emphasis on techniques and operations with freedom for deviations from accepted procedures.

In the introduction educational research was characterized as a multi-disciplinary and multi-method enterprise. This might be interpreted as researchers from many disciplines working side-by-side with their own methods on educational problems. It also could mean truly inter-disciplinary research making a co-ordinated attack on educational problems from a common frame of reference, where intra-disciplinary rules and concerns are subordinated to the common goal. Some educational problems can very well be tackled within a limited frame of reference, but others, and particularly those most important for macro-level policy decisions, are difficult to pursue if disciplinary rigidities are allowed to narrow the perspective. Broadening the frame of reference, however, tends to make research less neat and orderly and more open to methodological criticism. Here is another point where a proper balance must be reached in the training goals. Eide in a creative and provocative paper on educational research policy (1971), which inspired this and some other paragraphs, finds that this balance has not been achieved so far with training dominated by traditional academic values.

A basic notion in Eide's paper is 'informative criticism' as contrasted with 'prescriptive criticism'. This means an active search for alternatives to current practices and trying to change them through information rather than prescription. Informative criticism should be exerted by many groups in the society. 'But being potentially a function granted more discretion than any other, research can contribute decisively to the development of an attitude of informative criticism in all sectors, and at all levels of society'. This responsibility has implications for training goals. In addition to the critical function that is inextricably tied to disciplined inquiry the researcher also has a critical responsibility in relation to present practices in those areas of society where his research can be used.

Conclusion Research training in regular academic programmes at graduate level usually has to compete with the training requirements for teachers in higher education and professional specialists. All three functions, however, are best served by a programme that promotes in skilled specialists a depth of knowledge and understanding. This usually necessitates a concentration to a sub-area of a discipline, but the sub-areas should not be too narrow and they should be defined in a flexible way leaving room for individual choices. The dissertation is to be seen more as a training device than a contribution to knowledge.

In educational research three principal orientations can be distinguished among researchers and training programmes: methodology, disciplines, and educational practice. In many contexts team work by specialists from all three orientations is indispensable. If it is attempted to combine them in one programme and one person it seems most practicable to start from a behavioural science basis.

The steps and techniques of regular research operations in the educational field have been specified in a way that is most helpful for constructing training. In formulating training goals it should, however, not be forgotten that creative research, inter-disciplinary projects, and the application of 'informative criticism' may break some of these rules of procedure and still remain within the realm of disciplined inquiry.

STUDENTS

In the academic community, studies and research in education have a fairly low status compared both to other professional fields and most disciplines within the faculties of arts and sciences. This low reputation, which has had serious consequences for the recruitment of research students, has many roots. Teacher training has a weak connection with knowledge gained through disciplined inquiry, a fact that has been deplorably evident to those coming from a subject matter education in the disciplines. Many professors of education have had very little experience in empirical research and thus have not been able to function as models for research-oriented students and to create a favourable research climate. Unlike most science and arts disciplines education is not perceived by students at secondary or undergraduate level as a possible field of research. Until recently the field has had very limited economic resources, and where these have increased rapidly the research output, due to lack of competent personnel, has not always been of the intellectual quality and practical usefulness hoped for. The reputation for having money available may attract students to training in educational research, but not the other features as described here, and it is not sure that economic incentives if not combined with a research climate attract the right ones.

This may seem harsh; unfair to many individuals and a disservice to the field to make such conditions publicly known. But they are already well documented by many American writers (see for instance Berelson, 1960; Lazarsfeld and Sieber, 1964; Phi Delta Kappa, 1965; Buswell *et al.*, 1966; Cronbach and Suppes, 1969) and there is no reason to infer that Europe is better off from the fact that very few have followed the late Professor Wiseman's example (1962) and reported on the situation. In the past, the field has simply not been able to recruit top-level students in a number that corresponds to its importance for the society and to the resources that the society—at least in some countries—is willing to invest in it. An improvement is badly needed.

Desirable characteristics The first question then is: what kinds of students shall be recruited? Fortunately this is not entirely a matter of opinion even if the empirical results available come from the United States and its system of training and not from European countries.

Buswell *et al.* (1966) made a series of empirical studies on training for educational research. One of them is a ten-year follow up of the research output of persons receiving a doctorate in education in 1954. In total about 800 doctors answered a questionnaire of which 300 had received a Ph.D. and 500 an Ed.D. Only 12 per cent could list two or more research publications in the ten-year period, 13 per cent one research publication, and the remaining 75 per cent none. The percentage having at least one publication was 36 for the Ph.Ds and 18 for the Ed.Ds—a difference which is quite natural in view of the different objectives of the two degrees, the first being primarily a research degree and the second a degree for professional specialization. Both percentages, however, are low and mean that the majority of the doctors do not engage in further research. The average age on completion of the doctoral studies was thirty-nine years, which was nearly ten years more than in many science disciplines. Younger doctors were shown to be considerably more productive during the ten years after graduation than the older ones. Late decisions to start graduate work and the number of years of teaching experience were negatively related to productivity but these factors cannot be separated from age in the reported data. Having an undergraduate major in psychology was a positive indication for future research productivity, likewise to have taken the bachelor's degree in an institution granting doctor's degrees in education. On the other hand, the number of courses in education at undergraduate level correlated negatively with research output which most likely had to do with the practical emphasis of these courses as being requirements for teaching certificates.

The project also comprised a study of thirty-one researchers in education and related fields receiving most votes as outstanding scholars from a somewhat larger group identified through frequency of published papers and including most of those eventually nominated. 'In terms of their academic backgrounds the scholars in this study tended (p. 111):

1 To be graduates of liberal arts undergraduate programmes
2 To have attended one or more private institutions of higher education
3 To have earned degrees in two or more fields of study
4 To hold doctoral degrees from Columbia, Harvard, Chicago, Minnesota, California or Ohio State Universities
5 To have selected their graduate schools on the basis of its reputation for scholarly research and its outstanding research faculty
6 To have attended graduate school on a continuous full-time basis
7 To have completed the doctoral degree before age 30
8 To have published research before (or within one year of) completion of the Ph.D. requirements and consistently thereafter
9 To be somewhat alike on personality scales measuring theoretical orientation, ability to deal with complex ideas and autonomy but more broadly varied on scales measuring thinking introversion and estheticism.'

Just two of the thirty-one held doctor's degrees in education outside the field of educational psychology and testing, one in curriculum and one in educational administration, which was very meagre in relation to the great numbers of doctors each year with non-behavioural specializations.

Although these eminent researchers took their doctor's degrees long ago, a few of them as early as the 1920s, under conditions that are not typical for the present generation of graduate students, some of these characteristics may still be predictive of research productivity. It seems worth noticing that the group did not tend to come from teacher education but from the disciplines, they were young when taking their degrees, they had a considerable range in their studies, and they chose their graduate school for its research reputation. Similar points are made in the conclusions from the project in general (p. 2):

> It is increasingly apparent that potential researchers need to be identified, selected and encouraged while they are young; that

persons engaged in educational research should have a strong background in the liberal arts, rather than extensive courses in education; and that their grounding in the behavioural sciences should be strengthened as they study the philosophy and science of education.

The second major study of educational research productivity was carried out by Sieber and Lazarsfeld (1966) as a continuation of a more exploratory study a couple of years earlier (Lazarsfeld and Sieber, 1964). Both studies mainly dealt with organizational variables. The unit of observation was the institution, not the individual. During a three-year period only 6 per cent of the doctors from graduate schools of education were estimated to have entered research positions directly upon graduation. This was taken as a criterion of the programme's productivity for research and was analysed in relation to recruitment policies, research climates and training provisions. The proportion of researchers was higher when the graduate school was more selective, when teaching certificates or teaching experience were not required at entry, and when the proportion of doctoral candidates working for a Ph.D. (instead of Ed.D.) was high. Selectivity of the student body, however, was chiefly operative when the school had a favourable research climate and when apprenticeships were provided on projects (p. 338).

The low research productivity of existing doctoral programmes and the lack of qualified research personnel in spite of great numbers of doctors led to the establishment, under United States Office of Education, of a Title IV programme for graduate research training. The training takes place at selected graduate institutions. These receive extra funds for the training and the graduate students get stipends from Title IV.

In an AERA Task Force on Training report (Hopkins, Worthen and Soptick, 1970) the characteristics of 1969–70 Title IV trainees are described. From Fleury and Cappelluzzo (1969) (not seen by the author) the report cites five important recruitment variables: (1) age, (2) talent, (3) previous teaching experience, (4) academic background, and (5) grade point average. Data were collected on these. The 800 trainees in 1969–70 could be expected to graduate at an average age of thirty-one which compares well with the recommendations of Buswell *et al.* (1966). On standardized aptitude tests the trainees had average scores comparable to the highest scoring disciplines and professional schools and much higher than doctoral candidates in education in general. The trainees began their graduate studies shortly after their first degrees which means that they usually had not had much time for teaching experience—a negative factor for research productivity according to the earlier studies. The proportion recruited outside education was somewhat higher than in earlier studies and so was the proportion coming from positions which involved some research activity.

The Title IV trainees here described are a select group of students getting stipends and as such not directly comparable to earlier or coeval cohorts of doctoral candidates in education. But their composition shows that it is possible in education to recruit research students with characteristics quite comparable to those in the most highly regarded academic fields. And their number is quite impressive —nearly 800—so it is not just a small elite.

The next question to ask is naturally: what did they do to bring about such an improvement in student recruitment? But firstly the empirical results will be discussed and related to other information about desirable student characteristics.

The criteria of research productivity of the Buswell *et al.* and Sieber-Lazarsfeld studies could be questioned. The number of publications and the proportion of doctors entering research positions directly upon graduation are very crude measures of dedication to research. The proportions in the positive categories are small, especially in the Sieber–Lazarsfeld study. But where comparisons can be made the results are quite coincident in spite of clearly distinguished criteria and this lends more credibility to the conclusions drawn than two studies with identical criteria would have done. The main results are also supported by informal experiences reported by other authors and groups.

High academic talent is stressed by most of those who have written on student requirements—perhaps more so by Stanley (1962, 1966a, 1967) than by anyone else. Usually talent is operationally defined by tests such as Miller Analogies Test and Graduate Records Examinations, in which case there may be a risk of viewing talent too narrowly and too much from the convergent thinking perspective (cf. Guilford, 1967). If selection procedures are used in connection with admission to graduate studies, assessments of creative abilities also should be used to balance the more conventional tests in the information processing and problem solving area.

Another measure of academic promise is achievement at earlier levels. In discussing academic grades as predictors of performance in research training an *ad hoc* committee of the American Psychological Association (APA, 1959) warns that (pp. 174–5):

> A high grade record may be evidence of high intelligence, but it may also be evidence of a tendency to social conformity which may be undesirable for research. Indeed, many types of deviant behaviour may be assets in a research man. For example, rejection of authority, perseveration on 'pet' ideas, unwillingness to commit energy in subject areas of low interest, and general independence of thinking are all probably desirable characteristics for research. These same characteristics, however, may result in an appearance of undesirable deviation from the norm—for example, in a spotty grade record.

The findings of the study of outstanding scholars also touch general personality characteristics. More extensive studies have been made in other fields of research (cf. Super and Bachrach, 1957; Taylor and Barron, 1963; and Barron, 1969). In the Taylor–Barron report on scientific creativity characteristics of productive scientists are abstracted and brought together in a common list (pp. 385–6):

1. A high degree of autonomy, self-sufficiency, self-direction
2. A preference for mental manipulations involving things rather than people: a somewhat distant or detached attitude in interpersonal relations, and a preference for intellectually challenging situations rather than socially challenging ones
3. High ego strength and emotional stability
4. A liking for method, precision, exactness
5. A preference for such defence mechanisms as repression and isolation in dealing with affect and instinctual energies
6. A high degree of personal dominance but a dislike of personally toned controversy
7. A high degree of control of impulse, amounting almost to overcontrol: relatively little talkativeness, gregariousness, impulsiveness
8. A liking for abstract thinking, with considerable tolerance of cognitive ambiguity
9. Marked independence of judgment, rejection of group pressures toward conformity in thinking

10 Superior general intelligence
11 An early, very broad interest in intellectual activities
12 A drive toward comprehensiveness and elegance in explanation
13 A special interest in the kind of 'wagering' which involves pitting oneself against uncertain circumstances in which one's own effort can be the deciding factor.

It is difficult to judge to what extent these characteristics are important also for educational research productivity. For one thing, interest in education usually is thought to go together with social-personal interests. According to most typologies of interests and motivations (cf. Holland, 1966) these are at variance with intellectual and scientific interests. This would make it difficult to find the rare combination that leads to research in education, at least on classroom problems, rather than to research in sciences or, when the interest profile is reversed, to educational practice. If there is some truth in these speculations they should hold also for research in social work and in client-oriented fields of psychology. Such differences also can be behind the distinction between the methodology, discipline, and professional orientations as treated above.

The recommendation for undergraduate preparation in liberal arts rather than teaching has been commented upon already and will not be dealt with at length here. Worth noticing is, however, that this view is not only taken by people from the disciplines but also by representatives for the professional education side (cf. Cronbach and Suppes, 1969, p. 22)—probably not so often by teachers anyhow! A Swedish example of a similar concern may be cited. According to the proposal of a government committee *Pedagogikutredningen* (1970) an organizational integration of the departments of education (as distinguished from teaching methods departments) in schools of education and universities has been decided by the parliament. One of the main reasons for this integration, expressly stated both by the committee and in the government bill (*Proposition*, 1971) was the need to facilitate the recruitment of university students, especially in behavioural and social sciences, to research in education in teacher-training contexts.

The apparent lack of appreciation for teaching as preparation for educational research, which has been a recurring theme in this section, must not be interpreted in a superficial way as teaching *per se* making a person less apt for educational research. On the contrary, the experience as such is most likely to be of value but this has to be weighed against a number of other consequences. Recruitment from teaching should be stimulated. But those who are likely to come are just too few and too specifically prepared to form a main manpower source for large scale educational research.

The causation behind the empirical findings on teaching reported is complicated. Tentatively the following explanations are suggested:

1 Teacher training, especially for classroom teachers, tends to attract persons more characterized by social-personal than intellectual-scientific interests.
2 Teaching at primary and secondary levels does not receive the status and rewards that enable it to compete successfully for the intellectually most qualified students. This, however, is not likely to hold in all countries and all social groups.
3 As said before, teacher training usually has little contact with research either in the form of research-based procedures or personal models for doing research.
4 Teaching experience between undergraduate and graduate studies tends to delay entry into graduate school until a period in a person's life when many occupational and private responsibilities compete for time and interest; sometimes even until an age when flexibility has decreased and time begins to become too short for a significant amount of research production.
5 Being trained in a group where the majority have other professional aspirations than research also makes involvement in research less probable.
6 Teacher education has its special objectives and cannot afford to put in enough time for basic behavioural science to be a main channel of recruitment to educational research training.

Sieber and Lazarsfeld (1966, p. 349) recommend that 'the requirement of professional experience or of the teaching certificate for admission to doctoral candidacy in education should be eliminated for students who wish to specialise in empirical research'. Instead, field observations in school systems should be organized as a part of the graduate programme.

For a person not already involved in research it is difficult to know what research is like, and whether one's own interests and capabilities meet the demands made by graduate studies and dissertation work. Therefore it is desirable to let the prospective research students have some experience of research already at undergraduate level. This may function both as a recruitment incentive and as an instrument for self-selection. In addition, undergraduate research performances would be one of the best selection instruments for admission to graduate school. These aspects were stressed particularly much by the APA *ad hoc* committee (1959, p. 175). The requirement of a thesis at undergraduate level is obligatory in the Swedish system, and also for teachers who plan to go on to graduate studies in education. Most people in educational research find it so indispensable that they may not even have thought of another course of action.

Active recruitment policies This section can be brief as some procedures have already been described and others follow rather directly as implications from desirable student characteristics. From what has been said above it also follows that the main target for active recruitment operations are young talented students in the social and behavioural sciences, although some effort can also be aimed at recruiting from among prospective teachers.

The recruitment operations fall into two main classes (1) creating interest, and (2) supplying support. It seems important not to pass over the first of these two steps and attract people into the field primarily with economic incentives. Interest should preferably be developed into a genuine interest for research in educational processes and institutions and not for research in general, since the opportunities to emigrate to other fields of application after training are, if not legion, manifold.

In creating interest, the first condition seems to be to establish contact with young students and make the field of educational research visible to them. These opportunities vary to a great extent with institutional factors. Where education is studied at undergraduate level only in schools of education and teacher training colleges, reaching liberal arts students is a difficult task since it is highly dependent on the interest for educational matters of teachers and researchers in other disciplines—psychology, sociology, etc. In this case, it seems necessary to establish organized relations between education faculties and undergraduate departments in social sciences. Sieber and Lazarsfeld (1966) found that the research quality of the schools of education was higher when arts and science professors took part in the recruitment of faculty members in education. Maybe this organized co-operation could also have effects the other way around in making it more likely that students in arts and science faculties through their professors become interested in educational problems. This, however, is not a matter that could be left to contingencies but should be given constructive thought by those interested in promoting educational research.

A proposal for finding and recruiting graduate students by means of summer institutes was made by Stanley (1967). His proposal was specific to the educational and psychological statistics area, but could be developed for other areas as well. The target population was third-year undergraduate students (p. 19):

> The inducements would be (a) the opportunity to study statistics and experimental design intensively with instructors and graduate assistants well versed in these at the end of the junior year of college, preparatory to doing honors work the senior year; (b) eight semester-hour credits to transfer to one's college; (c) stipends adequate to compensate for income lost because of studying rather than holding a summer job; (d) eligibility to compete during the summer for several (hopefully, at least five) three-year graduate fellowships to be awarded to the most promising participants in the summer institute; and, probably not least, (e) the opportunity to enjoy the country-club summer atmosphere of Madison.

The situation is easier where education is studied in a disciplinary framework as a subject parallel to other behavioural and social sciences, both at undergraduate and graduate level. There it is possible to reach the student from the first day of his university life and have him spend most of his university education in an education department. This is the case in Sweden where education (or pegagogics) can be studied for from one up to four of the six semesters of undergraduate study and four years at the graduate level. This gives educational research a maximum of chances to become known to the students. But still the recruitment problem remains, since choosing education as a major subject at undergraduate level without acquiring a teacher competence (except possibly in psychology and education) calls for other professional opportunities. One such opportunity in Sweden is to attain competence as a professional psychologist. All prospective psychologists take at least one semester course in education together with courses in psychology and sociology. If they become interested in educational psychology, they have had the option to take a major part of their undergraduate and all of their graduate training in the education department. Many of those who are now active in educational research have started their specialization with the intention to qualify as professional psychologists. This has been of major importance for the empirical and policy-oriented trend in Swedish educational research. With growing professionalization of the training of psychologists, however, the departmental specialization is going to decrease and with that to some extent the chances to keep prospective psychologists in educational research training. Therefore, attempts are being made to develop training programmes for education specialists of different kinds, for instance educational technologists, that can be chosen with a fair promise of professional opportunities and help to serve as a basis for recruitment to doctoral studies. It will take some time, however, before such new specialties get the same status and attractiveness as professional psychology.

Leaving aside the institutional prerequisites for attracting students in their early career a general remark should be made about channelling student interest. If engaging the students in research on their own problems and perceptions as partners in an educational process, instead of dull course-work, education should have a unique chance to lay a solid foundation for motivation and interest which could be extended to other parts of the field. Is it presumptuous to suspect that activity-oriented pedagogy now is lectured upon more than practised in education departments?

Supplying support for research training is done through various methods and programmes. Usually there is a general system of stipends for graduate study. Assistantships in instruction or research, with time put aside for own training, also form a channel of support that often exists side by side with stipends. Then there are special programmes for supporting graduate study in education of which the Title IV programme of the US Office of Education is likely to be the most important. In Sweden, the National Board of Education practises a system whereby a number of graduate students are financed while they do research on problems having connection with contracted research projects. In addition, many graduate students have regular appointments within projects and are allowed to use work in the mainstream of the projects as dissertations. In their evaluations of the Swedish programme Passow (1968) as well as Passow and Postlethwaite (1970) stress the importance of systematic training activities as part of such arrangements. At somewhat higher levels of competence the Social Science Research Council finances a few research posts for doctoral study. Sieber and Lazarsfeld (1966) recommend that the US Office of Education automatically should offer contingency funds to every project that assumes the obligation to train a graduate student in conjunction with the project beyond the project's minimal needs for routine assistance.

All these different channels of support should be used to facilitate the recruitment to educational research training. It is important that both stipends and assistantships be combined with individualized training programmes under the supervision of competent researchers, not necessarily one of the few professors but rather full-time researchers in a suitable area of specialization. Assistants employed for instruction or in research projects should not be over-burdened with routine tasks. Instead, they should as much as possible be used for tasks that are in line with their own specialization, and which can also be credited as degree requirements.

The last few paragraphs would appear to obviate the need for a section devoted to recommendations, as far as this part of the paper is concerned. The general conclusion is: educational research needs young, talented people with a good background in disciplines, a realistic perception of what research is and a solid interest in educational matters. This may be a conclusion of such general quality that it is hard to see who would not endorse it for his own field of application. We shall therefore not get such researchers without competition.

PROGRAMMES, CONTENTS, AND METHODS

Some of the topics that could have belonged to this section have already been treated under 'Goals' since these often had to be inferred from programme construction and content. Some items dealing with the teaching-learning situation have been introduced in the section on students. What remains to be done here is to illustrate some programme characteristics and actual or controversial questions of content. In addition, some methods and procedures with particular relevance for research training will be discussed. In contrast to the section on students, little empirical data on the efficiency of various procedures has been found. This could be looked upon as just another example of the preoccupation in educational research with input and output variables leaving the teaching-learning process to take place without comparable guidance by research. As earlier in the paper, the United States and Sweden are heavily over-represented in the examples—the first because of its dominance in the literature on educational research training, the second because of the restricted range of the author's own experience.

Degree programmes The doctor's programme is the main instrument for research training in most countries. Ideally the training covers the three to five years that follow the successful completion of a first degree course, but since a great proportion of the doctoral candidates do not start directly after their first degree and often teach or do professional work during their studies the time lapse between the degrees tends to become twice as long as the ideal or even more (Berelson, 1960; *Forskarutredningen*, 1966). Attempts have been made to reduce this time and to produce doctors at an earlier age. This is important not least for their future research productivity. Four main remedies have been tried: organizing graduate studies in courses, providing more research supervision, cutting down the size of dissertations, simplifying the procedures of publication, and providing economic support in order to get more full-time graduate students. The Swedish reform will be used to illustrate how these measures can be employed.

As mentioned above, the two-level system of research degrees in Sweden with ideal time 3 + 3 years was changed in 1969 to a one-level programme for a doctorate in four years of full-time study from the first degree. The programme contains both course and dissertation work. The proportions, however, may vary between disciplines. In education and psychology, most universities have allocated half of the available time to course work, half to the dissertation. Within course work the proportion between common and specific parts also varies between disciplines and universities, but as a rule there are at least a number of general methods courses that must be taken by all candidates.

Providing more research guidance means increasing the number of professors (all levels), or cutting down the number of students, or both. The admission to the earlier system of individual studies was free, at least in principle, and the students got the guidance their professors had time to give. Now the target is a maximum of about six doctoral candidates working on dissertations per research supervisor. But in the behavioural sciences it will, even with high selectivity at admission, take time to come down to this figure, since the students in the old system are still abundant and rightly demand guidance. In addition to permanent members of staff, whose numbers have not increased as rapidly as was hoped, researchers on projects and in separate institutes are expected to function as research supervisors. Measures are being taken to institutionalize such contacts.

General recommendations to professors and doctoral candidates concerning a reduction in the amount of work submitted for dissertations have been reinforced by cutting down the number of pages for which the candidate gets printing support. Besides printed monographs, reprints of research papers published in journals and mimeographed reports can be used for dissertation purposes. The reprint form has already been used for a number of years and seems to be the most frequent form in natural sciences, medicine and technology. Its use in psychology is rapidly increasing. The grading of dissertations has been discontinued. Another means of reducing the work on dissertations might be to make the public discussion of the dissertation less demanding and formal, but not much has been achieved as yet in this direction.

Research support is given through stipends, which still are much too scarce, and through assistantships in departments. An assistant is supposed to need one extra year for his degree but because of the load of his other tasks this is generally considered to be unrealistic in comparison with the full-time students.

In the United States there are two doctoral degrees in education, Ph.D. and Ed.D. Ph.D. is primarily a research degree, Ed.D. more a degree for professional specialization with lower dissertation requirements. In institutions where both degrees are given side by side the two programmes do not, however, seem to be sufficiently differentiated, and according to Sieber and Lazarsfeld (1966, p. 287) the less research-oriented degree tends to influence the Ph.D. norms in the direction of lower research quality than in institutions that only grant Ph.Ds.

The Swedish government committee on educational research (*Pedagogikutredningen*, 1970) that proposed an integration between the departments of education in universities and schools of education also tried to construct an alternative type of doctor's degree for subject-matter oriented educational research. The study programme differences between this and the existing behavioural-science oriented degree in education are outlined in Table 2.1. Both degrees will be granted by the social science faculties of the universities with the integrated education departments responsible for the programmes—

Table 2.1: Swedish doctoral degrees in education

Behavioural-science orientation	*Subject-matter orientation*
3 years of undergraduate study at the university with 60 credit points* in education (major discipline) (includes 10 points for own research) 60 in other discipline(s) usually including sociology and/or psychology	3 years of undergraduate study at the university with 60 credit points in one discipline (major) corresponding to a school subject (includes 10 points for own research) 60 in other discipline(s) also corresponding to school subject(s)
4 years of graduate study with 20 credit points in methods of educational research 60 in other education courses 2 years of dissertation work in any field of education	1 year in a school of education with courses in education, teaching methods, and teaching practice. Together with a summer course the education course is equivalent to 20 credit points in education
	4 years of graduate study with 30 credit points in major subject-matter discipline 20 in methods of educational research 30 in other education courses selected for relevance to research on subject-matter teaching 2 years of dissertation work in curriculum, teaching methods or other area related to subject-matter teaching.
In total: Education as a discipline 140 Other disciplines 60 Research 2 years	In total: Education as a discipline 70 Major subject-matter discipline 90 Other subject-matter disciplines 60 Research 2 years Teaching courses and practice 3/4 years

* One credit point roughly corresponds to one week of course work (instruction, exercises, and reading).

as regards the new degree, in co-operation with the university department in the subject-matter field.

The programmes are clearly differentiated both in respect of prospective students, programme content and competencies obtained. The subject-matter oriented degree (pp. 74–6 and 145–9) is supposed to be useful both for subject-matter teachers at upper secondary level, methods teachers in schools of education, and researchers in subject-matter oriented projects. Whether it is also suitable as a training background for future professors of education will depend on the research productivity of the holders of the new degree, which according to a recent parliament decision will be tried out with a few major school subjects. As a member of the committee responsible for the proposal, the author is very anxious not to have contributed to importing the Ph.D.—Ed.D. dilemma into Sweden.

Intermediate research degrees requiring from one to three years of graduate study exist in some countries, for instance Masters and 'Licentiate' degrees. In some countries it is also possible to take an undergraduate or diploma programme with up to two years in education as a discipline, in which case a considerable part of the second year may be used for research. Partly due to lack of information, partly because the problems are likely to be similar to those for the doctor's programmes these degrees will not be explicitly dealt with in this paper. Just two points will be made. Sometimes the intermediate degrees have served as 'consolation prizes' for interrupted doctoral studies, and this has been detrimental to their prestige. Otherwise, in many professional fields, a two-year programme after the first degree would be even more appropriate than doctoral studies. Such programmes, however, should not be looked upon as research training and evaluated from that point of view. An example of a two-year professional degree is the recently established Swedish diploma for professional psychologists (*Psykologexamen*) which, when starting, became so attractive that it almost posed a threat to the recruitment of doctoral candidates in psychology and education.

Another example of a specialized intermediate degree, is a proposal by Stanley (1966a) for a 15-month (two summers and one academic year) programme for research specialists in school systems which could lead to a master's degree in educational research. The target group here is teachers who are interested in being promoted to positions as directors of research in local school systems. One of their future functions would be liaison with research institutes.

As mentioned in the goal section, the regular university programmes in education have been criticized for not having adapted themselves to the needs of large scale research efforts, particularly of the inter-disciplinary character. It is maintained that admission and degree requirements tend to be too rigid and too much influenced by intra-disciplinary value systems. Minor problems with high security are preferred to those that are socially important but involve a high risk. The training takes place in isolation from other disciplines and the field of application.

There is certainly much truth in this criticism but it is not possible to evaluate it properly here without more detailed specification and concrete examples. The stress on regular university programmes in this paper stems from two convictions. One is that educational research is such a difficult and expensive enterprise that it must be based on a thorough grounding in basic disciplines and methodology, which cannot be achieved just through a few research courses or through apprenticeship without the guidance of a basic training programme. The other conviction is that universities in general are flexible organizations—otherwise they would not still be here—with great potentialities for change in contents and methods, even if their freedom and flexibility now and then seem used for rigid decisions. This risk follows from the autonomy they have been granted and which is good for other purposes. According to these convictions it is better to adjust the regular programmes to forthcoming needs than to set up basic training programmes outside the degree system which is common to most disciplines and professional fields. Not least the recruitment problems call for such a reformative strategy.

Special programmes Basic research training accomplished by degree programmes is a long-term proposition. There are, however, a number of short-term needs as well as needs for updating of knowledge and skills among research personnel that are best served by special programmes. A few distinctions will be made and examples given in order to illustrate such programmes, beginning with those that are aimed at continuing education for people already in the field.

The AERA Task Force on research training identifies four objectives for a future in-service training programme (Sanders, Byers and Hanna, 1970, p. 1):

1 upgrade the skills of researchers who are now poorly trained;

2 maintain the high level of competence of researchers now entering the field;
3 teach new skills made necessary by innovations in educational techniques and products; and
4 broaden the base of personnel engaged in activities calling for the application of educational research skills.

They also mention several vehicles for an expanding training programme (pp. 2–3):

1 Pre-session courses, of the sort which have been successfully conducted by AERA, in a still greater variety of substantive areas;
2 Courses of longer duration, application to techniques and skills which require longer study;
3 Summer institutes, conducted by outstanding scholars with particular areas of expertness;
4 Conferences which would emphasise the generation and organisation of new knowledge;
5 Workshops for the teachers of educational researchers, emphasising methods of teaching specific techniques or methods;
6 Development of instructional materials and products for distribution to AERA members.

Special programmes can also serve to introduce educational research to teachers, subject matter experts, administrators, and similar groups who are going to work in research and development projects or who are responsible for the application of research results in their professional functions. A foundation for this should be laid already in basic teacher training and in the specialized professional courses for administrators, guidance personnel, etc. But special conferences and seminars are also needed. There must be numerous examples of this. A recent one is the IEA Seminar in Curriculum Development and Innovation held in Sweden over a period of six weeks of the summer 1971. Educational researchers functioned as instructors or consultants in curriculum theory, evaluation methods, individual and social change, and educational technology parallel to seminars and exercises in curriculum construction with the participants grouped according to subject-matter areas. Here the orientation in educational research was given in close connection with a specialized professional preparation. In other cases, the introduction is given in more general contexts, usually in conferences of short duration.

Another target group for special programmes are researchers with their basic training in other disciplines, for instance sociology, economics, history, philosophy, who like to engage in educational research. Some remarks about this group will be made later (see page 80).

Also technical and clerical personnel working in institutes and on educational research projects need both specialized courses and a general introduction to the aims and principles of educational research. A modest attempt in the latter direction was made in the Göteborg Institute where all personnel—teaching, research and support—spent a day together for information on all Institute activities with emphasis on research projects, and where this introduction was followed up in group work on selected problems related to the Institute's activities. There are surely many much more ambitious enterprises in this field but they usually do not get reported.

CONTENTS

In discussing the Glass-Worthen specification (1970) of research and development operations the idea of a contents × operations matrix was put forward in order to bring the items into a taxonomic model that could also comprise more subject-matter oriented goal specifications. But the contents dimension so far has only been touched on in examples of programme contents. To do more in this direction would mean constructing a model of the discipline of education and discussing what are the core contents that all research students should have and what could be optional. This is clearly not feasible within the framework of this paper, and the likelihood of getting consensus of such a proposition very little.

With this the question could have been put aside in favour of more concrete problems. But here an example could also be of some use as an illustration of *one* solution to the specialization dilemma. In the provisional plan for the behavioural-science oriented doctorate in education at Göteborg University the following distribution of the 80 credit points has been made (for the over-all plan see page 71):

General methodology		20
Theory of science and research design	5	
Research techniques (mainly data processing)	5	

Analysis of verbal information	5	
Analysis of quantitative information	5	
Theory and specialized methods in		60
Learning and cognition	7	
Development	7	
Individual differences	7	
Education and society	7	
Instructional processes	7	
Analysis and evaluation of educational systems	7	
Optional specializations	18	

In examining this specification, one should bear in mind that the students have at least three semesters of education (60 points) at undergraduate level behind them. During this time they have been introduced to all substantive areas mentioned and some general methodology. Three of the six substantive areas are mainly psychological, the remainder deal with macro- and micro-level perspectives of the educational process and institutions. Here also historical, philosophical, and economic aspects have their place. The optional part of the programme may seem small, but it should be remembered that the dissertation work which is truly specialized takes up as much time as all the course work together.

When scrutinizing the plan against recommendations in this paper, the author would have liked to have two more things included: opportunities to consult or minor research work in addition to the dissertation in order to broaden the experiences necessary for proficiency in some of the research operations specified by Glass and Worthen (1970), and organized observations of educational practices as recommended by Sieber and Lazarsfeld (1966). Room for these activities would have to be taken from the substantive courses—in the general rather than in the optional part.

Plans for special programmes are likely to give a picture of what parts of the research training have been weak in the past and where new developments, too difficult to attain just by reading, have taken place. Both reasons seem to hold for the abundance of methodology items in the plans. Experimental design, analysis of variance, multivariate analysis, psychometrics and scaling, and computer usage are such recurrent topics of specialized courses. These methods are difficult to learn for most people in the field because of lack of mathematical preparation. Paradoxically they are comparatively easy to teach, at least to those having a reasonable background, because the materials are well organized conceptually and lend themselves readily to exercises. Both characteristics make them ideal course stuff and no criticism is intended for their being emphasized so much.

The question is, however: is quantitative methodology the only aspect where training given and research produced are defective? Of course not. One could take the Glass–Worthen list of skills necessary for educational research and almost item for item point out skills that are not usually trained in a systematic way and which are learnt at best incidentally in dissertation research. On the other hand, many of these skills cannot be successfully taught by the lecture method in courses but must be practised, ideally in a research group working on a large project under the guidance of an experienced researcher.

Still not everything is made sufficiently explicit in the Glass–Worthen lists. The methodology section should preferably include what in the Göteborg plan has been called analysis of verbal information, that is the analysis of content and style of documents, interview and observation data, psycholinguistic methods and similar techniques of treating less 'hard' data. This can be taught in courses. Another topic, which is represented in the Glass–Worthen list but not often in training, is the planning, management, and logistics functions of research projects. Techniques and materials here could be imported from industrial and business administration courses.

Finally in this section, mention will be made of contents and techniques stimulating the production of ideas and hypotheses even if these may be the most difficult things to specify and to do anything about in training. As an example, the psychology department in Göteborg is trying a course in research creativity based on reports on the process of discovery in various fields, to mention just one, Watson's book *The Double Helix* (1968). Polanyi's essays (1969) on tacit inference referred to earlier would be another stimulating source. In the Phi Delta Kappa symposium (1965) the chapters by Bereiter and Mooney present interesting views on the preconditions of scientific discovery that also could be of guidance in this context. One source of ideas and hypotheses that should not be forgotten is naturalistic observations of the educational process (cf. Jackson, 1968) but these belong more to the next section on teaching methods.

Methods and institutional arrangements The trend in the direction of more organized course work at graduate level should not mean substituting conventional lecturing for the independent study that has predominated. It should mean that the expectations put on the candidates become more clearly defined than earlier and their studies organized in a way that they can complete their degree requirements within the time limits set. The methods of instruction, on the other hand, must vary with the goals and contents. In some more technical parts, as mentioned earlier, lecturing in combination with exercises would be well adapted to the needs of the participants. In others, probably the majority, independent reading followed by seminar or small group discussions would be more appropriate.

The examination procedures, too, should be adjusted to the level of the candidates. Where possible, individual or group reports, based on literature accessible, should be substituted for conventional questioning on memorized materials. These reports could also be used as exercises in concise writing which is a skill that seems to be lacking even among high level students in many countries. The checking of composition and style required cannot always be performed by the regular teachers and supervisors. Berelson (1960, pp. 247–8) mentions a scheme where special 'editors' review the writings of the students and have them revise and rewrite until their style has improved. In addition systematic training should be given in methods of oral presentation.

The main instrument for research training is active participation in research, i.e. not just doing what the supervisor tells you to do but being able to influence all steps in the research sequence. Krathwohl (1965, pp. 84 ff) classifies doctoral programmes according to the extent of participation in research: from thesis work only, via consulting, analysis and data processing, to research experience in addition to the dissertation. Cronbach and Suppes (1969, pp. 212 ff) stress the importance of doing research from the first year of graduate school if not earlier. A Canadian researcher, R. Edwards (1968), presents interesting views on research training where he stresses the step-wise establishing of 'research behaviour' that is likely to last even after graduate school. Besides research itself, an efficient learning experience is the supervision of undergraduate research. This might be given credit points counting for the doctor's degree and be substituted for course requirements.

One of the most important influences in research training is to have the candidates work in a research-oriented setting—that is an institution where good research is done and a favourable research climate created—with fellow students also dedicated to research. This is stressed by many of the authors cited here and in earlier sections, not least the APA *ad hoc* committee (1959, pp. 176–7). Learning from models is an important means and cannot be replaced by methodology courses. An ideal setting would be apprenticeship in a research group under the guidance of an experienced researcher and working side by side with fellow students—this in its turn complemented by courses and seminars where methodological and substantive problems can be treated in a more systematic way than with apprenticeship only (cf. Passow and Postlethwaite, 1970).

This ideal makes clear demands on research projects to engage in research training. This has been touched on already. In return the leaders of the research projects, whether university based or not, should receive an academic status and influence comparable to that of other supervisors of research training at graduate level—a question that we come back to in the career section.

As a substitute for teacher training and experience, field observations have been recommended as a part of the graduate studies. The main reason is that this arrangement should make it possible to recruit young undergraduates from the disciplines without giving up the demand for first-hand experience of education—notably from other points of view than that of the former pupil and student. Not much is known of techniques here—and similar enterprises in other contexts have often failed—but one thing seems to be sure, the field observations must be organized as an integral part of the graduate programme and they should be accompanied by seminars where experiences are examined from the point of view of the disciplines taught and research work considered. It should be a real challenge for those researchers with field experience to try to devise procedures for such training.

Another means of establishing contact with field problems is consultation with teachers who carry out classroom experimentation on an exploratory level. They often need help in designing and evaluating their experiments, and consulting with them could be a profitable learning experience, both from methodological and field orientation points of view, even if the work cannot as a rule be used for dissertation purposes. Such organized consultation has been described by Stanley (1964) and referred to earlier. It might be well to give credit points for such consultation, perhaps even make it a degree requirement alongside courses and the thesis.

EVALUATION

This section has been included mainly for the sake of completeness in the instructional technology model and cannot be developed in detail here. Evaluation can refer to the individual level and comprise, for instance, examinations, grading of performances for degree requirements etc. These have been touched on in earlier sections: the Swedish attempt to shorten the time of doctoral studies by means of *inter alia* the discontinuance of grading for graduate courses and dissertations, and the examination procedures mentioned above.

Evaluation can also mean an examination of the system of research training in relation to its goals. Such evaluations have been done, at least partly and in informal terms, in connection with reforms of the system of research degrees in various countries. One example is the Swedish *Forskarutredningen* (1966). Linked with such evaluation are empirical studies like Berelson (1960) on graduate education in general, Buswell *et al.* (1966) on research productivity in relation to training, Sieber and Lazarsfeld (1966) on the functioning of graduate schools of education, and some of the AERA Task Force reports (1970). Practically all of what has been quoted from quantitative evaluations, and most of the qualitative also, comes from the United States. But it is not necessary to make evaluations on a national basis. They could be made on an institutional level, and Berelson (1960, pp. 254 ff) recommends aspects to be taken into account at that level.

Recruitment of trained researchers from other fields

This section, too, will be brief—much briefer than its importance for educational research in the future. It will deal with the types of researchers needed from other fields and the conditions for their involvement in educational matters. Most of what is said is based on the assumption that these categories of researchers cannot be properly trained at pre-doctoral level in departments or schools of education but have to be specialized in their own disciplines before they enter educational research.

In principle most other disciplines and professional fields have some connection with education and could therefore be mentioned in this context. But such a broad conception is of little help, so an attempt will be made to single out the main groups of researchers that could be recruited for disciplinary or inter-disciplinary research on educational processes and institutions in addition to functioning as subject-matter experts in their respective fields.

Six such groups will be mentioned and commented on very briefly.

1 Psychologists, sociologists, anthropologists, and child psychiatrists, that is persons from the other behavioural sciences, whose role in educational research is evident. It should also be remembered that undergraduates in the same fields should be a major target in policies of recruitment to graduate studies in education.
2 Philosophers and historians have long been connected with educational research and their function in analysing values and institutions has increased rather in the rapidly changing world of educational reforms.
3 Economists, political scientists, and geographers are needed for research on educational institutions and have important roles to play in building up a scientific basis for educational planning and administration.
4 Statisticians and mathematicians are needed to refine research methodology and to adjust it to the particular demands of educational research.
5 Linguists should be able to exert a considerable influence on educational research in the basic processes of transmission of knowledge, communication, and understanding. The Cronbach–Suppes report (1969, pp. 218–19), for instance, suggests that researchers in the reading field should have their basic research training under linguists and not as traditionally under topic-oriented reading specialists.
6 Engineers and computer specialists have a place in the development of the hard-ware side of instructional technology, especially computer assisted instruction, even if their function might often be technical expertise rather than educational research.

Here, too, it seems best 'to get them young' which in this case means directly after completion of their doctoral studies, or even better at the selection of their dissertation topic in their disciplines. A post-doctoral programme introducing the special problems of educational research would at that time be feasible and also profitable to an extent that is more doubtful for persons already having gained research positions in their own discipline. The problems of making educational matters visible to researchers in relevant neighbouring fields are similar to those complicating the recruitment of undergraduates. Economic incentives are likely to be important since education is better-off at present in many countries than most social science and arts disciplines—perhaps not in so far as career prospects for the researcher himself are concerned but in obtaining money for other costs connected with research projects. The career problem remains to be solved since a researcher from another discipline choosing to work on educational problems may risk landing outside the promotion list of his own discipline.

Career structure

The last paragraph brings us directly into the career problem which can be seen both from individual and institutional points of view. The individual researcher likes to have an interesting job, with salary and chances of promotion comparable to those which persons with similar qualifications get, and with a reasonable measure of security in his appointment. Usually he is willing to trade some money and some security for the autonomy and interest that are characteristic of his job but not more than to a certain point. The institution (state, research council, foundation, etc.), on the other hand, likes to make use of his capacity as researcher during his productive years and, if possible, place him in another position when experience begins to outbalance innovative ability, to put it mildly.

Different organizational settings have different effects in these respects. Project research attached to small permanent organizations like university departments tends to favour the institutional need for flexibility. In addition, projects often have ample recruitment possibilities among graduate students and are well suited for persons holding their first jobs after degree. From the institutional point of view they are defective mainly if they tend to work without sufficient continuity and if they cannot compete for qualified researchers who instead seek permanent positions.

Separate institutes with predominantly permanent personnel may have all the continuity they wish for, but if not connected with a graduate department they may have difficulties in recruiting young research personnel. Their possibilities of replacing persons who have passed their research-productive age are not very great if special arrangements are not made for promoting them to positions where their experience can be better used. This is the negative side of the personal security aspect.

It is outside the scope of this paper to treat the organizational problems as fully and with similar documentation as the different aspects of training. The questions touched on in the last two paragraphs are of a general nature and have been studied and discussed by sociologists and organization experts in connection with both governmental and industrial organizations, not least research and development laboratories. Just a few amateurish remarks will be made here, largely reflecting the author's own convictions.

It seems that research is done most creatively and effectively in rather horizontal organizations with a minimum of hierarchical structure. Such a structure makes it possible for junior researchers to interact directly with seniors (not primarily in the literal, temporal sense) of similar specialization and interests instead of having to report through intermediate links in a hierarchical chain of responsibility. This is good not only for the training of the young researchers but also for keeping senior researchers alert and in touch with real research problems instead of hiding behind administrative routines. Everyone in the group contributes what he is capable of, ideally irrespective of seniority or formal competence (cf. Bruner, 1962). This conception of a group with a very low degree of formal stratification is also behind the experiments with self-governing groups in industrial organizations (cf. Thorsrud and Emery, 1969).

In university contexts such a pattern is at least easy to conceive, since professors at various levels are supposed to work directly with young people and not through intermediaries. But the risk of patriarchal instead of democratic relations in the group is evident, and another problem is to get enough positions with tenure to let professors use, say, half of their time to function as leaders or methodology experts in research teams within their own area of specialization. After completion of a project the persons can be regrouped to take up new problems or they can leave research for other responsibilities.

In separate research institutes the senior researchers usually are placed as heads of departments (or similar) and they tend to have their own staff, each with its stratification. Such departments often are charged with a responsibility to watch over development within a certain area or sub-discipline—a function which is not so easily performed in a clear-cut project organization. For carrying out problem-oriented research, a project organization can be superimposed upon such a departmental structure. There can be brought together persons from various departments according to the nature of the problem, often breaking through the stratification based on general competence and seniority for the benefit of functional requirements. Personnel from a general pool or hired on a temporary basis can be put into projects side by side with persons taken from the departmental structure. Such loosening of hierarchical ties seems to be frequent in innovative industrial organizations. Toffler (1970) in his provocative book *Future Shock* talks about the new 'ad-hocracy', replacing hierarchical bureaucracy, as being one of the factors behind the increasing rate of change in modern society.

What are then the implications for career structure of this prospect of research being done primarily in *ad hoc* project groups? This certainly is a matter for discussion, and the following should be regarded as one opening contribution. It seems that researchers in their most active years should not be placed as a rule in a fixed hierarchical structure of positions as department heads, deputy department heads, assistants to department heads, etc., but rather belong to a pool of research staff that can be grouped into projects with a low degree of stratification. This does not mean that all belonging to this pool can be treated equally as to salaries and tenures, but these should not necessarily follow from positions in the organization. They could be awarded in relation to length of employment, level of research competence, quality of performance, and responsibilities held in projects—to mention some criteria that seem relevant.

Such *ad hoc* groups cannot exist, however, without an organizational framework providing for finance, administration and support, perhaps also a follow-up of certain areas of research. Leading positions in this framework should be held by persons with personal research experience but not necessarily any longer taking part in actual research.

In a flexible 'ad-hocracy' it is important that researchers develop talents in addition to their research competence but without permitting these side-lines to take up too much of their time during their most active period of research. Each project must attend to some of its own finance, administration and support functions—in addition to liaison with those responsible in the overall organizational framework—and this provides opportunities for both natural selection and training for such functions. Each project should give research training to its junior members, and this function provides channels of transfer to teaching positions to be filled with research-trained personnel. Each project needs specialized documentation services in its own field, and this can become a preparation for the more general follow-up of an area that may be a function of the overall organization. These various research-related functions can be served by different members of a project and prepare them for a continuation of their research interests in research-related careers as institute directors, department heads, professors with primarily teaching functions, etc.

Norms for salaries and tenures vary so much between countries and types of organization that recommendations cannot be made. The following is a Swedish example of how the norms for an academic research career can be mapped out (*Proposition*, 1969):

> Graduate studies during which most doctoral candidates either are assistants in university departments or projects, or get stipends, usually on a yearly basis;
>
> Directly after Ph.D. 'research assistant' (junior researcher) during a maximum of two three-year appointments;
>
> 'Docent' (assistant professor), as a rule during a maximum of two three-year appointments;
>
> Professor or associate professor holding a permanent appointment.

If permanent positions are not available at the end of the 'docent' period, the research councils can establish research fellowships for highly qualified researchers. As a rule these are temporary. At each level, however, some persons are supposed to leave their research career for positions outside academic research. And since promotion is based on research qualifications and not on seniority short-cuts are both possible and frequent in expanding areas. At all levels persons following a research career have some teaching responsibility which at least partly can be performed as supervision of graduate students. As a rule persons following a research career have somewhat lower salaries than those in teaching or administrative positions at a comparable level.

In some fields academic research careers are often abandoned for research positions in specialized institutes or industries. Since it is important to retain them as supervisors of graduate research, a proposal recently has been made to establish part-time professorships for qualified researchers outside universities who are supervising graduate research. A similar system is already practised in some countries.

Appointments in research projects usually have a lower degree of permanency than regular career positions—most often one year at a time or a maximum of three years. Salaries are paid according to the level of competence comparable to career positions, sometimes with extra pay for administrative duties within projects, or on the basis of salary received in the person's regular position, if he is on leave from such a one. The latter principle can be very complicated indeed to apply in the case of a teacher having extra remuneration for administration or in the case of persons from outside having high salaries based on their regular responsibilities but who have a comparatively low level of research competence. Sometimes the hiring proposition can be baited with an academic degree or status.

In separate research institutes the career structure tends to follow the pattern of civil service appointments with salaries mainly coupled to positions, permanency mainly based on seniority in the organization and without the academic constraint of leaving the position after a fixed number of years. The pros and cons of such a career pattern have been discussed above.

Final recommendations

This chapter has aimed to present a number of questions for discussion among persons responsible for the administration of educational research. In some parts, the author has been able to document the presentation with experiences from other sources, including research. In other parts, mainly the author's own views and speculations have been reported and this pertains especially to the section on career structure.

We all hope that educational research on a large scale and with policy implications has come to stay. A vital question for us all is then the training and nurture of educational researchers. This training has to have a solid scientific and professional base and not just be performed through improvised courses of a technical nature. Therefore, we should support basic training in the educational research profession. Our best contribution is to open up training possibilities in our research institutes in close co-operation with those responsible for the academic preparation of researchers—the administrators of graduate programmes.

Included in this recommendation, but important enough to be stated explicitly in this context, is a recommendation to try to make part of this training international through supporting the exchange scheme which has been proposed by the Council of Europe but which until now has met with a fairly cool reception from those responsible in various countries. A condition for success is the readiness of research institutes to include resources for research guidance and participation in training programmes and projects. Another condition is that trainees should be supported long enough for them to become real participants rather than mere visitors.

REFERENCES

APA Education and Training Board (1959). 'Education for research in psychology', *American Psychologist*, vol. 14, 167–79.

BARRON, F. (1969). *Creative person and creative process*, New York: Holt, Rinehart & Winston.

BERELSON, B. (1960). *Graduate education in the United States*, New York: McGraw-Hill.

BRUNER, J. S. (1962). 'The conditions of creativity', in *Contemporary approaches to creative thinking*, ed. H. E. Gruber *et al.*, New York: Atherton Press.

BUSWELL, G. T., AND MCCONNELL, T. R., together with Heiss, A. M. and Knoell, D. M. (1966). *Training for educational research*, Berkeley, Calif: Center for Research and Development in Higher Education.

CRONBACH, L. J., AND SUPPES, P. (eds) (1969). *Research for tomorrow's schools*, London: Macmillan.

EDWARDS, R. (1968). 'The training of educational researchers: A North American viewpoint', *Bulletin of the British Psychol. Soc.*, vol. 21, 61–6.

EIDE, K. (1971). *Educational Research Policy*. Technical report, CERI, OECD (now published; quotation from manuscript version).

ENGEL, M. (1966). 'Thesis-antithesis: Reflections on the education of researchers in psychology', *American Psychologist*, vol. 21, 781–7.

Forskarutredningen (1966). 'Forskarutbildning och forskarkarriär', *Statens offentliga utredningar* 1966–67.

GLASS, G. V., AND WORTHEN, B. R. (1970). 'Essential knowledge and skills for educational research and evaluation', *AERA Task Force on Training, Technical paper* no. 5.

GUILFORD, J. P. (1967). *The nature of human intelligence*, New York: McGraw-Hill.

HOLLAND, J. L. (1966). *The psychology of vocational choice*, Waltham, Mass.: Blaiden.

HOPKINS, J. E., WORTHEN, B. R., AND SOPTICK, J. M. (1970). 'An analysis of the characteristics of the 1969–70 trainees in Title IV graduate research training programmes and a comparison with Sieber's study of 1966–67 trainees', *AERA Task Force on Training, Technical paper* no. 13.

JACKSON, P. W. (1968). *Life in classrooms*, New York: Holt, Rinehart & Winston.

KRATHWOHL, D. R. (1965). 'Current formal patterns of educating empirically oriented researchers and methodologists', in Phi Delta Kappa (1965).

LAZARSFELD, P. F. ,AND SIEBER, S. D. (1964). *Organizing educational research*, Englewood Cliffs, N.J.: Prentice-Hall Inc.

PASSOW, A. H. (1968). 'Bureau L4 and educational research and planning in Sweden', *School Research Newsletter* 1968:9.

PASSOW, A. H., AND POSTLETHWAITE, T. N. (1970). 'A further look at educational research and planning in Sweden', *School Research Newsletter* 1970:13.

Pedagogikutredningen (1970). Pedagogisk utbildning och forskning. *Statens offentliga utredningar* 1970 : 22.

PHI DELTA KAPPA (1965). *The training and nurture of educational researchers*. Sixth annual symposium on educational research 1964, Bloomington, Indiana: Phi Delta Kappa.

POLANYI, M. (1969). *Knowing and Being*, University of Chicago Press and London: Routledge & Kegan Paul.

Proposition no. 31 (1969). *Angående forskarutbildning och forskarkarriär m.m.*

Proposition no. 38 (1971). *Angående pedagogisk utbildning och forskning m.m.*

ROGERS, W. T., WORTHEN, B. R., AND SANDERS, J. R. (1970). 'An analysis of 1970 AERA Employment Service data', *AERA Task Force on Training, Technical paper* no. 8.

SANDERS, J. R., BYERS, M. L., AND HANNA, G. E. (1970). 'A survey of training programs of selected professional organizations', *AERA Task Force on Training, Technical paper* no. 11.

SIEBER, S. D., AND LAZARSFELD, P. F. (1966). *The organization of educational research*, New York: Bureau of Applied Research, Columbia Univ.

SJÖSTRAND, W. (1967). 'Education as an academic discipline', *Acta Universitatis Upsaliensis* C:12.

STANLEY, J. C. (1962). 'Doctoral students and research in educational psychology', *School and Society*, vol. 90, 375–7.

STANLEY, J. C. (1964). 'A paradigm for classroom experimentation', *American Psychologist*, vol. 19, 64–5.

STANLEY, J. C. (1966a). 'Preparing educational research specialists for school systems, a proposal', *Phi Delta Kappa*, vol. 47, 110–14.

STANLEY, J. C. (1966b). *Benefits of research design*. Final report to US Office of Education.

STANLEY, J. C. (ed.) (1967a). *Improving experimental design and statistical analysis*, Chicago: Rand McNally.

STANLEY, J. C. (1967b). 'On improving certain aspects of educational experimentation', in Stanley (1967a).

SUPER, D. E., AND BACHRACH, P. B. (1957). *Scientific careers and vocational development theory*, New York: Teachers' College, Columbia Univ.

TAYLOR, C. W., AND BARRON, F. (eds) (1963). *Scientific creativity*, New York: John Wiley.

THORSRUD, E., AND EMERY, F. E. (1969). *Medinflytande och engagemang i arbetet*, Stockholm: SAF.

TOFFLER, A. (1970). *Future Shock*, London: Bodley Head.

WATSON, J. D. (1968). *The Double Helix: a personal account of the discovery of the structure of DNA*, London: Weidenfeld & Nicolson.

WISEMAN, S. (1962). 'The tools of research—men and machines', Symposium: Educational research today III. *British J. Educ. Psychology*, vol. 32, 218–23.

WORTHEN, B. R., AND SANDERS, J. R. (1970). 'An analysis of 1968 AERA Employment Service data', *AERA Task Force on Training, Technical paper* no. 6.

Part two

Disciplinary perspectives

3 The philosopher's contribution to educational research

R. S. Peters and J. P. White

Introduction

Philosophy of education, like any other branch of philosophy, is concerned with problems about the meaning and inter-relationships of concepts and with the justification of assumptions—relevant, in this case, to the area of human endeavour, which we call 'education'. It is only to be expected, therefore, that a philosopher asked to discourse about the philosopher's contribution to educational research should begin 'It depends what you mean by "educational research" '.

In most of the literature on educational research there is an assumption, implicit or explicit, that educational research is a branch of psychology or social science. If this were so, then the philosopher could only contribute to educational research in so far as he concerned himself with the philosophy of these sciences—or in other words with questions about their concepts and methods. To take an example: many philosophers have worked on Freud's and Piaget's theories which are of obvious relevance to education. Questions are asked about the meaning of concepts such as 'unconscious mental processes' and 'assimilation'; and about the possibility of testing assumptions employing such concepts. Thus the philosopher could, even on this restricted view of 'research', contribute to educational research by helping to clarify and improve the theories employed by the scientists engaged on it. But then it might be asked: is not what the philosopher is doing, in working alongside the scientist, itself a form of educational research? And is the scientist himself not doing 'research' when he himself thinks about his concepts and methods, but only when he is actually doing experiments or conducting surveys? Is not a wider view of 'research' needed if justice is to be done to the more reflective side of scientific work ?

Of course our ordinary use of the term 'research' is not restricted in this way to enquiries in which hypotheses are subjected to observational tests. This would immediately rule out pure mathematics and most of history, as well as philosophy. And most of us would regard them as subjects in which research is possible. Indeed our ordinary use of the term 'research' would cover much more than this. For it would be perfectly good English to say that a man had better go and do a bit of research into train-timetables in order to find the best way to get from Oxford to Cambridge. C. A. Mace, in his *Psychology of Study*, maintained that 'research is, after all, just "search", looking for answers to questions and for solutions to problems.'[1] On such a broad view, which is enshrined in ordinary language, a man who tried to find out the number of grains of sand on Blackpool beach would be doing research—though it might well be pointless research.

Between the narrow view, which confines research to the attempt to test empirical hypotheses, and the much wider use of 'research' in ordinary language, there is the use of the term 'research' in academic institutions to refer to systematic and sustained enquiry carried out by people well versed in some form of thinking in order to answer some specific type of question. Philosophy, mathematics, and history count as research as well as the empirical sciences—and certainly Ph.Ds are awarded for all of them. We intend to interpret research in this way which is, to a certain extent, more restrictive than ordinary usage, but not so restrictive as the legislation of those who are unduly preoccupied with their eyes, ears, and finger-tips.

There is, as a matter of fact, an important philosophical lesson to be learnt from this preliminary probing into the meaning of the word 'research'. For it has revealed both that our concept of 'research' is a pretty fluid one and that there is a tendency to tighten it up in certain respects. There may be some point, for the sake of avoiding misunderstanding, in tightening it up in certain contexts; but it is absurd to introduce such a restrictive operation with the question 'What then *really is* research?' or 'Is research *really* possible in philosophy?' For, provided we get clear about the similarities and differences which enable us to use the *same* word 'research' rather differently in different contexts, what is the force of 'really'? What point is there, once we are clear about these distinctions, in asking the further question 'What does the word "research" really mean?' What *depends* on label-sticking once we are clear about the underlying facts?

Actually, of course, what often depends on being able to convince people that what you are doing 'really' is research is cash! But what lies behind this linkage of cash with certain sorts of enquiry that are accorded the title of 'research' which has now become honorific? Surely a conviction that some sorts of enquiry are so important that people should be paid to spend time on them. In this context, then, the fruitful question to ask is not whether philosophers are really doing research but whether their enquiries are important in trying to find answers to educational questions. We are glad to be able to report that even the Social Science Research Council, as well as the Department of Education and Science, are prepared to spend money on the philosophy of education. So, using this rather mundane criterion, we have a prima facie case for assuming that the philosophy of education has something of importance to contribute to the answering of educational questions—that it 'really is research'!

So far so good; but it could still be the case that the contribution of philosophy of education to educational research might be confined to clarifying the concepts and methods of those sciences such as psychology and sociology that are usually equated with educational research. The next question to be faced, therefore, is whether philosophy has something to contribute on its own which is independent of the contribution which it might make as the helpmeet of these sciences. To answer this question we must first ask 'What is educational research?' This depends on what we take education to be. If we take it to be the development of desirable states of mind involving depth and breadth of understanding,[2] then educational research is research which is connected with this end. We might, of course, call research 'educational' if it is merely concerned with what goes on in educational institutions. The difficulty with this, however, is that all sorts of things can go on in schools or colleges. On this criterion we could admit as educational research, for instance, research on the most nutritious school dinners that could be provided on a limited budget. But would this be educational research or research in dietetics? There would only seem to be point in calling it the former as well as the latter if, for instance, school dinners were thought to be so bad that they made the children incapable of being educated.

Philosophical research not geared to social science and psychology

If we grant that educational research is sustained systematic enquiry designed to provide us with new knowledge which is relevant to initiating people into such desirable states of mind, it is immediately apparent that these enquiries cannot be restricted to empirical enquiries. For how, by doing social science and psychology alone, could we answer questions about what is desirable and about the criteria which we could appeal to for deciding such questions? Now presumably we do not want just to moralize or to attitudinize about such matters. We want to get down to this question of the ethical foundations of education in a detailed, systematic way. And so immediately we have to do some research, to tackle these questions seriously with the help of moral philosophers in the concrete context of education. Underlying the whole question of the content of the curriculum lies the fundamental question in ethics, raised by the Utilitarians when they asked why poetry is preferable to push-pin. A curriculum is, of course, to be justified to a certain extent by reference to considerations extrinsic to education—e.g. the need for typists, scientists or statisticians. But it is also often argued that some pursuits are, educationally speaking, more worthwhile than others. How do we know this? How do we assess the claims of games alongside those of literature or music? Unless there are some good reasons for having some things on a curriculum rather than others, there is no rational basis for deciding on priorities on educational grounds, and teachers, generally speaking, are the arch-priests of an irrational cult.[3] Such questions may become increasingly important if teachers manage to attain more autonomy in determining the curriculum in their own schools.

This shows the relevance of a particular branch of philosophy, namely ethics, to education. But we are not arguing, of course, that the philosopher can answer questions about the content of the curriculum alone. He needs the help of psychologists, historians, and practical educators. To take a more straightforward parallel: a question such as 'Should corporal punishment be inflicted on children?' can only be adequately answered by drawing on psychological research about the effects of punishment, or the threat of punishment, on the character and behaviour of children. This example shows that explorations in ethical theory are not sufficient for answering an educational question; but it also shows that they are necessary. For the assumption that it is important to consider the effects of punishment, either on those punished or on others who may be deterred by the threat of punishment, presupposes an answer of a certain type to a philosophical question about the justification of punishment. It is assumed, in other words, that the justification of punishment is to be sought in its effects. Empirical probing into its effects presupposes that the utilitarian theory is justified about the *reasons* for punishing people and that the retributive theory is not, whatever the status of the latter as an answer to the question 'What do we mean by "punishment"?', to which it does provide a convincing answer. Philosophical argument is necessary to establish the merits of the utilitarian theory as providing an answer to the question 'What are the reasons for punishing people?' before the *relevance* of psychological research into the effects of punishment can be shown.[4] Philosophical research is thus necessary, though it may not be sufficient, to providing an adequate answer to the original question about the infliction of corporal punishment on children.

This example is a paradigm of how the philosopher can co-operate in an educational enquiry; for it shows *both* the lines along which work in a branch of philosophy, namely ethical theory, is crucial for education *and* the role of philosophy in mapping out the different types of question falling under the general problem of punishment. Much is made of the analytic aspect of philosophy these days. But we think that in the field of education philosophy also has an important synoptic function to perform in trying to get clear about how different types of enquiry are relevant and linked together in relation to particular educational issues. Without this preliminary clarification educational research of an empirical type would be both indeterminate and blind.

This point may sound obvious enough, but the extent to which it is neglected is depressing. On the one hand subjects like Latin or skills like reading are taught without any clear thought about how they fall under any concept of education. Or children are encouraged to go about gaily 'discovering' or 'experiencing' things on the completely indeterminate assumptions that this helps them to 'grow', become 'whole' or to 'realize themselves'. On the other hand pieces of psychology are eagerly pounced upon, and educational practice is geared towards them, without any clear thought about their relevance to education. At one time, for instance, Freudian theory was very popular in teacher training. But there was never any clear thought about the differences between an educational and a therapeutic situation and about the appropriateness of regarding mental health as an educational aim.[5] Then there was the period when psychological theories of 'needs' became incorporated into educational theory without any clear thought about the concept of 'need' and the possible ways in which a curriculum could be related to the 'needs of the child'.[6] Nowadays Piaget has, as it were, been 'discovered' by education lecturers in spite of the fact that his basic writings have been lying around for well over a quarter of a century. Concept-formation is all the rage. Whereas previously the manipulative play of the infant was thought to be significant for the emotional satisfaction which it afforded, it is now thought to be of great importance in concept formation. Whatever the evidence for these assumptions, the significant thing is that the shift of emphasis from emotional development and motivation to intellectual development has occurred largely because of the popularization of limited psychological theories. Attempts have seldom been made to assess the *relevance* of this psychological work to the highly complicated enterprise of educating children. This would require concentrated work of a philosophical sort on education and its aims and on the aspects of education that are relevant at different stages of development. This sort of work has not yet been done.

Countless questions in connexion with the nature and justification of the curriculum are also in need of philosophical examination. What is a school-subject? To what extent does it represent an accumulation of items which has a historical explanation rather than a rational justification? What degree of 'specialization' should there be at secondary school level?[7] Can moral education take place in a formal classroom situation? If there are distinct forms of knowledge such as mathematics, science, and history, should they be taught as such or as related to some common field?[8] At a time when many are advocating a 'topic-centred' curriculum for the non-academic child there is an appalling vagueness about the educational point of this exercise. Is it to motivate children better? Is it because the areas covered by the 'topics' are thought to contain a body of knowledge that every child should possess? Is it an exercise in moral education? Without some clarity about the point of this how can such experiments ever be assessed—unless they are rather negative containment operations to keep children busy while they reluctantly stay on at school.[9] Here again there are countless empirical issues which cannot be settled without preliminary philosophical analysis.

So far the place of philosophical research has been indicated in relation to the content of education. An equally strong case can be made for its necessity in relation to educational *procedures*. Since the 1931 Hadow Report much has been made of 'activity methods' and 'learning by experience'. But there have seldom been vaguer or more indeterminate concepts in the history of educational thought. Such methods are contrasted with formal instruction, which is often equated with sitting children down in rows on forms. Omnibus pronouncements are made about the ineffectiveness of 'rote learning' and the desirability of learning by 'discovery'. Yet 'discovery' is used in at least three different senses[10] and careful attention is seldom paid to the different sorts of things that have to be learnt.[11] Imitation and practice are obviously very important in the learning of skills; they are not so important in the learning of history. Again it is often said that there is no alternative but to 'indoctrinate' children in moral values; but the distinction between 'instruction' and 'indoctrination' is never clearly made.[12] And how does 'imparting' something differ from 'instructing' someone in something?[13] Is 'teaching' a specific sort of activity?[14] Another modern slogan is that learning should arise from the interests of the child. But does this mean his permanent interests, if he has any, or what he happens to be interested in at the moment? And how is 'interest' related to 'attention'? Should not the teacher consider, too, what is in a child's interest which may be something quite different from what the child is interested in?

Embedded in these procedures are principles which prescribe how children should be treated. Obviously, for instance, the principles of freedom and respect for persons are implicit in the procedures of the child-centred movement; a belief in authority is perhaps implicit in more 'formal' methods. Philosophical questions of far-reaching importance have to be raised about the meaning of such concepts in general and in relation to the educational situation; there is also the question of the justification of such principles, both in general, and in their application to the dealings of adults with children. There are, finally, questions of a similar sort about the distribution and organization of education which are raised by talk of 'equality of educational opportunity', 'the development of individual potentialities', and 'democracy in education'. The whole area of social philosophy as applied to education is opened up by such questions.[15]

So much then for philosophical research which is not explicitly geared to social science or psychology. Much of it is, as yet, at the programmatic stage, because the philosophy of education in any precise sense has only just got off the ground in this country. To a large extent the general woolliness of educational theory, which is one of the reasons for its low standing in academic circles, is due to the general lack of rigorous thinking about educational concepts and arguments which has characterized it in the past. We must now turn to philosophical research which is more specifically geared to social science and psychology.

Philosophical research geared to social science and psychology

(a) The first place where the philosopher might be able to help the social scientist is in the clarification of his aims. Handbooks on empirical educational research commonly assert that there are two kinds of educational research: basic (or fundamental) research and action (or operational) research. Basic research aims at the development of explanatory theory, action research is concerned with 'on the spot' improvement of current educational practices. Sometimes writers on educational research stress one sort of research rather than the other. Those who favour action research often do so because they have lost patience with basic research on account of its lack of applicability to the problem of the teacher in the classroom.[16] On the other hand, those, like Travers,[17] for whom the aim of educational research is the construction of theory, see little in common between action research and scientific research proper: much of action research, for Travers, is 'no more than good management'.

There is some point in both these charges; but they are directed against extreme examples of both sorts of research, neither of which may properly be called empirical research at all. Having lopped off the extremities, we may see that there is a large area of empirical research, where the division between 'action' and other research can usefully be made, and where a case can be made for both types.

(i) Let us see what substance there is in the first charge, that basic research is concerned with the development of pure theory, which is of no practical value. The object of attack here is, for instance, research carried out under the banner of one of the current psychological systems, like behaviourism or Lewinian field theory. In so far as these systems are aiming at the development of psychological theory after the model of physical theory, criticism of basic research of this sort is justified—not, however, on the ground of its demonstrable inapplicability to practical concerns (for physical theory often finds unexpected application in technology), but on the more radical ground that it is not at all clear that the social sciences or psychology *can* be theoretical sciences, in the sense that physics is theoretical—that is, that they can ever include overall theories which explain lower-level laws. For the phenomena of human behaviour require logically disparate types of concepts for their description and identification, and hence for their explanation. Actions can never be reduced to mere bodily movements; the difference between remembering and imagining can never be brought out by reference to the processes involved in either. Knee-jerks require a very different type of explanation from running a race, discovering from devising a scientific experiment, and toothache from laughing at a joke. D. W. Hamlyn's dismissal of theories of perception in psychology may perhaps be generalized to cover all social and psychological phenomena: 'If generalizations are all that can be produced about such phenomena, there is no place for theories either.'[18] The 'theories' of, for example, Hull, or the new school of information theorists as applied to human psychology, are more metaphysical treatises than empirical theories in their attempts to redescribe human nature in physicalistic concepts. Neither is it the case that research into Programmed Instruction provides a counterexample to the thesis that behaviourism is of little help to educational research, on the grounds that 'teaching machines are an example of the technological application of basic science (i.e. Skinnerian behaviourism)', as Skinner claims.[19] For, as he admits in his next sentence, 'It is true that current machines might have been designed in the light of class-room experience and commonsense, and that explanations of why they are effective can be paraphrased in traditional terms.'[20]

(ii) Just as doubts may be legitimately expressed about the empirical nature of many of the 'theories' in psychology, so, too, some of what passes for action research may be non-empirical. Travers may be right in claiming that it has, in some cases, little to do with scientific research. Let us take, for instance, the case described by Michael Young.[21] This is a geography lesson in which a hundredweight of clay was used to make an island, shaped into hills, valleys, cliffs, etc., and laid on a sheet of white paper. Sections of the island were cut off with a wire cutter and placed on the sheet. The outlines of the section were pencilled in. In this way the children learnt what is meant by a contour map. Young calls this the 'simplest model for "action research"—trying an idea out in the classroom and seeing if it appears to work'.

On this account, it may seem as if whenever a teacher has a bright idea for a lesson and tries it out on the children, she is doing research. But this is not always, or indeed usually the case. If she systematically tests her method of teaching by experiment (e.g. by using control groups, and by comparing the results of using this method with those obtained by using other teaching methods), then this might well be called empirical research in that some controlled confirmation was sought for her rational expectations. If, on the other hand, she is not interested in testing her ideas *in this way*, she cannot be said to be engaged on empirical research. This is not to say that she is not interested in testing her ideas *in any way*. The good teacher is always thinking out new ways of presenting her subject and rejecting those that are unsatisfactory. But much of this testing is done *a priori*, from reflection on the logical and epistemological priorities[22] in teaching her subject and on her knowledge of what sorts of things her class will respond to. The crucial test of her ideas is, of course, whether they will work, that is, whether the children succeed in learning what she teaches. But this is not a scientific test, because no attempt is made to control the variables involved. If an idea works, a teacher does not usually look further into the precise reasons why it works. If she can get her children to learn, her job, qua teacher, is done. Only when she looks more systematically into the reasons can she be said to be doing research.

If we rule out as forms of empirical research both the 'theoretical' research described in section (i) and what the teacher does who just tries out a new idea with no attempt at systematic testing, this does not mean that there is *no* point in distinguishing between 'action' and other sorts of empirical research. Let us compare, for instance, the work on the Initial Teaching Alphabet carried out by the Reading Research unit of the London University Institute of Education with Bernstein's work on the influence of the sorts of linguistic codes, into which children are initiated at home, on their educability.[23] Both studies are concerned with testing a causal hypothesis, in the first case the hypothesis that the unsystematic nature of English spelling may be an important cause of reading failure; and in the second case the hypothesis that an important cause of the poor scholastic performance of many working-class children is the 'restricted' language code which they have been taught. But the methods of testing these hypotheses are different. The ITA project compares the results of using traditional orthography and ITA in a number of infants' schools over a number of years; Bernstein's work analyses tape-recordings of children's speech to discover the elements that differentiate one speech-code from another and correlates the findings with other variables. It is clear that while both sorts of research face difficult problems in controlling variables, the ongoing form of research, of which the ITA project is an example, faces peculiar difficulties in this respect. How can one control for teacher-ability in the experimental and control groups? Will the teachers using ITA tend to be more enthusiastic because they are using a new method? Will the parents of children learning ITA be more interested in their children's progress for the same reason? J. D. Williams discusses these and several other difficulties in this sort of research, with special reference to the NFER project on teaching arithmetic.[24]

If ongoing studies of this sort are what is meant by 'action research', it is clear that what distinguishes action research from other research is not that action research is 'practical' while other research is 'theoretical'. All empirical educational research is practical in the sense that it can be seen as relevant to educational practice, and theoretical in the sense that the investigator is not himself concerned with the question 'What ought we to do?', but with the question, 'What are the facts?' and 'How can we explain them?' Neither is 'the critical feature of action research that it is not primarily concerned with the application of the findings beyond the group studied'.[25] The ITA project and the NFER project on teaching arithmetic are both concerned with problems of general application. The planning of the geography lesson described in the previous section may have had just one particular class in mind; but we have seen reasons why this should not be called empirical research. What *does* distinguish action research from other research is the added difficulty of controlling variables faced by any form of 'on the job' research. Some of these variables are impossible to control in 'action' research for moral reasons—for there are certain things that we would not do to children when trying to educate them—even in the interest of controlling the relevant variables. No teacher, for instance, would by being systematically unkind to a group of children in order to test the effect of this sort of interpersonal variable on their learning. In this respect the problem of controlling variables in action research is somewhat similar to problems encountered in making psycho-therapy 'scientific'.[26]

The above discussion is relevant to Michael Young's argument that new ideas on teaching methods are often the product of passing fashions, and that, to prevent this, all innovations should be tested by research. 'You can easily have innovation without research—the fashions which periodically sweep through the educational world are witness to that. You can, and almost always do, have research without innovation. This book urges—it is the principal theme—that the two should be brought together.'[27] The problem is to see *which* innovations need to be tested by research. While there is room for research on something like the ITA project, not all bright ideas that teachers have, as we have seen, are subjected to a direct empirical test; at best their use under practical conditions constitutes an indirect test of their validity. Other new ideas, such as the new emphasis on 'creativity', which Young mentions, may require conceptual analysis as much as empirical test, as we shall argue below in section (e).

(b) Closely linked with the philosopher's distrust of explanatory theory in the social sciences is his insistence that the latter are not based merely on external observation, as the physical sciences are. As Winch[28] points out, understanding social phenomena is qualitatively different from understanding physical phenomena. External observation is not enough: the student has to enter imaginatively into the phenomena in question if he is to make sense of them. The anthropologist describing the behaviour of a primitive tribe, the psychiatrist studying schizophrenia, have to understand the conceptual schemes of the tribesmen or of the schizophrenic from the inside. For human actions are not simply bodily movements, which can be identified by external observation alone; their identification normally depends on identifying the intention behind them. So understanding human behaviour involves understanding how men see what they are doing. Bantock[29] has shown how the failure to take this into account has affected educational research. He points out, for instance, that the use of the questionnaire method in educational research often fails to do justice to Winch's point. While a student of the effects of television on the child might well get useful information by asking 'For how long did you watch television last night?', getting the child to complete the sentences 'A good husband is a man who . . .' and 'A good wife is a woman who . . .' in an attempt to find out whether television affects the child's ideas about what makes a good husband or wife,[30] does not take into account the way the child understands the question, which, if it differs from child to child, robs the final classification of children's replies of most of its value. (c) As Bantock gives one or two other interesting examples of this overemphasis on external observation, we will say no more about this but pass on to another point: that social scientists sometimes reach a conclusion by empirical evidence, which could with much less trouble have been reached by philosophical reflection. This confusion between logical and empirical issues has been discussed in the field of general psychology in, for example, D. W. Hamlyn's critique of the Gestalt theory of perception in his *Psychology of Perception*. The so-called 'figure-ground hypothesis', for instance, which has been the subject of many experiments, is not an empirical hypothesis, but is true in virtue of what we *mean* by an object of perception: we would not call anything an object unless it could be distinguished from everything else that formed its background (pp. 55–6). Hamlyn has recently discovered a further example of this confusion between the logical and the psychological in research which is more educationally relevant.[31] This is Piaget's work on how young children learn the concepts of elementary physics, the 'conservation studies', in which empirical research revealed that children who saw water poured from a short, fat jar into a tall, thin one said that they thought there was more in the latter than in the former, whereas in fact the quantity of water remained unchanged. Only gradually did the children proceed from the more concrete notion that identity depends on height to the more abstract one that it depends on volume. Hamlyn maintains that there is no need to resort to empirical studies to see that children's concept-learning proceeds from the concrete to the abstract; it is something that could have been discovered by reflection. Such a progression is presupposed in the notion of normal human development. Given that we are talking of normal human children it could not but be true that they develop in this way.[32] If this is indeed a conceptual truth, then there is no *point* in further observations to prove the hypothesis (just as there would be no point in taking a poll of bachelors to prove the hypothesis that all bachelors are unmarried). If one accepts Hamlyn's argument on this crucial Piagetian 'discovery', it remains to be seen how much of Piaget's work on other topics has supported conclusions that embody logical truths of this kind.[33] In brief the relationship between the logical and the psychological aspects of teaching particular subjects such as mathematics, science, history, and music has yet to be explored. To what extent must teaching depend on the logical features of what is being taught and to what extent are psychological generalizations possible about such matters?[34] To what extent is 'intellectual development' a matter of the conceptual and logical structure of the different forms of thought such as mathematics, science, and morals and not a matter for psychologists at all?

More clarity about such matters is necessary not simply as an aid to efficient teaching; it is also of crucial importance in the training of teachers. One finds frequently in colleges of education, especially those concerned with the training of primary teachers, a state of cold war between the education lecturers and the subject lecturers. This is partly, of course, a power struggle; it is partly also a reflection of deep-seated insecurities in that education lecturers tend to know a lot about small children but very little about subjects, whereas subject lecturers, whose experience has been predominantly in secondary schools, know a lot about a subject, but little about small children. But underlying this struggle is a fundamental lack of clarity about the logical as distinct from the psychological aspects of learning. This is only exacerbated by the works of Piaget and Bruner, which are widely read, in which such questions are systematically confused. This is a crucial area in the philosophy of education where fundamental research is needed.

(d) Since Piaget's work is at present influential in educational circles, it is worth mentioning another argument cited in Hamlyn's article,[35] which illustrates a rather different point. This is that conclusions which could have been reached by philosophical reflection are sometimes reached not after empirical enquiry as in (c), but by using a speculative model. Hamlyn's example is of Piaget's theory of concept formation. Piaget argues that intelligence grows by the concurrent 'accommodation' of the subject's intellectual structures to perceived objects and 'assimilation' of these objects to the intellectual structures —a process of mutual modification of subject and object which is found also in biological processes like digestion. Piaget upholds such a theory as against the associationist abstractionism of S-R schools and against the innate-ideas view of the Gestaltists. But what are in dispute here are not three different psychological, i.e. empirical, hypotheses, but three philosophical positions about the origins of our concepts, which go back at least as far as Kant, Locke and Plato respectively. Piaget's own notion is the Kantian one—which is also the correct one—that in order to form our empirical concepts we need not only experience of phenomena in the world, but also a conceptual scheme which we bring to our experience and fit over it (cf. assimilation). He could have reached this conclusion by reflection, and thereby avoided the misleading implications of his biological model, which are analysed in Hamlyn's article. The biological model, in other words, is simply a piece of pseudo-science.

(e) So far, we have not explicitly mentioned one of the most important ways in which the philosopher can help the empirical educational researcher. By drawing attention to the use of words for whose application no clear criteria are provided, he can save the scientist much time which might otherwise have been spent on testing hypotheses whose meaning was unclear. We will take as an example the work that has been recently done in the field of creativity. It has been claimed that certain schoolchildren are more 'creative' than others and tests have been devised to determine who they are—the so-called 'creativity tests', stemming from Guilford and applied to schoolchildren by Getzels and Jackson in their recent book.[36] Now when philosophers have objected to the use of intelligence tests to test intelligence,[37] this has not been because they have not been fairly clear what is meant by the phrase 'he is an intelligent child'; it is because they have questioned, for instance, whether a low score on the tests does not in many cases indicate a lack of interest in solving anagrams and extrapolating from a series, rather than low intelligence. But the problem they face when they turn to creativity tests and other work on creativity is what 'creativity' itself means. As the word is used in recent literature it appears to have a number of different meanings in different contexts.

Some say, for instance, that young children's paintings, which have been produced as an exercise of 'free expression' without guidance by the teacher, manifest creativity. A creative piece of work, in this context, seems to mean one which is not in conformity with expected rules. Now a child is sometimes also said to be showing creativity when he produces unusual answers to the question 'What may a brick be used for?' in a creativity test.[38] In both these cases the productions of the children concerned manifest departures from conventional expectations. But there is a difference of intention between them: the child artist is not—usually at any rate—intending to produce unconventional pictures, while the other child *is* intending to produce unconventional uses for a brick. This presupposes that he knows what the conventional uses are. So while *knowledge* of rules and conventions is built into the concept of creativity in the second case, as well as the production of something that is actually different from conventional expectations, no such knowledge is implied in the case of the child artist's creativity.

Of further interest, however, to the educational philosopher is the relevance of *either* concept of creativity to education. For if education is initiation into desirable states of mind, there is not necessarily anything desirable in getting children to think up ideas which are merely different from usual expectations. Mental homes, after all, are full of people who can do this. The sense of 'creativity' relevant to education is that in virtue of which we might call E. M. Forster a 'creative writer' while denying the application of the term to, say, Agatha Christie. That is, we call Forster a creative writer not merely because he has produced something original, in the sense of different from conventional writing, but also because his work is valuable according to criteria of aesthetic value. Similarly, Einstein and Darwin may be called creative scientists because they produced valid hypotheses of great scientific value. If, as educators, we want to encourage creativity in children, this must be in the third sense of the term just given. Encouraging creativity in children must be encouraging them to produce ideas or pieces of work which are not only new, but valuable, according to the different criteria of value enshrined in different forms of thought. (It is another question how far children can be creative in this sense, given that creativity in any discipline presupposes an initiation into that discipline. It is a further question still how far, assuming that children can be encouraged to be creative, creativity should be emphasized at the expense of other educational aims, like teaching children to appreciate others' work, rather than create work of their own.) Given, too that creativity in this third sense is specific to a particular discipline (for criteria of value differ from discipline to discipline) it is hard to see how one can talk, as Getzels and Jackson do, of 'highly-creative' people as if creativity were a general trait.

A more constructive role for philosophers of education?

A fair comment on philosophers in the past has been that they often indulged in criticism of social science and psychology without troubling to inform themselves about what was going on. This criticism, however, would not be fair in relation to the modern generations of philosophers many of whom have written about developments in psychology, history and social science in a very informed way. A more apposite comment on their work would be that they always seem to be critical, as it were, after the event. They do not work with psychologists or social scientists in clarifying theories that are being launched; rather they shoot them down when they are aloft. It would, therefore, be quite in place for a social scientist or psychologist to remark rather irritably that if philosophers are all that interested in the concepts and methods of social science and psychology, and if they think that they have relevant remarks to make about them, they should make them at a stage when some account can be taken of their comments.

In 1967 a concentrated colloquium was held in Chicago in which four eminent American psychologists were walled up for five days with four philosophers in the attempt to get clearer about problems to do with the explanation of human behaviour.[39] One of the convictions which united the philosophers was that their concern about concepts was not indicative of an interest in verbal subtleties for their own sake. Rather they were attempting to see through the words in order to get a better understanding of how things are and how best they were to be explained. Indeed one of the philosophers recalled how Lavoisier's initial ambition to revise chemical nomenclature had insensibly led him to a complete reconstruction of chemical theory. But Lavoisier was not interested in terminology just for its own sake. And how could we have *improved* it without regard to facts? The notion that the philosopher is only interested in destructive criticism or in making purely verbal points is one that is connected more with the modern 'image' of the philosopher than with the substance of his activities. In our view most of the best work in British philosophy since the time of Thomas Hobbes has been generated by the stimulation of analytic acumen and constructive imagination by excitement about developments in mathematics and the sciences and worry about social and political change.

This close connexion between philosophy and other theoretical and practical activities applies as much in the philosophy of education generally as it does in that particular portion of it that is concerned with the philosophy of psychology and the social sciences. It would be hopeless to have people doing research in this field who are not well trained in general philosophy; but it would be equally hopeless to have people without first-hand experience of teaching and without a vital concern for how things are and ought to be in our educational system. Perhaps in one respect we have an advantage for pursuing this kind of co-operative research in educational departments. Teaching and research in the 'pure disciplines' are so organized in universities that this sort of co-operation in research is not always easy to contrive, even if the requisite good-will is present on both sides. In educational research, however, it is not so difficult because departments and institutes of education and research institutions are coming increasingly to reflect the obvious truth that education is a 'field' or a collection of practical activities to which philosophy, psychology, social science and history must necessarily contribute. There must, therefore, be co-operation at the outset between representatives of the different disciplines which are directly relevant to education if any clear-cut answers to educational questions are to be obtained. Research projects are beginning, therefore, to include philosophers from the start. The research, for instance, which was done on moral education by the Farmington Trust in connexion with the Oxford Department of Education, was directed by a philosopher working in conjunction with a sociologist and a psychologist. Philosophers were involved in the attempt to formulate the objectives of comprehensive schools in the large-scale research into comprehensive education which was undertaken by the NFER under the sponsorship of the Department of Education and Science. A philosopher was on the committee for determining criteria of curriculum evaluation set up by the Schools Council. It is to be hoped that it will become normal practice for educational research to be conducted by interdisciplinary research teams and that such teams will include someone with a philosophical training.

These developments are indicative of two things which could be of great importance to the future of the philosophy of education. On the one hand they show that there is a growing realization that the philosophical dimension of educational research is an important one and that there are crucial questions in research that are not purely empirical. On the other hand they show that, though philosophers have abandoned the view that they are spectators of all time and all existence whose job it is to make oracular pronouncements about the purpose of life and of education, they need not restrict their activities to commenting critically on the theorizing and practical endeavours of others. They have also a more constructive role to play in the development of policy based on clear-headed research.

NOTES

[1] C. A. Mace, *The Psychology of Study*, London: Penguin, 1963, p. 108.
[2] R. S. Peters, 'Education and the educated man' in R. F. Dearden, P. H. Hirst and R. S. Peters (eds), *Education and the Development of Reason*, London: Routledge & Kegan Paul, 1972.
[3] See R. S. Peters, *Ethics and Education*, London: Allen & Unwin, 1966, ch. v; 'The justification of education' in R. S. Peters (ed.), *The Philosophy of Education*, London: OUP, 1973.
[4] Ibid., ch. x.
[5] See R. S. Peters, 'Mental health as an educational aim' in T. H. B. Hollins (ed.), *Aims in Education*, Manchester University Press, 1964.
[6] See B. P. Komisar, ' "Need" and needs-curriculum' in B. O. Smith and R. H. Ennis, *Language and Concepts in Education*, Chicago: Rand McNally, 1961 and R. F. Dearden, ' "Needs" in education' in *British Journal of Educational Studies*, November 1966.
[7] See H. S. Broudy, B. O. Smith, and J. R. Burnett, *Democracy and Excellence in American Secondary Education*, Chicago: Rand McNally, 1964.
[8] See P. H. Hirst, 'Liberal education and the nature of knowledge' in R. D. Archambault, *Philosophical Analysis and Education*, London: Routledge & Kegan Paul, 1965.
[9] See P. H. Hirst, 'The curriculum' in *The Educational Implications of Social and Economic Change*, Schools Council Working Paper, No. 12.
[10] See R. F. Dearden, 'Instruction and learning by discovery' in R. S. Peters (ed.), *The Concept of Education*, London: Routledge & Kegan Paul, 1967.
[11] See R. S. Peters, 'What is an educational process?' in ibid.
[12] See J. P. White, 'Indoctrination' in ibid.
[13] See M. Oakeshott, 'Teaching and learning' in ibid.
[14] See I. Scheffler, *The Language of Education* (Springfield, Illinois: Thomas, 1960) ch. iv.
[15] See R. S. Peters, *Ethics and Education*, Parts II and III.
[16] See, for example, J. W. Best, *Research in Education*, Englewood-Cliffs: Prentice-Hall, 1959, pp. 8–11.
[17] R. M. W. Travers, *An Introduction to Educational Research*, New York: Macmillan, 1958, p. 66.
[18] D. W. Hamlyn, *The Psychology of Perception*, London: Routledge & Kegan Paul, 1957.
[19] B. F. Skinner, 'Why we need teaching machines' in *Harvard Educational Review*, vol. xxxi, Fall, 1961, 397.
[20] On this, see I. Scheffler, 'A note on behaviourism as an educational theory', in *Harvard Educational Review*, vol. xxxii, Spring, 1962, 210–13.
[21] M. Young, *Innovation and Research in Education*, London: Routledge & Kegan Paul, 1965, pp. 89–91.
[22] On this point, see D. W. Hamlyn, 'The logical and psychological aspects of learning' in R. S. Peters (ed.), *The Concept of Education*, London: Routledge & Kegan Paul, 1967.

[23] B. B. Bernstein, 'A socio-linguistic approach to social learning' in J. Gould (ed.), *Penguin Survey of the Social Sciences, 1965*, London: Penguin 1965.

[24] J. D. Williams, 'Some problems involved in the experimental comparisons of teaching methods', in *Education Research*, November, 1965.

[25] H. H. McAshan, *Elements of Educational Research*, New York: McGraw-Hill, 1963, pp. 13–14.

[26] For further discussion of these problems see R. S. Peters, *Brett's History of Psychology*, London: Allen & Unwin, rev. ed. 1962, pp. 751–61.

[27] M. Young, *Innovation and Research in Education*, London: Routledge & Kegan Paul, 1965, p. 8.

[28] P. Winch, *The Idea of a Social Science*, London: Routledge & Kegan Paul, 1958.

[29] G. H. Bantock, 'Educational research: a criticism' in *Harvard Educational Review*, vol. xxxi, 1961, 264–80.

[30] H. T. Himmelweit, *et al.*, *Television and the Child*, London: Oxford University Press, 1958, p. 247.

[31] D. W. Hamlyn, 'The logical and psychological aspects of learning' in R. S. Peters, (ed.), *The Concept of Education*, London: Routledge & Kegan Paul, 1967.

[32] See D. W. Hamlyn, op. cit., for details of this argument.

[33] Even if this thesis is accepted there might still be point in performing Piagetian type experiments in order to communicate such conceptual truths clearly to teachers and parents, who, for various reasons, are more prepared to take notice of this form of demonstration. It could be the case, too, that many adults are still in their thinking about learning, at a very concrete stage. The concept of 'normal development' may therefore have to be fixed more determinately by many such examples of children developing 'normally', in the only way, logically speaking, that they could develop. [We owe this point to Mr R. Cave and Miss M. Bradley who raised it in discussion at the Cambridge Institute of Education.]

[34] See P. H. Hirst, 'The logical and psychological aspects of teaching a subject', in R. S. Peters (ed.), *The Concept of Education*, London: Routledge & Kegan Paul, 1967.

[35] D. W. Hamlyn, op. cit.

[36] J. W. Getzels and P. W. Jackson, *Creativity and Intelligence*, New York: Wiley, 1962.

[37] A. MacIntyre, 'Purpose and intelligent action', in *Proc. Arist. Soc. supp. vol.* 1960.

[38] Cf. Getzels and Jackson, op. cit. See also J. P. White, 'Creativity and education' in *British Journal of Educational Studies*, June 1968.

[39] Their deliberations were later published in a book edited by T. Mischel called *Human Action*, New York: Academic Press, 1969. A subsequent meeting was also held in 1969 and published as T. Mischel (ed.), *Cognitive Development and Epistemology*, New York: Academic Press, 1971.

4 The psychologist's contribution to educational research

J. D. Nisbet and N. J. Entwistle

Peters and White in their contribution to this book define educational research as sustained systematic enquiry designed to provide us with new knowledge which is relevant to initiating people into desirable states of mind. Other definitions include 'information-generating processes which are predictive and theoretical and not merely data-collecting' (Floyd Robinson); and 'the thorough and methodical investigation of educational phenomena leading to discovery of verifiable facts and relationships which are fundamental to the systematic understanding and explanation of phenomena' (R. Oxtoby). All these definitions stress contribution to knowledge: essentially they put educational research into the category of pure research. This is certainly one form of educational research, though in this form it is difficult to distinguish it from psychological or sociological research.

If, instead, educational research is defined more narrowly, the boundary becomes more clear between pure research in the social sciences and educational research in the area of the applied sciences. A definition in these terms would take the form: educational research consists in careful, systematic attempts to understand the educational process and, through understanding, to improve its efficiency. This shift of emphasis from 'understanding' to 'improvement' is likely to be disputed by many who are active in what they claim to be wholly respectable educational research which does not aim at 'improvement'—such as historical studies or comparative education. For such studies, a broader definition must be accepted and a broad definition may be appropriate in certain types of discussion. If the discussion is in practical terms, with reference to conditions as they are, it may be more realistic to define educational research in the more restricted sense set out above, as an applied branch of study. A definition which includes the notion of 'improvement' is increasingly being applied (often implicitly) in deciding priorities in educational research. Though the following quotation comes from a statement of policy by the Malmö school of education in Sweden, the point of view is certainly shared by educational research organizations in many other countries:

> The following principles have been used as general guiding lines in our choice of research problems. First: the project should be of such a kind that its results have a reasonable chance of being of some importance and consequence for decisions and actions related to current Swedish school problems. This means, for instance, that certain types of comparative and historic research tasks have to be ranked low on our priority list. Second: explicitly or implicitly, the projects should raise problems that have some general interest; at least some aspects of a project should be of interest even to educationalists outside Sweden. As far as possible we like to aim at general theories about the relationships between actions and consequences in educational situations. Nothing is more likely to be practical than theories of this kind, in the long run. The too specific tasks—e.g. construction of tests or study material without any such general problem attached—would not be listed among the primary jobs of our research department.

The second of the principles stated provides the answer to those who fear that this narrow definition of education might be dangerously restrictive. The definition implies for the research worker an active involvement in improving the effectiveness of educational methods. If misused, this involvement might be contrary to the best traditions of disinterested research. But it would be unrealistic to suggest that the majority of research workers in an applied field are disinterested in the practical effects of their research findings. They do care and, especially in the context of education, it is surely right to feel this way.

The role of the psychologist varies for different meanings of the term, 'educational research'. Clearly, for pure or basic research, which might equally be classified as 'psychological research', he has a central role to play. In applied research, his role is too often underrated. Here, too, at least in the present state of knowledge, his contribution is of the first importance. Sometimes this contribution is made by a psychologist, so designated as a member of a research team: at other times, this contribution is made by others who, for this purpose, must think as psychologists. The implication is that thorough training in psychology is an essential element in the training of a research worker. (Perhaps the same argument can be extended to sociology; but that is another question.)

The psychologist is not merely an auxiliary in a research team, called on to apply, or advise on applying, tests. This is perhaps the best known of his contributions to research, and it represents an important basic element in a research project. This is the 'psychometrist' role. The solution of problems in education requires the collection of relevant information, and usually this involves measurement or special techniques of assessment. It is a common error to assume that measurement means testing. Recent years have seen the development of standard procedures for a whole range of techniques —the assessment of personality by inventories, attitude scales and projective methods; procedures for the design of questionnaires and structured interviews; techniques for recording interactions in small groups. The psychologist in educational research now has a responsibility to widen the area of inquiry, which in the past was too often restricted to the knowledge-transmitting function. To quote again from the Malmö statement of policy:

> In many countries both the school itself and school-related research has had what might be termed a built-in intellectualistic one-eyedness. The measurement of knowledge, the grading and the assessment of intelligence have been given focal attention, whereas individual diagnosis, mental hygiene, education to develop study interest and adequate study habits etc have very often been given only occasional attention. Perhaps this has been natural from the point of view of research economy; in the field of achievement measurements we usually feel most certain that we can produce clear results within a short time span. But it ought to be self-evident that, in spite of this, research should not confine itself exclusively within the barriers of this 'easy' field. Exploring new areas should be especially important in a country like Sweden, where the school plans have underlined

the personality-developing function of the school so emphatically.

At a more general level, the psychologist also contributes a skill in interpreting data. He has—or should have been given in his training—experience of common fallacies, statistical traps and self-fulfilling prophecies. One common fallacy, for example, is the 'naming fallacy': one assumes that a test called a 'reading test' measures reading ability, whereas it may measure speed of working; or that a non-verbal test is independent of verbal ability, though the instructions are printed; or that one has eliminated the influence of social class, by partialling out 'father's occupation on the Registrar-General's Scale', which leaves a considerable amount of the variance uncontrolled. The two commonest statistical traps in educational research are probably regression, and homogeneity of variance caused by a selected sample and resulting in spurious attenuation of correlation coefficients. The self-fulfilling prophecy is well-known, but still crops up in experimental designs which produce spurious and predictable results, and in failure to control for 'Hawthorne' effect. All these are points which the psychologist must put forward, not merely in interpretation of findings but in anticipation at the planning stage. More positively, he has useful concepts for thinking about data: validity and reliability, for example, or dimensions of measurement, and the whole range of concepts formalized in statistical procedures—critical ratio, t, χ^2, variance, and so on.

But the third and most important level at which the psychologist influences and contributes to educational research is at the level of concepts and theories. The concepts of psychology provide a *language* for handling educational problems. One might say that psychology provides both the vocabulary and the grammar of educational discussion. Admittedly, the psychologist has no exclusive claim to providing this language. The philosopher and the sociologist may equally claim that educational discussion should be conducted in their languages. But in this generation, most of the thinking on education is based on psychological concepts.

This can best be demonstrated by noting the changing pattern of official reports on education. In the nineteenth century, naturally enough, reports contained no explicit psychological evidence. Conclusions were reached after detailed examination of expert witnesses, whose opinions were often recorded for posterity to ponder over. The first report to acknowledge the influence of psychological research findings was from the Hadow Committee (1926). The reorganization of the whole educational system by dividing at age 11+ into primary schools for children and secondary schools for adolescents was justified by appeals to research evidence on the onset of adolescence. But the actual research findings on which this decision was supposed to be based are not presented in the report. Five years later, however, the Hadow Report on primary education did contain an appendix in which Burt was allowed to explain the psychological evidence presented to the commission. The body of the report shows traces of psychological thinking, but the predominant influence is still the committee's instinct for what would be right for children in primary schools. Again in the Norwood Report there is a notorious misuse of psychology to justify the continuance of a system of education which was largely the result of a series of historical 'accidents'. The tri-partite division into children who were good at logical reasoning, those who had high level technical skills and those who were less well endowed followed no clearly defined psychological evidence. The tendency to find convenient psychological and sociological research findings to explain present practice can still be found in recent reports, but more weight is now being placed on objectively evaluated research. The change began in 1948 with the publication of the report, *Standards of Reading Ability*. This report was the first one to use sophisticated sampling techniques, and the results showed clearly that many current assertions about illiteracy were exaggerated. In 1954 the report on *Early Leaving* provided an outstanding example of the use of a survey in which statistical evidence was used meticulously to develop the case for change. The effect of social class on early leaving from secondary school courses was demonstrated by a well-designed investigation, and the publication of the report was followed by a remarkable lengthening of the average school life. Possibly this would have happened in any case: the resulting trend towards staying on at school has certainly upset projected estimates of numbers seeking higher education. In the sphere of educational reports, *Early Leaving* could be said to mark the coming of age of statistical surveys.

Since then each report has had its accompanying survey. The Crowther Report on education between 15 and 18 used its surveys to support the argument of an untapped reserve of ability. The Robbins Report used statistics extensively to support its recommendation for expansion of higher education. Newsom and Plowden also have shown conclusions which reflect at least some of the statistical results of their own empirical enquiries. But still the recommendations ignore inconvenient findings. For example, the Plowden Report in its discussions over the relative advantages of 11, 12 and 13 as the age of transfer to secondary education does not mention that, although primary school head teachers, in their questionnaire survey, considered 12 to be the best age, secondary school heads were equally strongly opposed to this change. Again, in spite of its extensive social survey, the Plowden Committee stated that there was 'no evidence of the value of nursery schools and so we will accept the opinion of experienced teachers that they are of value'.

Today, no large-scale report on education is adequate without its supporting survey. All aspects of educational innovation—programmed learning, curriculum development, examination reform, and so on—are expected to be firmly based on experimental findings which in turn rest on procedures borrowed from psychological inquiry or from the other social sciences. The administrator has quickly learned to use the vocabulary of psychology; the teacher also is learning to do this, though more slowly. Too often, however, they are merely using the language, without mastering the ideas.

The Newsom Report, for example, included a survey based on two independent and interpenetrating samples each of seventy-five secondary modern schools, stratified by size, sex and region, together with a selection of twelve comprehensive schools and a supplementary sample of twenty schools in the slums (to allow a special study of this category). The heads of these schools were first asked to comment freely on their schools and their problems. They also completed four questionnaires, on pupils' time-tables, on staffing, on school buildings and equipment, and on examinations. A reading test (the same as that used in the 1948 survey and in two later follow-up studies) was given to all the pupils. Finally, a variety of more detailed information was collected for a one-in-three sample of the fourth-year pupils in the same schools. Some of the material thus assembled was worked into the text, but there is also a considerable section of part three of the Newsom Report which touches the depths of triviality. The sample of pupils was divided by the reading test score into a top quarter, a middle half and a bottom quarter, and for each group a typical boy and girl are described—John and Mary Brown, John and Mary Jones, John and Mary Robinson. John Jones, for example, 'is probably about 5 ft 4½ in. in height though he is quite likely to be any height between 5 ft 3 in. and 5 ft 7 in. and, of course, may be even taller or shorter'.

This kind of material is a parody of the psychologist's contribution to educational research, but at least its irrelevance is obvious. Less obvious is a different kind of weakness in the use of psychological ideas in popular thinking about education. Those who have acquired merely the vocabulary of the social sciences, but are untrained (or self-trained) in psychology, are liable to be influenced by unstated assumptions in the concepts and vocabulary which they use and take for granted, e.g. 'discovery', 'activity', 'self-expression', children's 'needs', 'intelligence', 'mental health', 'creativity' and, currently, 'Piagetian stages'. The psychologist, one would hope, has been trained to *think through* these concepts, and so to be on guard against naive over-simplifications. People seize on the word which applies a closure to their problems—e.g. dyslexia as the 'cause' of failing to learn to read (when it is merely a classical term for poor reading), or minimal but undetectable brain injury as a 'cause' of poor performance.

Peters would not be trapped by such circular arguments, and he might claim that sorting out the logic is really the philosopher's contribution. But, for certain terms in common use in education, the philosophical attempts at clarification begin to look like academic wrangles in semantics. It is more helpful for the teacher to have an operational definition. The term, 'free activity', for example, could be elucidated either by an understanding of the component words, or by a description of what children actually do during periods of 'free activity'. The latter description would help teachers to communicate more effectively, and it would also help the linguistic philosophers to decide whether the words used described the activity appropriately. Psychologist and philosopher make important, though different, contributions; but the psychologist, like the philosopher, is concerned with helping teachers to define their terminology, and to analyse their interpretations of education more clearly.

The point which is being made here is closely related to the argument in Waismann (*How I See Philosophy*, 1968), when he analyses the philosopher's contribution to science. What he says about philosophy can be applied, in our context, to the role of psychology in educational research: 'A philosophy is an attempt to unfreeze habits of thinking, to replace them by less stiff and restricting ones. Of course, these may in time harden, with the result that they clog progress . . . . The liberators of yesterday may turn into the tyrant of tomorrow' (p. 34). In short, we do not need to show that psychology can contribute to educational research today: we need to make sure that we fully understand the terms and ideas of psychology which we use, or they may limit our thinking just as drastically as half-understood religious notions have limited it in the past.

All this has important implications for the training of the psychologist as a research worker in education. It is clearly not sufficient merely to teach him basic psychological theories and techniques of research. These two components are essential, but so also is a third—experience in handling research data, in reading and criticizing research, in discussing and analysing ideas and concepts. Within the syllabus of training, this means establishing a bridge between theories and techniques. This is no different from what has been accepted traditionally as a main objective of university education, but it needs to be stated specifically, and to be taught deliberately.

5 Research in the history of education

Brian Simon

A committee on the Role of Education in American History was formed in the United States over ten years ago, following on a complaint by historians that imperfect knowledge of educational history had had an adverse effect on 'the planning of curricula, the formulation of policy, and the administration of educational agencies' in the post-war crisis of American education.[1] This may be seen as a criticism of the neglect of education by historians, or of the history of education as so far written. It may also be taken as a welcome recognition that the historical approach is indispensable to an understanding of the nature of education and the direction in which it is developing.

This was once generally accepted in England. For instance, pre-war official reports were prefaced by a scholarly historical introduction: the three Hadow Reports and the Spens Report are examples. More recently it has been usual to depend on what might be called a psycho-sociological commentary of a generalized kind, accompanied by somewhat casual enquiry into practices in other countries. It would be interesting to look into the reasons for this. But that neither the Crowther Report (1958), the Newsom Report (1963), the Plowden Report (1966), nor at the other end of the scale the Robbins Report (1963) based discussions on a firm historical foundation, marks a deterioration in the precision and relevance of educational thinking as a guide to policy making.

This is not to suggest that study of the history of education should be framed to guide politicians in drawing up policies. It is to underline that study of the historical formation of educational institutions, administration, subject-matter, teaching methods, is relevant for all concerned with the effective development of education. More generally, historical research can assist towards an understanding of current ideas and practices which often remain unexamined even while they daily shape developments in schools and universities. Attitudes to education have often been much influenced by different disciplines as they have emerged on to the stage and been propagated in various ways. That a number of schools of psychology have taken root, sometimes directly at war with each other, that sociology speaks with more than one voice and often in opposition to psychology, that history presents various interpretations in a multiplicity of branches, that the scope of philosophy has been newly defined and redefined—all this has led to confusion of thought about education. It is not, therefore, enough for specialists to criticize educationists for this confusion and advocate a more concentrated dose of the same medicines as a remedy. Self-criticism is also in order and efforts to repair the damage.

If, then, it is claimed that the historical approach is essential to understanding any field, in this case the complex field of education, historians must make good that claim. They must be capable of studying not merely the external structure of the educational system but aspects of educational practice and the operative ideas which have helped to shape curricula and teaching, forms of internal school organization, and attitudes to children generally. Investigation of the almost geological layering of ideas and practices at different stages—from nursery school to university—is, perhaps, one of the most useful tasks the historian can undertake. For this facilitates an objective approach both to practical problems and the tools used for their solution, as well as to the different techniques and theories which have come to bear directly or indirectly over the years up to the present. To state the matter in this way is to suggest a more conscious approach to the history of education than there has yet been.

I

Criticism of the inadequacy of historical studies to date can justifiably centre on the lack of a clear approach to the field, or the narrowness with which 'education' has been defined and described. In general, it has been defined too exclusively in terms of formal instruction, from the standpoint of the administrator or educator, so leaving aside the innumerable other agencies which exercise an influence on the physical, moral and mental development of the young; or, to extend the scope still further, the population as a whole. In other words, there has been little attempt to assess education from the point of view of those experiencing it, or subject to its influence.

The historian of education who concentrates on describing the enormous expansion of the organized educational system in the modern age, and the increasing enlightenment of educational thought and practice, may end by presenting a picture of schooling and its influence directly at odds with the actual position on the ground.[2] It is not that what is said is inaccurate in detail, but that it may be woven into a whole which patently fails to correspond to, or cover, the facts—and so is an inadequate guide to the teacher in the classroom and the framer of policy alike.

The point may be put in another way by saying that standard accounts of the development of education lack breadth and depth, in terms of a psychological and sociological understanding of what education is and does, and also in terms of historical understanding. It is on the latter point that criticism has concentrated in America where inflated ideas about the efficacy of the public school system, undermined in the difficult post-war conditions, were again rudely shaken by the Soviet sputnik of 1957. Three years later there appeared a critical study by a leading historian, Bernard Bailyn, prepared under the auspices of the Institute of Early American History and Culture. Pointing to the limitations of influential historical accounts, the writer proposed that historical study of education should cover 'the entire process by which a culture transmits itself across the generations'.[3] In so doing, he drew attention to key aspects altogether left aside by concentration on formal schooling, notably the family as a primary educational institution, apprenticeship as a major educational agency over many years, and the many institutions bearing on adult education. To open up the perspective in this way made clear the great gaps to be filled:[4]

> the needs and opportunities for study are manifest, indeed limitless, shifting and multiplying with the historians' angles of vision and with developments in other areas of American history and those related fields of social inquiry that affect the understanding of historical processes.

In a rejoinder an historian of education—Lawrence Cremin of Teachers' College, Columbia University—accepted the main criticism, but pointed out that the confusions laid bare were not merely those of the historian of education but reflected differences among historians themselves—of a kind that still persist in various forms. Moreover, to define 'education' as the means whereby a culture transmits itself is to set the further task of defining 'culture'. Is this to be understood in the anthropological sense of 'enculturation' or should one not rather see 'true education' (or 'true culture') as 'the deliberate, self-conscious pursuit of certain intellectual, ethical and aesthetic ideals' while at the same time being ready to grant that 'nondeliberate influences are often, if not always, more powerful and pervasive and that the educational historian must be concerned with both'?[5]

Here the argument borders on matters with which philosophers of education in this country are concerned, when, for instance, they define 'education' as 'passing on something worthwhile in a morally unobjectionable way', rather than passing on just anything at all. But were the historian to be bonded by definitions of this order in selecting evidence he would, it might be argued, pass up his task as historian. Indeed, one of the chief weaknesses of the history of English education is that its selected starting point has been the landing of Augustine in Kent in 597, with the Latin prayer book and the Latin grammar, from which there has naturally followed a history not so much of *education* as of grammar schools.

The historian attempts to assess the educational forms at different stages of social development, and how they are modified or changed, in the light of the needs they met and the ideas they embodied at the time, rather than in terms of the moral and intellectual values of the 1960s. For one thing, there is no other way of arriving at an understanding of how current values themselves have taken form and root, to exercise in turn an influence on educational institutions—and also to define an approach to the history of education which is now justifiably seen as narrow and lacking in historical perspective.

But Bailyn's reference to opportunities for the historical study of education 'shifting and multiplying with the historians' angles of vision . . . and with developments in related fields of social inquiry' that affect understanding of the historical process, indicates the difficulties in store, rather than providing any clear guide to work on a broader canvas. It is not as if historians were agreed on the relation of the social sciences to historical enquiry; on the contrary, they differ sharply on this matter. Some who continue to see history as a *record* of unique events cannot easily envisage any drawing together with sociology.[6]

More concretely, when the historian of education turns to history for points of reference he finds a rich and variegated collection of historical studies under a wide variety of headings which historians have not yet managed to bring together. The central core might, perhaps, be called politico-constitutional history, divided by nation and by period, the deficiencies of which have been remedied by outgrowths of economic history and latterly social history, or, more particularly, local history; while numerous other aspects now have outlets in specialist journals, from ecclesiastical history to the history of transport. Then, of particular moment to the history of education are other special branches—each of which has developed more or less separately—such as the history of art, science, law, technology, medicine and so on. In short, material relating to education in a formal or informal sense is to be found scattered in many separate sectors which have yet to be absorbed fully into the mainstream of history. Where, then, is the historian of education to take his stand?

The problem has not been posed here as it has been in America, for academic historians have paid little attention to education as a factor in British history, just as universities here are less cognizant of the rest of the educational system than are American universities. But there is the beginning of a recognition that only certain aspects of education have been investigated and that it deserves much more attention. It could hardly be otherwise given the present educational explosion which is bringing the educational services into the position of the chief growth or investment industry. This naturally directs attention to the role education may formerly have played in economic and social development, particularly among historians who are now interpreting developments since the industrial revolution in terms of growth. The process has been aided by the development of sociology which brings on stage for attention all ranks of society, down to the lower depths, and insists on attention to the society as a unitary whole. This exposes the weaknesses of a history which has interpreted events primarily from the standpoint of government and paid all too little attention to social structure.

Complacency about the historical record as so far established has also been seriously undermined by the emergence of what is sometimes called the third world, or the drawing together into one world of areas hitherto rigidly separated in historical studies. In short, it is

now recognized that a history concentrating on Europe, or written from a European standpoint, provides an inadequate background to understanding developments in the world of today, or is a deficient account of the world of yesterday. In much the same way, a history of education which concentrates on the educated, or is written in the light of particular academic values, is an inadequate background to understanding the overall problems of education whether in developed or developing countries.

The point to be recognized here is that for most of recorded history a minority has regarded the majority as ineducable, whether for reasons of low estate, political and economic expediency, genetic inadequacy, or whatever other argument has served at different periods. Today—recognition of the human right to education apart—it is becoming clear that the illiteracy of the majority in a technological age is a contradiction in terms. Moreover it poses dangerous problems and action taken in highly industrialized countries to rescue neglected sections of the population is paralleled by efforts to eradicate illiteracy throughout the world. In the process it has become apparent that certain directive theories are misleading, that new patterns of education are desirable, that new technological aids can help to realize them on a mass scale. All this has established a new angle of vision, a new perspective.

Accordingly, it is required of the history of education that it should cover what is now recognized as the field of education, or all those influences which have a formative effect on the individual and social development of people. If this seems an impossible task, it may be recalled that the schoolchild himself is subject to such influences and to understand them is a prerequisite to that appreciation of the scope, or limitations, of formal schooling which has been lacking from historical surveys of education in the past—as from much current educational practice. That the historian has been too exclusively concerned with the organization of institutionalized education—and the ways in which different institutions, or pioneers, consciously and deliberately set out to inculcate certain knowledge or skills, a particular outlook, morality, or values—accounts for the present imperfect knowledge of the facts of life at the receiving end, and, in particular, among those barely touched by the formal machinery of education.

The lesson to be drawn is that, rather than analysing the machinery of the educational system on the one hand, and the ideals of educators on the other, as has been customary in educational studies, historical study should focus on the process of education. This implies much more attention than formerly to actual educational practice at different levels and to the operative influences shaping it—whether political or economic, psychological or social, and so on. It also implies a recognition that formal education is only, as it were, informal education raised to a new level and biased in particular ways, so that its nature or effect—however powerful as techniques improve—can only be adequately appreciated if the wider framework is constantly kept in mind.

Here one of the main difficulties, as has been suggested, is the present state of historical studies. So long as historians differ fundamentally in approach, or fail to bring different aspects of history into meaningful relation, so long is there no clear framework of reference for the history of education, which has links with so many aspects of life from the economic to the ideological. Inadequacies in the history of education as so far written are not only to be attributed to its place among educational studies, and a consequent tendency to preach an educational creed in the light of selected historical material rather than taking the historian's stance. They also result from deficiencies and divisions in academic history and its lack of attention to education as a key factor in the historical process. To take a particular instance, the history of English schooling has been much influenced by an ecclesiastical history of a strongly high church colour which is only now being rewritten, just as it has inherited from general history a strong constitutionalist bias. That this last is now being amended is one of the main reasons why the attention of historians has been directed to education as a social function. But welcome though the new interest is, in the circumstances it also has its dangers.

No department of history in any English university makes a special study of this centrally important question, despite the proliferation of special studies. This means that there is little concentrated thinking about the subject, as opposed to attention to it from particular angles—a weakness brought to light when work on the history of education is reviewed in historical journals by experts uninformed about the subject except from the particular angle that is their own. More research from different standpoints—by economic historians, say, on the one hand, or historians of ideas on the other, by seventeenth-century historians with their particular preoccupations and conflicts or nineteenth-century historians with theirs—is unlikely to clarify a general perspective. It may, rather, result in a new form of lopsidedness, reflecting disparate or uneven development as between different branches of history. The danger is the greater given what has been called the academic research industry and the attraction of a relatively underdeveloped field for those seeking subjects for theses or papers.

It may be suggested, therefore, that the historian working in education should try to keep a watching brief on the subject as a whole and guard its interests. For instance, he should judge as a contribution to the history of education researches which are elsewhere evaluated as contributions to economic, ecclesiastical, or sixteenth-century history. This, in turn, implies care in accepting conclusions which may fit in with other findings in a period or area but take insufficient account of what went before and what came after in the history of education. It implies also distinguishing interpretations which rest on a tacit acceptance of sociological determinism—a current trend among some historians—or, on the other hand, on a particular theory of psychological spontaneity. The history of education is a branch of both social and intellectual history and not to be elucidated solely in terms either of social or psychological structure. This would merely repeat old mistakes in a new form.

More particularly, while the specialist historian may have chiefly in mind a contribution to a particular sum of historical knowledge, the historian working in education has special preoccupations because he *teaches* the subject. To this extent the need to contribute the historical element to operative knowledge about education provides his framework of reference.

This, it may be suggested, can be a useful guide to coherent development of the subject, by comparison with special scholarly interests pulling in one particular direction or another. To recognize the obligation to educational studies and practice is not to encourage a repetition of former errors. Rather it indicates a means of overcoming them. Every generation tends to rewrite history, or to look afresh at the past with the eyes of a present which has concerns peculiarly its own. This is no hindrance to objectivity so long as the fact is duly recognized and allowed for, much as is the intervention of the experimenter in natural science. By contrast what has been harmful is the aspiration to present the one and only correct interpretation for all time—which then becomes so much a part of educational thinking that it is not even recognized as the interpretation of a particular generation whose perception of the historical process is conditioned accordingly.

With these considerations in mind, the future direction of research can be considered in more detail from the point of view of the historian working in education.

II

First, what is the point of departure in terms of work already done? When the history of education became established at the turn of the century there were some sound scholars at work in the field whose contribution is still respected by historians—for instance, W. H. Woodward, Foster Watson, J. W. Adamson, whose main concern it was to seek for the roots of modern education in the sixteenth and seventeenth centuries. To this extent the situation differed from that in the United States where it is the complaint that the early history of American education was interpreted by educationists concerned to magnify the importance of the emergent teaching profession, and exhort it to realize certain ideals, rather than qualified to engage in historical scholarship.

On the other hand it is remarkable that so little has been done to build on the foundations laid that the main works of the authors cited were not significantly added to for over half a century. It is also remarkable that, despite these scholarly contributions, there should so long have been adherence to the unreliable interpretations of A. F. Leach, on the part of historians generally and not merely historians of education. Indeed it is to the latter that amendment of the position is due and there is now a sound foundation for future work.[7]

Medieval historians have taken more account of education than others, since the universities take a central place in the history of this period and studies of the great religious foundations cover educational functions. But it can, perhaps, be complained that little has been done to bring together widely scattered evidence about schooling and other educational forms, so that the works of Leach remain in use for want of an alternative.[8] American scholars have contributed most to intellectual history at this period, or discussion of the university curriculum.[9] Meanwhile there has been too little attention in England to materials which throw light on university developments, a point underlined in a recent study of King's Hall, Cambridge. Even from Cambridge it can be complained that studies of 'English collegiate history have been blurred by that kind of parochialism from which amateur productions are prone to suffer', and that 'there has sometimes been a facile disregard of those impersonal forces of change, both social and economic, which underlay and largely determined the major upheavals and deflections in this field'.[10] No doubt there are historical reasons for the reluctance to consider Oxford and Cambridge colleges, or those universities, as social institutions, but the fact has left many gaps to be filled and there are rich archives yet to be drawn upon. It is a reproach that student notebooks and other illuminating sources in college and university libraries have been used mainly by American scholars.[11]

I do not propose to go over again ground already covered in an earlier paper which included a preliminary bibliography.[12] But to reiterate thus far, it remains the case that research relates mainly to nineteenth-century developments and that the eighteenth century, or the period 1660–1760, is still a neglected period. But here again there has been a questioning of long accepted views about the charity school movement in such a way as to open up what has been another closed subject for fresh research, particularly at the local level.[13] It is to the development of local studies that we can best look for solid evidence on which to base generalizations which have formerly been too easily arrived at on the basis of studying the documents of central organizations; and, as researches into local history are now multiplying, it may be hoped that many of them will relate to the educational field. Meanwhile there is some reason to think that the very existence of such records as those of the SPCK and the National Society, by comparison with the lack of easily accessible information about other educational initiatives, may have resulted in a comparable lack of balance in assessing respective contributions. There are other similar examples, and historians, nose down for primary sources or documentary evidence, have been too little alive to this ever-present danger. It may be added that new contributions to ecclesiastical history help towards a more disinterested approach.[14]

While the period from 1780 has attracted more attention, it is only necessary to look at new surveys of modern history to realize how inadequate is the coverage of education. For instance, in *The Age of Revolution: Europe from 1789 to 1848* (1962), Eric Hobsbawm has chapters on nationalism, the labouring poor, 'the career open to talent', and on developments in the arts, science, secular and religious ideology. Under each of these headings education enters in, but under none is there an adequate account of educational developments on which to draw. On the other hand, one sentence suggests a new direction for educational inquiry: 'The chief result of opening education to talent was . . . paradoxical. It produced not the "open society" . . . but the "closed society" of bureaucracy.'[15]

Some historians of the Victorian age are turning attention to the question of bureaucracy, with which the development of the professions is closely allied. Different professions have also been studied, the very establishment of which hinges on recognized forms of education, but there remains a vast field for investigation. Here, it might also be suggested, is a new angle of approach to the history of higher education, in terms of the professionalizing of the scholar, whether from the inception of universities or anew in the modern age. No doubt scholars do not easily think of themselves as having restrictive practices, like any trade unionist, but in a sense they form the oldest trade union of all and one of the most traditionalist.

It is, however, on the periphery of the organized educational system that there are the most neglected aspects. For instance, the study of English apprenticeship and child labour, published in 1912, which was inspired by the Webbs has long needed supplementing.[16] And English historians have paid virtually no attention to the unit on which civilization, or education, has been so largely based down the centuries, the family.[17] The lack is only beginning to be remedied by demographic study in the wake of that pioneered by French social historians. More relevant to the educationist, perhaps, is the kind of material drawn on to illustrate 'the secularization of the parish' and the corresponding 'spiritualization of the family' in Christopher Hill's *Society and Puritanism in pre-Revolutionary England* (1964). This provides a background for explaining what Bailyn considers the 'extraordinary provision' of the Massachusetts statute of 1641 laying on parents the duty of ensuring their children's 'ability to read and understand the principles of religion and the capitall lawes of this country'.[18] In this context, the family might be seen as an integral part of the organized educational system.

III

Criticism of the parochialism of studies in the history of English education brings to attention the need to develop a comparative approach in historical terms. It might be said that a European coverage is almost built in so far as study of medieval education is concerned, though effective grounds for comparison may be lacking.[19] The Renaissance and the Reformation are also seen as European phenomena up to a point, though too little attention has been paid to studies published abroad.[20] But once past this point national history tends to set in, and with it insularity.

This comes easily to the historian of English education in the modern period, given peculiar features differentiating the course of development from that on the continent generally, despite some national differentiation there. But it remains the case that there cannot be an adequate evaluation in terms of linear development in each nation separately, that comparison with other societies is necessary and desirable. For instance, the classical curriculum at the secondary stage was a European phenomenon from the sixteenth century, but did any particular divergences develop over the years? Closely related is the matter of introducing modern subjects. A study of the development of scientific and technical education in France after the revolution throws into sharp relief the failure to establish any form of organized education for the scientist in England a century earlier, when the Royal Society was established, which had a negative effect on the development of science.[21] Or, again, developments in schooling in later seventeenth-century England cannot be fully assessed without consideration of innovating tendencies associated with dissent which were excluded at various points up to the Restoration but found a fertile soil on the American continent. A comparative study of divergent developments in England and America after 1660 would be illuminating, but as little attention has been given to the accumulation of studies of the American scene as to the post-Restoration period in England itself.[22]

What can be done to distinguish broad lines of development is indicated in a short book by an Italian economic historian, C. M. Cipolla, *Literacy and Development in the West* (1969). This, incidentally, indicates the deficiencies of the synoptic survey of education in history which may begin with the Sumerians inventing a form of syllabic writing in the third millennium BC and obscure the fact that in 1750 some 90 per cent of the population of the world could neither read nor write. This is the end point of policies relating to popular education during the preceding centuries, which the historian of education has neglected to investigate, and the starting point for a study of literacy and popular education in the nineteenth century.

Cipolla's brief survey highlights many problems inviting further research and points some interesting lessons. For instance, he suggests that there was little or no development of literacy in England accompanying the rapid advance of industrialization in the period 1750–1850, in sharp contradistinction to the parallel advances of literacy and industrialization at a later date on the continent and in the United States. It may be that industrialization in England was not hindered because it was possible to live on past capital in the form of the relatively high level of literacy attained by the close of the seventeenth century.

To make this point, however, is also to recognize that there is no capital to fall back on to remedy the relative lag in higher education in this country today, by comparison with both the United States and the USSR. This, in turn, directs attention to the lack of studies of the nature of university education in its relation to social and economic needs over the past century. Even less has been done to elucidate the development of teachers' training, pivotal though this is to an understanding of educational developments and standards.

The development of technical education in relation to industrialization also remains to be investigated, in comparative terms. The Royal Commission on Technical Instruction, which reported in 1885, represents a peak in terms of attention paid to developments abroad, but how far were outside examples influential?[23] What accounts for the main differences in approach from the 1860s when highly successful technical high schools were set up in Germany and Switzerland but nothing comparable is to be found here? To what extent were old forms of apprenticeship continued, or revived in a new guise, and what was the role of trade unions in this matter? How far was the rate of technological innovation later a function of new educational approaches? In a study of the causes for the high rate of innovation in the United States, by comparison with Britain in the 1890s, H. J. Habakkuk discusses many possible factors, but there is no analysis of differences in terms of scientific and technological knowledge in relation to different forms of education; though economic historians are now showing a growing interest in the whole question.[24] More generally, war has been the midwife of technological development, and educational legislation, in many countries. What is there to be learned from this?

On the other hand the development of popular education, or literacy, cannot be seen merely as a function of industrialization.

After all, by comparison with England, Scotland provides an example of relative economic backwardness associated with a higher development of literacy and popular education.[25] What role did nationalism play in the nineteenth century, in Britain and on the continent, for instance in eastern Europe? Certainly it was one of the factors stimulating developments in Wales and there are interesting comparisons to be made between the development of secondary education in Wales and in England. To what extent did the higher incidence of secondary schooling in Wales contribute to maintaining the teaching profession in England, and so limiting the development of secondary education here during this century? This is only one of many questions. In Ireland an educational system was early imposed before there was any home model on which to draw.[26] How far did this experience play back on later developments in England, besides shaping the future in Ireland itself? This raises the whole question of colonialism, in terms both of its effect in modifying English institutions and of planting systems on the English model in Asia and Africa which persisted up to the establishment of independence. That newly developing countries are planning educational systems which obviate the former trend towards separating elementary and secondary education and confining the latter to a mainly academic pattern helps to highlight earlier attitudes and policies imported by colonial regimes.[27]

Demographic studies of the level of literacy in pre-industrial England, now under way, depend largely on such materials as signatures to marriage licences, but to interpret ability to sign one's name in terms of functional literacy is a complex and uncertain matter involving various assumptions.[28] There is, therefore, a good case for filling out the picture from other sources which help to gauge the level of operative literacy. Moreover, as Cipolla notes, while it is important to know how many people could read, 'it is no less important to know what people read and to what purposes'.[29] Only a beginning has been made in investigating popular reading matter. The contribution of schooling to reading habits might be approached by way of analysing the sum of materials to which the English child was exposed at different points in elementary school. Equally, more could be done to discover the teacher's equipment and the attitudes learned on the job, as evidenced in school and other records. This would be to get nearer to the stuff of education for the majority. Elementary school logbooks and school attendance records also indicate the extent to which attendance was affected by seasonal work, by epidemic, by family circumstances, but little has been done to collate and compare information from different agricultural and industrial areas from this point of view.[30]

A French historian, Philippe Ariès, has raised many points of interest in a wide-ranging study of childhood before the revolution—*L'enfant et la vie familiale sous l'ancien régime* (1960). This has much to say about the treatment of children in educational institutions, as well as in the family and society at large. Explaining his approach Ariès notes:[31]

> how difficult I have found it clearly to distinguish the characteristics of our living present if not by the differences which separate them from the related but never identical aspects of the past. Similarly, I grasp the specificity of the past to the extent that it does not altogether resemble our present. Historians of short periods can neglect without undue risk this dialectic of past and present. But it is integral to studying those customs and feelings which vary only over a 'long period'.

There may be some doubts about the way general conclusions are drawn from the kind of evidence studied—the depiction of children in works of art, their toys, games, dress, treatment in school—for the aim is to trace the *idea* of the family rather than legal and economic aspects. And historians of short periods may feel an urge to supply details lacking in a boldly outlined picture which has some comparative features, though the main materials derive from France. But there can be no doubt that a long neglected field is opened up. That parts of it have already been cultivated is demonstrated in the valuable work of Iona and Peter Opie on nursery rhymes and children's games. More recently a study of childhood in England since the Tudor age has appeared which, though weak on the interpretative side, collates useful information about the treatment of different categories of child—the orphan, the pauper, the delinquent and so on.[32] There remains much to be done in this area.

With the new perspective, and studies of the 'long period', there is a tendency to periodize into two main ages: pre-industrial society, or as it is sometimes called traditional society, and modern industrialized society, accompanied by a demographic revolution, which marks the advent of a new social structure. With this the new educational task is set of bringing a whole population within the orbit of compulsory, institutionalized, education. There is here an important turning point. But though the educational system, and its increasingly differentiated components, now moves into the centre of the picture, it must be remembered that 'universal, compulsory, education' only gradually supplements, and never entirely replaces, less formal educational influences.

IV

This brings us back to a problem already raised, the terms of reference of the historian of education and whether he should be concerned with 'enculturation' by comparison with 'true education': that is, the conscious and deliberate pursuit of intellectual or ethical ideals, or the passing on of something 'worthwhile'. As has been suggested, to approach the matter on this plane, by way of definition, is not a useful avenue for the historian.

For instance, an example may be taken of the deliberate inculcation of certain ethical ideals. 'If I died a good girl I should go to heaven', a small child working in the hellish conditions of the early nineteenth-century coalmine told one of the Commissioners on Child Labour in the mines. 'If I were bad I should have to be burned in brimstone and fire: they told me that at school yesterday, I did not know it before.' But it was not only in school that children were exposed to teaching of this kind, nor were working-class children alone subject to it. All who attended the chapels of certain denominations, or even the average Victorian family prayers, heard much the same kind of thing; and that so many children died young was a reason for regarding adequate preparation for death as worthwhile. For the historian of education the problem is to make the link-ups necessary to assessing the scope and effect of such teaching. Or, from another angle, he may analyse the components of an outlook which found it ethical, and morally unobjectionable, to torment mentally children already undergoing daily physical torment. How widely did this outlook prevail, what other attitudes were co-existent with it, how were these brought together or modified? If these matters are to be investigated in relation to the educational process account must be taken of circumstances outside the schools and not only within them.

That what is taught inside schools corresponds to what children learn outside them may be one of the measures of the effectiveness of formal education. Educators, whether today or in history, are concerned with people rooted in homes, localities, occupational groups, social classes. Whatever they may aim to perform these remain conditioning influences. In other words it is impossible to draw a distinct line between school and non-school experience; the one conditions the other, both then continue in parallel, or out of school experience may engender passive resistance to the offerings of the school. This rules out easy assumptions about what is, or is not, education.

In the same sense more account should be taken of what might be called non-academic experience in school. For example, from one point of view it might be said that the gathering of children in school in the sixteenth century to be taught the established religion must have been a powerful stabilizing force. On the other hand, the gathering together of peer groups from different ranks in the social order, the exposure to teachers whose views differed from those of parents, the receding of the age-old authority of the elders of the family in consequence, may have had an opposite effect; though, again, this may have been mitigated by the increasingly conscious attitude to education in the puritan family and the fresh assertion of parental rights and duties. In short, there must be an all-round appreciation of the circumstances.

It would be easy could we simply outline the curriculum which was supposed to be followed in school, according to statutes laid down, assume it was always followed, assume children absorbed it uniformly and then state that these were the ideas with which the new generation was equipped. Not only does some knowledge of psychology prevent such an assumption but there is a variety of evidence indicating that officially approved ideas were not always those disseminated by schoolmasters and that different people developed ideas other than those taught to them, or made these ideas over in their own way. Here the classic example is the use made of the literacy acquired in Sunday school by some members of the early nineteenth-century working class. Over and above this, there is the major point that up to the nineteenth century the way of life of the majority was little affected by formal teaching of any kind, and perhaps changed little in some areas over a long period, but none the less formative influences were brought to bear.

It is worth recalling here the approach of the economic historian George Unwin, who held that the term 'education', though generally confined to specific aspects, 'applies in a large sense to the whole process of class formation'. It was from this point of view that he discussed the educational functions of medieval guilds not only in terms of technical training but the socialization and political training of the urban middle class as well.[33] On the other hand a modern study directly concerned with the formation of a class—or rather the 'making of the working class' since the process was an active one—takes in education in the more specific sense of the word and examines the effect of religious teaching, in particular, in relation to other formative influences.[34] There are lessons to be learned from both these methods of approach.

Looking back on past errors, it would seem that historians generally have paid too little attention to enculturation, as opposed to following up 'progress' or social change. This suggests a need to come to terms with social anthropology in the attempt to find viable ways of tracing the educational forms in the community which have been supplemented by formal instruction administered in organized schools, though never altogether replaced. The same approach assists towards understanding school communities, which can be among the most traditionalist of institutions outside primitive society. Moreover, current studies of present-day schools indicate how fruitful anthropological techniques can be in apprehending the total educational situation, or the influence exercised on schoolchildren by factors which are normally not counted as educational—such as teachers' attitudes and pupil groupings in and out of class.

The amalgamation of different techniques becomes easier if their relation to the understanding of human behaviour is stressed rather than the differences which distinguish disciplines. As a social anthropologist has noted:[35]

> Although their practitioners often view them as alternative and incompatible ways of arriving at satisfactory explanations of human behaviour, sociology, history and anthropology (to mention only three possibilities) represent little more than partial techniques for attacking a problem. Serious scholarship will do well to avoid the irrelevant question of into whose domain a solution falls.

This is a point of view the historian of education can readily adopt. However, the problem is not so much the domain into which solutions fall as the difficulties attendant on using techniques which incorporate a specific, and sometimes specifically a-historical, approach: the primary example here being sociology. Some historians have borrowed sociological techniques without an adequate appreciation of this danger, or for that matter of the refinements of sociological investigation. This is a chief cause of resistance to 'sociologizing' on the part of other historians, though there is now a general recognition, even in conservative historical quarters, that the lessons taught by sociology cannot be ignored. It must be recognized that, since sociologists often tend to offer explanations in terms of interacting social forces at a given moment leaving historical formation out of account, techniques may reflect this. Simply to borrow these methods, in particular to apply them to investigations of pre-industrial society, is to run the risk of obliterating the historical approach; or, at best, of greatly oversimplifying the issues.[36]

An example illustrating some of the pitfalls is a paper investigating entrants to industry from 'public' schools after 1870. While the details are interesting and the analysis careful, doubts are raised by an over-simplified model postulating control of the late nineteenth-century public school by 'the aristocracy'.[37] Another instance is an attempt to rewrite the history of nineteenth-century developments in sociological terms, to avoid undue emphasis on Education Acts as turning points. For this purpose a particular sociological theory is applied, one of several which might as well have been chosen, with the end result that the points emerging for emphasis are the same as before.[38] Besides being encumbered by theoretical presuppositions which direct attention to certain types of evidence rather than others, this kind of approach usually lacks the necessary precision in historical terms to inspire confidence.

There are obvious reasons why the 'public' schools should latterly have received so much attention. They appeal strongly to the sociological investigator for here an interest in the formation of élites (an important question) can be satisfied and there are also what might almost be called 'sociological' methods of education.[39] But it is important to avoid the supposition that to administer this (or any other) form of education automatically produces the desired effect—according to the simple formula stimulus-response, advocated by a particular school of behaviourist psychology, which usefully chimes in with the sociological picture.

To bring in psychology is to recognize that historians, for their part, have tended to absorb ideas from this field in a somewhat random way, including some already dated on the home ground and others which have never been generally accepted. Since the Reformation in Europe has been attributed in large part to Luther's relations with his parents, or tendency to anal-eroticism, the way has been opened for further speculative adventures. There is already a tendency to import interpretations from the Freudian armoury into discussions of puritan upbringing and they are likely to enter in more generally as investigation of the family takes a more important place. Here it is worth pointing out that, from the historical point of view, the long reign of psychological theories deriving from biology appears now to be drawing to a close, suggesting the possible dethronement of the influential psycho-sexual interpretation of child development with its non-intellectual tendencies. This, incidentally, is an important area for study in itself, for bio-psychology has had an immense influence on educational thinking and methods through theories about child development ranging from the aridities associated with 'intelligence' testing to lush accounts of 'inner life' or spontaneous 'growth'.

It is worth noting here J. McV. Hunt's view that the development of rational methods of infant education designed to compensate for deprived home environments was arrested in America early in this century by the opposite tendencies of psychometry, Freudianism and a composite approach deriving from Dewey. Now that there is a reversion, to meet pressing needs, it is realized that there are few direct observations of children on which to depend, by comparison with an enormous volume of speculation. How far might the same be said about this country? It has recently been argued that in England Freudian ideas operated to encourage observation of children but that thought about child development ossified in the early 1930s at the point reached by Susan Isaacs.[40] The growing point of psychology today is a concern with cognitive development which opens up more profitable modes of investigation for the historian in so far as a leading idea is the relation of language and mental development.[41]

Attention is also directed to the broader social aspects of education by efforts to discover what sections of the population were to be found in schools and colleges at different periods. This is not an easy task before the modern period and there have been some premature conclusions about the composition of the student body at the universities in the seventeenth century, no less questionable because based on a certain deployment of statistical information. Quantification is not in itself a guarantee of objectivity; the theoretical approach, the selection of evidence, above all its interpretation, continue to count.

For the modern period there is a great deal of material as yet virtually untouched and some preliminary studies indicate that it can be illuminating.[42]

It is not only universities and grammar schools that can be investigated in this manner. There is much information about attendance at elementary schools. There are also specialist institutions well worth study, military and naval schools, for instance, which had a considerable influence in pioneering mathematical and scientific studies.[43] In this connection biographical evidence has been too little drawn upon, valuable though it can be in illuminating family habits in selecting schools and the experience of individual children in them. A study based on some local collections of correspondence brings to light—among a good deal else—that as early as 1789 north country parents were sending small boys aged six and eight on a long and difficult journey to a preparatory boarding school in the south, primarily to ensure that they lost the local accent.[44] Or, again, the great realist novelists of the nineteenth century have much to say on education, and their own way of evaluating it in broad terms in the manner in which they introduce their characters, besides having direct comments. 'You see all you public schoolboys have a kind of freemasonry of your own and outsiders are looked on by you much as I look on rabbits and all that isn't game', says Mrs Gaskell's Squire Hamley, of long pedigree but small means and homely ways, to his son. 'I'll have no one here at the Hall who will look down on a Hamley, even if he only knows how to make a cross instead of write his name.'[45]

Such various materials can be drawn upon in various ways and there is no need to quarrel over the particular techniques used. Rather the need is to throw light on dark corners of the history of education without either introducing preconceptions or claiming for a useful conclusion on a limited front more than it stands for. Above all the historian must resist the attempt to describe education solely in terms of 'sociological formation', as a reaction from previous neglect of this aspect, or for that matter in terms of ideological formation, a sociological concept which tends to eliminate the individual and the psychological. The historian working in education is in a better position than most to draw attention to its complexities and the oversimplification that may result from single-minded adherence to a partial technique or approach—the more so if he is ready, as it has been suggested he should be, to forfeit some of history's cherished peculiarities to make way for a more comprehensive and relevant history of education.

V

It would be mistaken to think that psychology and sociology are the only disciplines relevant to education, because they are the ones at present established as such among educational studies, besides history itself and philosophy in its 'spectatorial' role. Government, politics and law cover matters of the greatest moment to education and failure to take these aspects into account in discussing the evolution of educational theory and practice leads to false conclusions.

It cannot be denied that governments have educational aims, or that politicians introduce policies which shape developments in a particular direction, sometimes other than that desired by those conducting education. As a new course is set, so the character of education changes, ideas are modified, a new stage is reached. In other words it is fruitless to confine discussion solely to the level of educational institutions and ideas current here. It is only necessary to recall, as some recent studies have done, the direction given to education in Nazi Germany on the basis of a bio-sociological doctrine of the 'higher race' which implied picking out as peculiarly degenerate the 'egalitarianism' associated with democracy; an idea which survives in vestigial form wherever the doctrine of 'higher intelligence' is propagated.

There are as many different ways of looking into the politics of English education as there have been few studies from this point of view—whether by examining parliamentary debates on bills and the amendments accepted in the course of debate, private office papers of the Board or Ministry of Education bearing on the formulation of legislation and even the specific clauses of Bills, through local administration, the influence of the local and specialist press, the activities of teachers' unions, the educational programmes of political parties, the controlling actions of the bureaucracy and so on.[46]

Much can be done if there is a focus of research at particular centres, as is illustrated by the volume of related higher degree work at the School of Education of Manchester University, centring on national and local administrative or political history in the nineteenth century. It is from here that Norman Morris has suggested that interpretations of educational policy in mid-nineteenth century in terms of *laissez-faire* run directly contrary to a reality which can be better understood in terms of seeking effective means of ensuring social control on the traditional pattern; not least in the matter of forming the moral outlook of working class children as an essential accompaniment to introducing a modicum of literacy.[47] This challenges the standard picture of educational policies such as payment by results and brings to the forefront 'social control' and the ways it has been exercised as a matter for investigation.

To turn to the legal angle, a complex matter, the gaps there have been in the record are indicated by recent studies in the law of charity, in the sixteenth and seventeenth centuries and up to today.[48] The *cy-près* doctrine, and how it was interpreted in the courts at different times, is central to an understanding of nineteenth-century developments. The law of charity as it relates to educational trusts is another phenomenon unique to England which has profoundly affected educational policies; there are fruitful opportunities for comparative study here, with France and other continental countries.

That little has been done to develop study of local government since the days of the Webbs may help to account for the almost complete lack of attention to the local government of education, important though it is. For example, the local director of education (or chief education officer) is one of those officials whose publicity value is in inverse proportion to the influence he has exercised in this century on developments in all the chief urban centres and every county area; so he remains without biographers. The same cannot be said about headmasters of public schools. Here is another example of inadequate, or unbalanced, cultivation of the field, likely to result in false emphases.

To move into other fields, it has already been suggested that historians of education could pay more attention to the history of medicine and paediatrics, which bears closely on conditions of child development, and there is growing attention to measures relating to public health. How often has a new understanding of the needs of the handicapped contributed to a deeper understanding of the normal child and the efficacy of educational methods in raising standards? Then it is only necessary to mention ecclesiastical history, and the history of religion, to bring to mind extensive records which are a mine of information and new treatments of ideas which exercised a formative influence on the organization and content of schooling over centuries. Recent developments in the history of science are of much interest to the historian of education, particularly as they relate to educational methods proposed in the seventeenth century and the opening up of the curriculum in the nineteenth. More generally, there has rarely been a measuring of current educational programmes against current developments in the humanities and sciences, with the aim of assessing how new subjects reach the stage of pressing for an entry to the university and school curriculum, the ways in which they then take a place among already established subjects, the modifications attendant on fitting into the given framework, and so on. This would throw an interesting light on the time lag usually involved, the way selection is made of one subject and not another, the officially approved span of knowledge stabilized and what it emphasizes or what it omits. Here is an essential prerequisite to appreciating the particular position in this matter today, whether in schools, colleges or universities.

VI

The curriculum—the central feature of formal education as it were—is the point of most interest to practising educationists, but as yet virtually a virgin field for historical study. It is, of course, a complex matter to investigate in an all-round way and pre-eminently one to be approached from various angles. It might be said that the structure of the school curriculum depends in varying degree at different times on outside pressures (political and vocational), academic factors (the structure of knowledge as reflected in the organization of university departments and the examination system which shapes work at the secondary stage etc.), the internal school situation (traditional habits and their modification in terms of timetables, the teaching force, its abilities and methods etc.).

To take a particular example, in the late nineteenth century classical studies appear to have gained a new lease of life as a fit medium for upper-class education of a distinctive kind, a matter to be assessed by closer study of the nature of the classical curriculum in the eighteenth century, the assessments and recommendations of Victorian commissions, the extent to which these were adopted in the reformed public schools. What effect did this have on the teaching of modern languages? Are current problems here in any way related to Thomas Arnold's attempts to solve the discipline problem at Rugby, by insisting that all his teachers taught French whether or not they knew how to, in order to dispense with the proverbial Frenchman who could not keep order in class? The result was, in this case at least, that classicists taught French by the only method they knew, the grammatical method developed in their own field which was not necessarily adapted to teach a modern language for use. There is a mine of information in the reports of the nineteenth-century commissions on subjects then figuring in the curriculum for they called on evidence from various sources and recorded it at length.

Of particular importance are the battles fought over the introduction of science, which resulted in admitting scientific studies only on a 'side' of their own in schools and as inferior partners to the traditional 'humanities' in universities. If the argument about the resulting 'two cultures' has so far been little more than a storm in a Cambridge teacup there are matters deserving of serious historical investigation here. It may be that the problem dates back to the foundation of the Royal Society in London in 1660, well away from the established centres of learning which both despised and feared the new 'natural knowledge'. Consequently it became accepted that humane learning could get along without science and that science has nothing to do with human values, as opposed to contributing to the development of 'useful arts' or manufactures. It is in this tradition that some scholars still firmly believe that to let science in at the door is to let values out, an attitude which precludes dispassionate consideration of a key issue.

Closely associated with the curriculum, its operative aspects in effect, are teaching methods, didactics, pedagogy. Why is it that pedagogy developed so particularly in Germany, spread through Europe generally, but has been virtually non-existent as a systematic branch of study in England? What was the influence of pedagogical ideas of a philosophical bent when they were imported—for instance, those of Herbart? Were they absorbed or watered down to tally with English empiricism? There has recently been an interesting study bearing on this question from Australia, by R. J. W. Selleck which, like all good studies, raises as many new questions for investigation as it answers.[49]

In general, do new ideas once introduced replace the old, or are they taken in to make a new whole despite contradictions? The latter would seem to be the case for there are layerings of ideas to be found in different institutions, subject to their openness at different moments to a new point of view. For instance, an amalgam of ideas and practice, often contradictory, has accumulated in the primary school as it has grown out of the old tradition of elementary instruction—as the chapters in the Plowden Report bearing on the curriculum indicate—and this calls for historical investigation. On the other hand, pedagogy is not a matter to which grammar schools of the modern age have paid much attention, given an assumption that children ought to absorb the given curriculum and need to if they are to pass on to university. The supposition that long-established practice needs neither defence nor explanation in educational terms, while developing practice is open to criticism for its very disturbance of stagnant waters, has been the foundation of all conservative resistance to educational change down the years.

It might be argued that curriculum and teaching methods hang together more than has been supposed, and that both depend more than is sometimes realized—given the stress on freedom of the school in the English system of education—on overall methods of social control. Thus it is possible to discern at certain stages a relation between administrative structure and the appropriate pedagogy, in terms both of directive theory and the details of practice. Payment by results, for instance, operating from the early 1860s to the mid-1890s, imposed a specific internal structure on every grant-aided elementary school—the 'standard' system, which in turn conditioned the content of education and methods of teaching. The rationale of these methods in psychological terms was to be found mainly in the theory of associationism, while there was another rationale tying up the system as a whole at the level of political philosophy. Again, during the period 1920 to 1960, economic and political pressures worked in the direction of restricting access to grammar schools and universities, and the appropriate psychological theory, corresponding to the organizational forms introduced, was the doctrine of 'intelligence', conceived of as innate and unchangeable; a doctrine which in turn operated to dictate different teaching methods adapted to different levels and a specific form of internal school organization (streaming by ability). Here was another entire 'system', in terms of government policy, administrative directives, educational organization, content, method and overall theory, apparently impregnable to change from any quarter, the more so since the operative psychological theory was believed to be scientific. The breaking down of this system has resulted in a move to establish control at the level of higher education, up to the late 1960s an area of rapid expansion, by the establishment of a 'binary' system which approximates closely to the former bipartite system at the secondary stage.[50]

While the development of English education is easily seen in terms of social control, in the sense of ensuring stability, a comparison with American developments reveals a quite opposite assessment of the social function of education. Thus Bailyn sees its role in American history as 'an agency of social change, a powerful internal accelerator'. Education 'has released rather than impeded the restless energies and ambitions of groups and individuals' by responding sensitively to social pressures, and operated to propel the American 'away from the simple acceptance of a pre-determined social role and to nourish his distrust of authority'. There is a useful emphasis here on the two-way role of education which 'not only reflects and adjusts to society' but also 'turns back upon it and acts upon it'.[51] In so far as English sociologists tend to rule out this second aspect, which is always present and uppermost at certain periods of English history, they substitute for the reality a conjured-up picture of human incapacity in face of impersonal social forces and fail to cover the fact of social change. This static outlook may be reinforced by confining study to the external structure of the educational system and ruling out investigation of the intellectual content as unimportant. To the extent that a sociological orientation favours this oversimplification, it reverses the trend of the history of education which has been in an opposite direction.

Here it may be recalled that in its beginnings in this country (for instance in the work of R. H. Quick) study of the history of education was much influenced by German scholarship and incorporated a considerable degree of 'philosophizing'. Then there was a turn to investigating the structure of the educational system and particular institutions, and to a lesser degree educational practice. Now there is a move towards considering the process of education. The task is to find adequate ways of doing so, complicated though this may be, and avoid any tendency to regress. This will bring the history of education once more into close connection with the practice of education. For, though the study of educational institutions gained from a closer attention to the historical context, the tendency to concentrate on the details of structure and administration has not provided matter of the most interest to educational studies.

VII

This paper could not hope to cover all aspects of future research into the history of education. Attention has therefore been concentrated on methodological problems which now loom large, taking account of what can be learned from recent advances in different sectors of history and the need for a reorientation of studies in such a way as to ensure a coherent, and relevant, development of the history of education.

While it is clear that much work needs to be done before a more comprehensive history of education comes into being, it is possible to move more steadily towards this end if from now on the wider framework is constantly kept in view. This implies, for one thing, more co-operation in research, if possible more planning, and a readiness to co-ordinate different viewpoints rather than insist on one or another. Leaving other disciplines aside and taking history alone, what the economic historian finds of interest in the development of education, or the sociologically oriented historian feels is the necessary pattern of research, or the historian of a particular period is moved to investigate, represents only a foray into an extensive field. That field as a whole is the object of study of the historian of education and it is his task to keep its interests and needs to the fore in this sense.

In recognizing the limitations of the various disciplines bearing on education, their partial approach and techniques, the historian must be most alive to the defects of his own. Historians have evaded the problem of co-ordinating the study of history by proliferating branches in all directions and leaving unsolved problems hanging in the interstices between them. This is why the relatively organic branch of local history is of great importance to the historian of education. But unsolved problems cannot be evaded and it is healthier to recognize than to ignore them. One of the points to be borne in mind here—given differences among historians about the nature and tasks of their subject, and particularly whether or not it can be scientific—is that science does not conflict with humanity so much as with preconceived ideas. In other words, science does not prove this or that but rather disproves, after which there is operation with what remains until that in turn may be disproved. In essence, this is the method followed in history, where, also, the main danger to guard against is insistence on having said the last word.[52]

Above all, the historian working in education, and so teaching the history of education, sees his subject as one that can enrich the thought or deepen the understanding of the active educationist, and this modifies his attitude to research. It has been forcibly argued by an historian of art that the academic industry of research, conceived of on narrow lines, 'threatens to become the enemy of culture and of cultural history'. There is a danger that the enthronement of disciplines in the educational field, and the pursuit of research in terms of the internal structure of these disciplines, may not so much enrich educational studies as deflect attention from matters central to education itself.[53]

> It cannot be repeated sufficiently often that the so-called 'disciplines' on which our academic organisation is founded are no more than techniques; they are means to an end but no more than that . . . It will be a sad day when we allow the techniques we have learned or which we teach to dictate the questions which can be asked.

The key point remains, then, the ability to ask relevant questions, or help towards answering the questions insistently posed in education. The historian can contribute to this process in the measure that he is well informed about the whole span of education and uses his techniques with humanity in such a way as to enrich working knowledge of this all-important field.

Postscript

Since this paper was written, in the summer of 1969, there have been several contributions to the subject as discussed here. Lawrence Cremin has published the first volume of a three-volume study of American education, sponsored by the American Historical Association and the United States Office of Education, *American Education. The Colonial Experience 1607–1783* (1970). This represents a working out of new approaches to writing the history of education and includes a comprehensive bibliographical essay, pp. 577–668. Another derivation from the Bailyn discussion is a paper by J. E. Talbott of Princeton University, 'The history of education', *Daedalus*, Winter (1971), 135–50. Of greater relevance to historians of education in this country is a stimulating paper by Asa Briggs 'The study of the history of education' which surveys relevant developments in historiography under the following headings: local history, comparative history, quantitative history (or 'cliometrics'), social history, 'history from below', history of administration and government; and is published in the new *History of Education Journal*, 1972. Two additions to studies of the family are Alan Macfarlane, *The Family Life of Ralph*

Josselin: A seventeenth century country clergyman. An essay in historical anthropology, 1970, and Peter Laslett, *Family and Household in the Past* noted as forthcoming in the same author's *The World we have Lost*, 2nd edition, 1971.

NOTES

[1] P. H. Buck *et al.*, *The Role of Education in American History*, New York: Fund for the Advancement of Education, 1957.

[2] 'The history of education is the history of a gradually widening conception of what education itself is', for instance, is a generalization which fails to cover a comparison of the advanced ideas of the seventeenth century with some of the more backward attitudes towards popular education in the nineteenth century. It occurs in the preface, by W. R. Niblett, to a much used textbook, S. J. Curtis, *History of Education in Great Britain*, London: University Tutorial Press, 1948, and frequently reprinted.

[3] Bernard Bailyn, *Education in the forming of American Society: needs and opportunities for study*, University of North Carolina Press and Oxford University Press, 1960, p. 14.

[4] p. 53.

[5] Lawrence Cremin, *The Wonderful World of Ellwood Patterson Cubberley: an essay on the historiography of American education*, New York, 1965, pp. 43–5, 74–5.

[6] An interesting example is a series of lectures on the teaching of history beginning with a broadside criticism of traditional approaches by a sociologist; none of the historians takes up the points made as opposed to debating how to bring together unique events according to the principle of 'colligation' advocated by the philosopher W. H. Walsh. W. H. Burston and D. Thompson (ed.), *Studies in the Nature and Teaching of History*, Routledge & Kegan Paul, 1967.

[7] Kenneth Charlton, *Education in Renaissance England*, Routledge & Kegan Paul, 1965; John Lawson, *Medieval Education and the Reformation*, Routledge & Kegan Paul, 1965; Joan Simon, *Education and Society in Tudor England*, Cambridge University Press, 1966; with extensive bibliography. See also a paper which builds on the work of that indefatigable Cambridge historian, John Venn, Laurence Stone, 'The educational revolution in England 1560–1640', *Past and Present*, no. 28 (1964).

[8] And have, like some other out of date works, been reprinted. While reprints of texts which have long been difficult to find are to be welcomed there is some disadvantage in the renewed circulation of secondary works without any explanatory preface to 'place' them and indicate to students how they have been supplemented or corrected.

[9] There is a useful select bibliography in Helene Wieruszowski (ed.), *Medieval Universities*, Van Nostrand, 1966.

[10] A Cobban, *The King's Hall within the University of Cambridge in the Later Middle Ages*, Cambridge University Press, 1969, pp. 2–3.

[11] For instance, W. J. Costello, *The Scholastic Curriculum at early Seventeenth Century Cambridge*, Cambridge, Mass., 1958; A. Dejordy and H. F. Fletcher (ed.), *A Library for Younger Schollers*, Urbana, 1961.

[12] 'The History of Education', in J. W. Tibble (ed.), *The Study of Education*, Routledge & Kegan Paul, 1966.

[13] Joan Simon, 'Was there a charity school movement? The Leicestershire evidence', in B. Simon (ed.), *Education in Leicestershire 1540–1940*, Leicester University Press, 1968.

[14] e.g. P. T. Marsh, *The Victorian Church in Decline*, Routledge & Kegan Paul, 1969.

[15] Loc. cit., p. 191. While many stimulating suggestions are to be found in this book, the treatment of education in a recent and valuable history of England is disappointingly perfunctory, despite the American author's special knowledge of the subject: R. K. Webb, *Modern England from the 18th Century to the Present*, Allen & Unwin, 1969.

[16] O. J. Dunlop, *English Apprenticeship and Child Labour*, New York, 1912.

[17] See Joan Thirsk, 'The Family', *Past and Present*, no. 27, 1964; also Keith Thomas, 'Anthropology and History', *Past and Present*, no. 24, 1963.

[18] Bailyn, p. 26.

[19] A recent comparative study is Gordon Leff, *Paris and Oxford Universities in the Thirteenth and Fourteenth Centuries: an institutional and intellectual history*, Wiley, 1968.

[20] For instance, E. Garin, *Educazione in Europa 1400–1600* (Bari, 1957) and the collections of documents edited by the same author which supplement the work of Woodward. Another very relevant study, from America, is M. U. Chrisman, *Strasbourg and the Reform*, Yale University Press, 1967.

[21] Maurice Crosland, *The Society of Arceuil: a view of French science at the time of Napoleon I*, Heinemann, 1967.

[22] There are useful bibliographies on the history of American education in the books by Bailyn and Cremin already cited.

[23] An interesting paper indicates the possibilities here, George Haines IV, 'German influences on scientific instruction in England 1867–1887', *Victorian Studies*, vol. 1 (1958), 215–44. The question is investigated in the recent surveys by W. H. G. Armytage of American, French, German and Russian influence on English education.

[24] H. J. Habakkuk, *American and British Technology in the Nineteenth Century*, Cambridge University Press, 1967. A number of the papers delivered at the Fourth Congress of the International Economic History Association, held at Indiana University in September 1968, bore on the relation of education to economic growth.

[25] Though former assessments of the provision of schools in Scotland are now under review. Considerable attention is given to the question in T. C. Smout, *A History of the Scottish People 1560–1830*, Collins, 1969.

[26] A recent study is Donald H. Akenson, *The Irish Education Experiment*, Routledge & Kegan Paul, 1970.

[27] Among many new studies which contribute to an understanding of the peoples of Africa and their societies, as opposed to presenting them as merely 'the objects of outside manipulation', is L. H. Gann and P. Duignan (eds), *Colonialism in Africa, Vol. I: The history and politics of colonialism 1870–1914*, Cambridge University Press, 1969.

[28] R. Schofield, in Jack Goody (ed.) *Literacy in Traditional Societies*, Cambridge University Press, 1968.

[29] Cipolla, p. 109.

[30] But see David Rubinstein, *School Attendance in London 1870–1904: a social history*, University of Hull Publications, 1969, with bibliography.

[31] Loc. cit., pp. i–ii. The book has been translated under the title *Centuries of Childhood*, Cape, 1962.

[32] I. Pinchbeck and M. Hewitt, *Children in English Society, Vol. 1: From Tudor times to the eighteenth century*, Routledge & Kegan Paul, 1969. This study has been long in the making and, with one or two exceptions, the bibliography does not extend beyond 1955. The second volume (1973) brings the account up to the mid-twentieth century.

[33] George Unwin, 'Medieval gilds and education', in R. H. Tawney (ed.), *Studies in Economic History: the collected papers of George Unwin*, Macmillan, 1927, p. 92.

[34] E. P. Thompson, *The Making of the English Working Class*, Gollancz, 1963, from which the example quoted above derives, p. 377.

[35] Jack Goody (ed.), op. cit., p. 25nn.

[36] As, it may be suggested, does Laurence Stone in an ambitious survey, 'Literacy and education in England 1640–1900', *Past and Present*, no. 42 (1969); this dismisses studies of the history of education to date as primitive, only to draw on selected examples as and when it suits the exposition of a particular theme. See also a paper by a nineteenth-century historian, 'The study of the history of education' (*History*, vol. liv, no. 180, 1969) which assumes the subject 'arrived' with a special number of the new *Journal of Contemporary History* (1967) devoted to 'Education and social structure' in Europe and America, and remained within the given limitations.

[37] David Ward, 'The public schools and industry in Britain after 1870', *Journal of Contemporary History*, vol. 2, 1967. There might profitably have been attention to earlier work, such as the two-volume study of the 'public' schools by E. C. Mack (1938–41).

[38] This point, about P. W. Musgrave, *Society and Education in England since 1800*, Methuen, 1969, is made by Richard Szreter in the *History of Education Society Bulletin*, no. 3 (1969); see also the latter's paper 'History and the sociological perspective in educational studies', *University of Birmingham Historical Journal*, vol. xii, no. 1 (1969).

[39] A recent study is R. Wilkinson (ed.), *Governing Elites: studies in training and selection*, Oxford University Press, 1969.

[40] W. van Eyken in an introduction to Maya Pines, *Revolution in Learning: the years from birth to five*, Allen Lane, The Penguin Press, 1969, which summarizes current developments in the United States. Cf. D. E. M. Gardner, *Susan Isaacs: the first biography*, Methuen, 1969; J. McV. Hunt, *Intelligence and Experience* (1961).

[41] Drawing in the main on researches by Soviet psychologists which have had much more impact in the United States than here, particularly since the translation in 1962 of a key work, L. S. Vygotsky, *Thought and Language* (Book Centre), first published in 1934, marking a very different trend in psychology in the USSR from that then current in England and America.

[42] F. De Dainville, 'Collèges et fréquentation scolaire au XVIIe siècle', *Population*, xii (1957). See, for other papers by this author, Robert Mandrou, *La France aux XVIIe et XVIIIe siècles* (1967), pp. 279 ff., 'Les Modèles éducatifs'. See also, W. M. Mathew, 'The Origins and occupations of Glasgow students 1740–1839', *Past and Present*, no. 33 (1966); H. Jenkins and D. C. Jones, 'Social class of Cambridge alumni in the eighteenth and nineteenth centuries', *British Journal of Sociology*, i (1950).

[43] There is a comprehensive bibliography of studies by Trevor Hearl in *History of Education Society Bulletin*, no. 2, 1968.

[44] Edward Hughes, *North Country Life in the Eighteenth Century: the north-east 1700–1750*, Oxford University Press, 1952, pp. 364–5.

[45] Elizabeth Gaskell, *Wives and Daughters*, ch. 22, set in the early nineteenth century before the Reform Bill and the railway age.

[46] Such sources are drawn on in an interesting study of Scottish education, John Stocks, 'Scotland's *ad hoc* authorities, 1919–1930' in History of Education Society, *Studies in the Government and Control of Education since 1860* (1970).

[47] Norman Morris, 'State paternalism and laissez-faire in the 1860s', in ibid. For a list of Manchester theses, see *History of Education Society Bulletin*, no. 1, 1968.

[48] Following on the studies of philanthropy by W. K. Jordan and David Owen comes an authoritative legal study, Gareth Jones, *History of the Law of Charity 1532 to 1827*, Cambridge Studies in English Legal History, 1969.

[49] R. J. W. Selleck, *The New Education: the English background 1870–1914*, Pitman, 1968, which distinguishes the practical educationists, the social reformers, the naturalists, the Herbartians, the scientific educationists and the moral educationists as co-operating and contending trends.

[50] Brian Simon, 'Classification and Streaming: a study of grouping in schools in England, 1860–1960', in Paul Nash (ed.), *History and Education* (1970). See also, for an interesting study in contemporary history, J. R. Lukes, 'The binary policy: a critical study', *Universities Quarterly*, December 1967.

[51] Bailyn, op. cit., pp. 48–9.

[52] For interesting comments on the objectivity of the historical approach, by comparison with the supposedly value-free approach of some sociologists which provides an umbrella for importing certain values, Hugh Stretton, *The Political Sciences*, Routledge & Kegan Paul, 1969: 'While the social scientist tries to understand people better than they do themselves, the diffident historian is more ambitious—to understand them as well as they understand themselves' (p. 187).

[53] E. H. Gombrich, *In Search of Cultural History*, Oxford University Press, 1969, p. 46.

6 Research on the sociology of the school and of teaching

Frank Musgrove

Society is studied by historians and anthropologists; special attributes of societies are studied by demographers, political scientists and economists. The distinctive concern of sociologists is with institutions, the elements which make a society: the church, family, political party, the school, and the legal system. The sociologist is interested in continuity and change in these various institutions; he is interested in their structure and function and the way in which they are interrelated and interlock to preserve the unity of society as a complete system. Thus changes in educational aims and provisions would be examined in the light of changes in the family, the church and the economy. The sociologist is also interested in social tension; although the model of interlocking and integrated institutions often seems to distract his attention from considerations of conflict. (Even crime may be—and has been—interpreted as a normal aspect of the social structure, a vocation to be studied in the same terms as teaching or banking.)

In their concern with institutions sociologists often seem to lose sight of the individuals who constitute them. They may, indeed, maintain that it is not individuals, but social positions, which constitute institutions. A series of individuals may occupy these positions and move on, but the institution may remain substantially unchanged. An institution is seen as an organization of roles around some central activity or social need. Nevertheless, as Max Weber insisted, sociological concepts can be reduced in the last analysis, if not the first, to the actions of individuals. This is what sociologists are essentially concerned with: social acts, the social relationships of people, the way they behave toward one another because of their positions in a social system.

Sociologists claim their specifically sociological modes of explaining behaviour. 'Social facts' are to be explained by other social facts. Sociologists resist 'reductionism' whereby social phenomena are reduced to psychological terms. (They often show less concern when psychological facts are 'reduced' to sociological terms.) One of the founders of modern sociology, Émile Durkheim, maintained that 'Every time that a social phenomenon is directly explained by a psychic phenomenon, one may be sure that the explanation is false'. His explanation of suicide-rates was in terms of social categories and circumstances.

A wide range of behaviour has been 'explained' by sociologists without reference to the personality or motivation of the people engaging in the behaviour. Migration, social mobility and 'acculturation' have been interpreted in terms of social circumstances rather than the will or desires of individuals. A topical issue may illustrate this point. A 'social fact' of grave concern in Britain today is the death-rate on the roads, particularly at holiday times. Of course this fact is made up of scores of individual actions and impulses. But the rate appears remarkably constant in spite of attempts to influence individual road users by appeals through the mass media. The rate of road deaths at Whitsuntide is a social fact explicable in terms of other social facts: the volume of traffic, the affluence of society, legal restrictions, and institutionalized holiday arrangements. If we wish to change one social fact we must change the other social facts related to it.

In studying social institutions sociologists have often employed the comparative method. Max Weber employed this method on the grand scale when he investigated the influence of religion on economic activity in China, India and Protestant Europe. In recent years S. N. Eisenstadt has compared the relationship between age-group organizations (including schools) and family systems in a wide range of contrasted societies. The comparative method can be used to study institutions and organizations within a particular society. Our understanding of our educational arrangements would gain much from such an approach, for we need to compare school with school and schools with other social organizations. Comparative studies would tell us how schools differ in their morale, 'social climate', and academic effort according to their size, recruitment (of staff and pupils), internal organization, external relationships and avowed purposes. Sociological research can tell us how schools are like, and how they differ from, other social organizations. What are the unique characteristics of schools? What features do they share with industrial work-teams, hospitals, families, army units, concentration camps?

A variety of concepts has been developed and refined by sociologists which guide their collection of data and analysis of social behaviour. (These essential tools are often dismissed as 'jargon' by non-sociologists.) Concepts such as primary group, secondary group, reference group, anomie, status (or social position), role, social integration and culture help us to understand social bonds and the way one man is related to others. Thus the notion of anomie, developed by Émile Durkheim, describes a particular state of social integration characterized by 'normlessness': individuals are not closely bound together by clearly defined and generally accepted rules and expectations. A culture (or subculture) describes how men are bound together and marked off from others by a shared normative system, common values, understandings and agreements. 'Role'—a central concept in contemporary sociological analysis—similarly describes the way in which a man is related to society, the kinds of behaviour that other people can rightfully expect of him because he occupies a particular status or social position.

These concepts, though much discussed, have been little used in empirical investigation in England. It is the purpose of this chapter to suggest ways in which some of these concepts might be employed in investigations of social relationships in schools. We still have little systematic knowledge of schools which has been obtained from investigations in which sociological concepts have been employed as tools. Our main source of information about the social character of schools is still autobiography and the novel.

Sociological enquiry in the field of education has been much concerned in the past with broader issues of social mobility. This work has been conducted, in the main, by demographers. Their work has thrown light on the processes of social mobility, the influence of education on the country's class structure. (They have shown curiously little interest in the effect of education on geographical mobility, the redistribution of talent and its concentration in particular areas.) A notable outcome of this interest and endeavour was the volume, *Social Mobility in Britain*, edited by D. V. Glass and published in

1954. Stemming from the same tradition we have more recently had J. W. B. Douglas's books *The Home and the School* (1964) and *All Our Future* (1969), reports on a follow-up investigation of a sample of the nation's children which was initiated by the Population Investigation Committee. The Ministry of Education shared this interest, and the report, *Early Leaving* (1954), was a major contribution to knowledge in this field.

All this work is of interest and relevance to the class teacher. It has illuminated the relationship between social background and educability. Douglas's work has demonstrated once again how unfavourable home circumstances, particularly lack of parental interest, exert a powerful influence on children's performance and prospects. Among borderline candidates for grammar school places the interest of parents appears to be particularly important. And levels of interest are closely related to social-class position: 'The parents who are most interested in their children's education come predominantly from the middle classes, and those who are least interested from the manual working classes.'

The general sense of these sociological investigations is well known and widely accepted by teachers in the schools. But to have a general sense of these findings is not good enough; they must be known in all their detail and with all their qualifications and reservations. Otherwise we are in danger of accepting a naive and debilitating sociological determinism: the social-class background of children may be used by teachers for quite improper predictive purposes. Mays found some evidence that this was happening in the back-street schools of Liverpool. In *Education and the Urban Child* (1962) he reports 'an unduly pessimistic attitude on the part of teachers' which appears to be based on the theory that if extra attention succeeded in gaining selective places for any of the borderline children in these working-class areas 'it would be an unwise policy since this would be at the expense of similar children coming from "better" homes in the better-off neighbourhoods'.

The child from the 'poor' home is a worse educational risk than the child of similar abilities from the 'good' home. But many, even border-line, children from lower-class homes do well academically. The Ministry's report on *Early Leaving* showed that 12 per cent of those children from the homes of unskilled workers who were in the bottom third of the grammar school intake had risen to the top third five years later. And Douglas argues that the efficient primary school can nullify the effect of home background. 'By improving the level of teaching in the primary schools it seems that the waste of ability through lack of interest and stimulation at home can be much reduced and perhaps eliminated.' Sociological investigation has shown that the home is a potent influence on a child's academic promise; it has not shown conclusively that the efficient school is incapable of compensating for the deficiencies of parents.

Substitutes for research

Sociological research can help the teacher to develop insight into the personal relationships which are at the heart of his job, rather than to hazard predictions about the academic prospects of his pupils. It can also provide information which has a direct bearing on administrative action and policy decision. There are urgent practical reasons why it should be undertaken.

We do not lack substitutes for actual investigation. The most dangerous substitute is the application to schools of research findings which have come from studies of other types of organization. Less dangerous, perhaps, but scarcely more profitable, are histories of those aspects of the school which we wish to understand.

There are many possible illustrations of the historical substitute. One will suffice. The contemporary influence (or alleged lack of influence) of teachers over pupils has been interpreted by Floud in historical terms.[1] In the affluent society, it is claimed, their moral authority is eroded (although their extraneous power as social selectors may be enhanced). Claims about the authority of teachers today are made by reference to an alleged authority in the past, when they commanded respect as teacher-missionaries. Today, it is argued, an all-graduate profession might command similar respect as teacher-crusaders.

No datum line is established from which change and decline are measured. It is not clear what teachers in the past are being compared with teachers today. The secondary modern teacher may have less moral (and social) authority than the gentlewoman teaching in a nineteenth-century Ragged School; he almost certainly has more than the Victorian elementary school teacher whose training (at public expense) never escaped the shadow of the Poor Law.

But historical analysis, however well performed, is unlikely to answer the question at issue: what are the personal, social and professional attributes of teachers which command respect today? In what terms are teachers evaluated by pupils and parents? Our statements are little better than guesswork until we have actually investigated pupils' perceptions of teachers of different kinds and the respect which they accord them. Notions which have been found useful in the investigation of other social institutions, and which have been put to some empirical test, are applied to schools with some adjustment and modification to suit what appear to be the special circumstances of the case. Interesting and even useful hypotheses about school life are advanced as statements of fact.

The role of the teacher, says Wilson,[2] is diffuse and affective. It is becoming even more so. The notion of roles which are diffuse or specific on the one hand, and effective or affectively neutral (or instrumental) on the other, is developed by Talcott Parsons[3] and other American sociologists. This distinction has proved fruitful in the investigation of institutions such as the family. Relationships in the modern family have been shown to be diffusely concerned with a wide range of obligations and services, and 'affective' in the sense that their most important purpose is to promote feeling, emotion, gratification. Clearly it would be illuminating to investigate schools in these terms: to compare, for example, the affectivity and instrumentality of headmaster and deputy-headmaster roles.

The diffuseness of the teacher's role is asserted by Wilson from common-sense impressions of the teacher's job and comparisons with common-sense impressions of the doctor's job and the lawyer's job. But common sense can be dangerously misleading. If we want to know whether teachers' roles are in fact specific or diffuse, we can find out by systematically observing their behaviour, by asking them to define their work, and by asking others who condition and determine their work to define it. The range of relatively distinct tasks in which teachers habitually engage, and the range of tasks which they regard as necessary and obligatory, will provide some indication of the diffuseness or specificity of their role.

In an attempt to discover how diffuse are teachers' conceptions of their roles, the author carried out an enquiry with his colleague, Philip H. Taylor, with five hundred teachers in grammar, modern and primary schools.[4] Teachers were asked to indicate on a check-list the tasks and objectives which they considered important and essential to their work, and tasks which they considered of little importance or no part of their business. As we might expect, diffuseness of role conception varied according to type of school and, in the case of primary schools, with the social character of the area. Grammar school teachers had a more restricted role conception than secondary modern school teachers; primary school teachers occupied an intermediate position. Junior school teachers in working-class areas had a more diffuse role conception than teachers in middle-class areas. Tasks and objectives which teachers rejected were entirely in the 'affective' field of personal relationships and social training. Moral and intellectual objectives were most generally accepted.

This enquiry cannot tell us whether teachers today accept a more diffuse role conception than at some time in the past; and it cannot tell us whether their role is more diffuse than that of doctors or lawyers. It was interesting, however, that teachers generally rejected the notion that they are social selectors, helping able children to social advancement. Both Floud and Wilson have emphasized this aspect of the teacher's role. Of course teachers are necessarily social selectors; but they appear to be unwilling to think of themselves in these terms. In general they conceive their role in narrowly moral-intellectual terms, particularly in the grammar schools.

This enquiry was a minor exercise in the substitution of enquiry for assertion. We need similar (but more elaborate) enquiries to test other assertions made by Wilson. He claims that the teacher's role is becoming not only more diffuse but more 'affective', principally because of alleged changes in family life which cause the teacher to take over more 'parental' functions. The family, he claims, is 'associationally in decline'. Research by the author indicates that pupils in both modern schools and grammar schools—but particularly in the latter—see their schools in predominantly 'instrumental', their families in predominantly expressive or affective, terms. They expect school to prepare them for the future, and feel that it does; they want their homes to afford emotional security, and to a remarkable extent seem satisfied that this is what they get.[5] This investigation of children's perceptions of home and school lends no support to the view that the school is taking over 'affective' functions from the home, or that the family is 'associationally in decline'.

There are severely practical reasons why we should have reliable information about the origins of teachers' role conceptions and conflicts. If teachers are at odds in their notion of their functions with the public, parents, administrators and inspectors, we might expect their frustrations to lead to low morale and reduced effectiveness. American research in a military academy shows how instructors' role-conflicts and ineffectiveness go hand-in-hand.[6] This looks rather like a discovery of the obvious. But the relationship between teachers' role-conflicts and their proficiency is still far from clear. It may be that some kinds and levels of conflict stimulate thought and effort. 'It is possible that contrary to common belief some role incompatibility is associated with some measure of teaching success.'[7]

American research has shown how teachers' role conceptions and conflicts are systematically related to certain differences among schools and among communities.[8] This is doubtless the case in England,[9] although English teachers are in general more protected from the communities in which they work. While it is important that we should conduct our own studies in this field, it is perhaps of greater urgency at the moment that we should investigate the consequences for teachers' role conceptions and conflicts (and efficiency) of the widespread reorganization of secondary education which is now taking place or is planned for the future. Reorganization often requires the teacher to reformulate his notion of his task, to redefine his objectives and revise his values. The ex-grammar school teacher who finds himself in a comprehensive school when he would wish to be elsewhere faces problems of adjustment which administrators need to understand.

Empirical investigations of the teacher's role are needed so that the teacher can more fully understand himself. Sociological studies of the teacher's behaviour in the classroom can show how apparently private predicaments are in fact the outcome of the social structure in which he works.

The teacher who feels that he is an inadequate disciplinarian may define his problem as personal failure, attempt to conceal his difficulties, and to seek a purely personal solution. Colleagues may be reluctant to share their deepest anxieties. The teacher refrains from the disciplinary action (for instance, sending a pupil to the headmaster), which reveals that he has a disciplinary problem. Sociological studies of the teacher's classroom role, conducted along lines pioneered in American high schools,[10] would enable teachers to view their problems in analytical rather than moralistic terms; and might perhaps liberate them to seek a solution through discussion and concerted action with their colleagues. Empirical investigations of schools might help to solve or lighten teachers' problems by providing them with a new perspective; the investigation of roles may help towards a more realistic definition of the roles themselves.

Power in the school

At the centre of the sociologist's interest is power. Sociological investigations of schools will concern themselves with the structure of authority, the manner and basis of task allocation, the influence of pressure groups inside and outside the school, the nature of the headmaster's authority and the way in which it differs from the authority of his deputy; the cleavages and camps among pupils and staff which are based on age and seniority, formal stratification, subject allegiance, or simply physical isolation or proximity. (A thorough sociology of school architecture is long overdue, to throw light on the social consequences of annexes, the accessibility of the Office, the location of the deputy-head in a corner of the staff room or in a separate suite with or without telephonic communication.)

Current interest in curriculum innovation has prompted a handful of enquiries into decision-making in schools.[11] 'Empire-building' in a technical college has been shown to be particularly fruitful.[12] Interest in 'pupil-participation' has also prompted studies of school councils and the realities and unrealities of their power.[13] 'Involvement' may lead less readily and surely to 'commitment' than Etzioni supposed.[14] Curiously, we know virtually nothing about the staff meeting in its various forms and guises; and very little about the formation and influence of external pressure groups. Old Boys' Associations are virgin research territory.

We do not lack unsubstantiated assertion about the nature and exercise of power in schools. These have a long history and are to be found in abundance in Willard Waller's classic *Sociology of Teaching* (1932). 'Typically the school is organized on some variant of the autocratic principle,' says Waller. Far from the total personal involvement which Wilson maintains is the teacher's lot, Waller asserts that the teacher can only be effective if he is personally meaningless. 'Students would hate teachers more than they do if it were not for the fact that distance between the teacher and his students makes the teacher relatively meaningless as a person.' It is the nature of schools to be despotic. 'The generalization that schools have a despotic political structure seems to hold true for nearly all types of schools, and for all about equally, without very much difference in fact to correspond to radical differences in theory. Self-government is rarely seen. Usually it is but a mask for the rule of the teacher oligarchy. . .' But it is a deeply troubled despotism. 'It is a despotism in a state of perilous equilibrium' threatened from within and without.

All this is exhilaratingly tough-minded and will have an immediate appeal to anyone who has ever taught in a school. But is it true? Waller reaches his conclusions from the general impressions of an active life and from novels. Other people (including the author) could counter with quite contrary impressions. We have no systematic studies of the realities of power in schools.

The truth is certainly less simple than Waller imagined. Schools are 'bureaucracies', and the exercise of power within them can be studied as it has been in other bureaucratic organizations. It is conceivable that schools might have developed along non-bureaucratic lines, as collections or colleges of professional men, tutors hired by clients to give particular courses of instruction. In fact they have evolved as bureaucracies in which performance is controlled by directions from one's superiors instead of the surveillance and self-imposed standards of one's colleagues.

Schools today have most of the salient characteristics of bureaucracies as described by Max Weber. Their complex activities call for the co-ordination which bureaucratic arrangements efficiently provide. The regular activities in which the school engages require a time-table, officially prescribed duties for members of staff, a division of labour maintained by specialized experts. The organization of offices follows the principle of hierarchy; and the operation of the school is largely governed by a consistent system of abstract rules and the application of these rules to particular cases. Employment in schools is based on technical qualifications and is protected—unlike the non-bureaucratic employment of domestic tutors in the past—against arbitrary dismissal.

The increasing bureaucratization of schools over recent decades is not difficult to demonstrate. It is implicit in successive salary awards which have recognized, defined and accentuated hierarchical pyramids of teachers. The requirements of external examinations have increased time-table complexities and have limited the teacher's freedom to decide how and what to teach. The consequence of bureaucratization for the nature and quality of interpersonal relationships within schools—between members of staff and between staff and pupils—is a largely neglected field of sociological research. But schools vary considerably in their degree of bureaucratization; and we should expect the way in which power is exercised to vary accordingly.

Cohen has recently shown how the head teacher's conception of his role tends to be more bureaucratized in our larger schools.[15] This is not surprising and is in line with what has been discovered about the effect of size in other kinds of organization. What is perhaps more surprising is the indication in some American research that teachers may find a sense of support and power in highly bureaucratic school systems.[16] Perhaps it is because they 'know where they stand'. Underbureaucratization may be experienced as neglect: one's superiors are not checking up and so may be presumed to have lost interest. But we know virtually nothing about levels of bureaucratization in relation to educational productivity. The sense of security which arises from well-established routines, a clear chain of command, and everybody knowing 'who is who', may be a recipe for complacent mediocrity. Organizational uncertainty and ambiguity may pay more handsome dividends.[17]

Educational institutions have, from their very nature, certain built-in resistances to bureaucratization. In particular, their avowed concern for personality and individuality conflicts with Weber's contention that an officer of a bureaucracy must act in a spirit of 'formalistic impersonality'. Nevertheless, it is possible that 'formalistic impersonality' is today more widespread in our schools—particularly those geared to a rigorous programme of external examinations—than teachers would be prepared to concede.

Perhaps one of the surest defences against the pressure of bureaucratic authority in schools and other educational organizations is the natural disloyalty (or 'higher' loyalties) of academic men. A bureaucratic organization requires experts if it is to function efficiently; it also needs loyal officers if it is to achieve stability. American research in universities and social work agencies, for example, suggests that employees with very high professional qualifications often feel a stronger loyalty to their profession than to the organization which employs them.

American university teachers with the highest qualifications and academic reputation have been shown in one enquiry to feel less committed to their college and more willing to leave for advancement than less distinguished teachers. These 'cosmopolitans' value the good opinion of other academics throughout the country more than the approval of their immediate colleagues. Their 'reference group' is the nation-wide community of scholars rather than the academic community in which they work. 'In short, there seems to be some tension between an organization's bureaucratic need for expertise and its social-system need for loyalty'.[18]

A similar picture emerges from a study of a social work agency. Employees who have the highest professional qualifications are more likely to look outside the agency for intellectual stimulation and to be willing to take employment with another agency. 'These findings confirm the hypothesis derived from other studies that a professional orientation is inversely related to organizational loyalty.'[19]

A study of American nurses does not support this view;[20] and it seems likely that when professional performance is only visible to one's immediate colleagues, 'cosmopolitans' are no less loyal than 'locals'.[21] Teachers in English schools who can figure prominently in the affairs of professional and academic associations, who write text-books and hold office in regional or national organizations, may enjoy a greater measure of independence than teachers who have neither scope nor talent for such activities. The tradition is no longer appropriate which requires them to feel guilt when they tell their headmaster that they are applying for another job. It is possible that headmasters and others responsible for appointing subordinates may often unconsciously favour the less distinguished and qualified candidate. His loyalty and stability are more assured. The need for stability and loyalty may outweigh the need for skill and expertise.

But in general the power of educational hierarchies is likely to be moderated as subordinates are ever more highly qualified for their work and as opportunities for qualified men expand. What is urgently needed is an empirical study of the exercise of power in schools which differ in the proportion of highly qualified and otherwise professionally distinguished teachers they employ. Despotism is more likely in a private school staffed by unqualified teachers than it is in a grammar school of high academic distinction.

There are other reasons why the universal despotism alleged by Waller is unlikely to characterize our school system. It is of obvious importance that we should try to discover the organizational arrangements which increase the autonomy of teachers and pupils, encourage spontaneity, innovation, and the free exchange of ideas within our schools between members of staff and between staff and pupils.

Markedly bureaucratic systems which are characterized by a pronounced hierarchical ordering of staff and formality and constraint between staff and students may further some objectives of a school but may seriously impede the attainment of others. Efficiency of day-to-day administration may be promoted, but a variety of educational experiences may be rendered impossible. In the field of staff relationships, pronounced hierarchical arrangements may limit the free flow of ideas and suggestions and so make more difficult the solving of common problems; in the classroom teaching and learning are unlikely to be a genuine enterprise of joint discovery, even if such an enterprise be attempted. Bureaucracy in its classical lineaments is the organizational framework for the authoritative transmission of established knowledge.

In a period of rapid change in the organization of education we need research into the human consequences of our re-arrangements and innovations. The trend towards more bureaucracy is strong but not irresistible; the problems of 'de-bureaucratization' are great but not insurmountable. Indeed, the abolition of payment-by-results more than half a century ago was a major achievement of debureaucratization and decentralization which had profound consequences for the exercise of authority by inspectors, head teachers and class teachers.

Decentralization (within a particular school, a local authority, or on a national scale) means that subordinates need to refer less often to higher authorities before they take action. There is some American evidence that in a decentralized school system class teachers engage in far more experimentation, develop more spontaneous relationships with pupils, and show more initiative in curricular development.[22] Of course the 'abolition of 11+' is a measure of decentralization, at least for the primary schools. We could profitably investigate and compare the personal relationships in schools before and after abolition, and in schools which have been relieved of 11+ examinations and those which have not.

Contemporary organizational changes raise a host of research problems of crucial concern to teachers. What are the consequences for communication, initiation of action and innovation of the even more formal hierarchies of our schools? How do distinctions of rank influence the exchange of opinions and the efficiency of problem-solving at staff meetings? Does the staff meeting delegate important problems to working parties of equals—or should it do so in the interests of greater efficiency? In a large school, does communication tend to be 'vertical', or do men of equal rank in different departments tend to confer together and short-circuit the flow of ideas and information which should percolate to all levels? Do junior members of staff feel left out of discussions which they feel concern them?

What are the effects on school life of the bureaucratic arrangements made necesssary by the Certificate of Secondary Education examination? It is as important in evaluating the effect of this examination to study its impact on personal relationships in schools as it is to study its effect on the level of academic performance. The administration of the examination gives assistant teachers a measure of independence, importance and authority vis-à-vis their headmasters; and if schools avail themselves of the opportunity to devise their own syllabuses, the class teacher is free to work with his pupils in the manner he finds most effective. The CSE may prove to be not a bureaucratic strait-jacket, but one of the most important measures of debureaucratization in the recent history of education.

Other measures which at first sight appear to move away from an hierarchical ordering of education might conceivably lead to more constraint, rigidity and autocratic exercise of authority in our schools. Highly selective organizations in general need to exercise less rigorous authority in order to control their members than open institutions. By increasing the selectivity of a school (in terms of academic ability, the social standing of parents, or other criteria relevant to the school's objectives) control can be relaxed. (In the same way open prisons can function with some measure of success at least in part because they enjoy a selective intake.)

But non-selective schools, less selective sixth forms and universities, are likely to find that 'democracy' entails greater coercion. As the first form, sixth form and university open their doors more widely, it is less possible to assume that the values, motives and commitments of entrants accord with the organization's aims. When most people go into the sixth form, instead of a carefully recruited minority, it is probable that the relatively equal and informal relationships between teachers and taught which have prevailed in the past will be impossible to maintain.

The culture of the school

Many sociologists have suggested that the teacher will gain a deeper insight into his condition if he looks at his school through the eye of the anthropologist. The social nature of schools might be illuminated if they were studied and compared as tribal communities with distinctive cultures marking them off from the wider society. Waller writes of the 'separate culture of the school'. In any school, he says, there are 'complex rituals of personal relationships, a set of folkways, mores, and irrational sanctions, a moral code based on them. There are games, which are sublimated wars, teams, and an elaborate set of ceremonies concerning them'. This culture is susceptible to anthropological investigation.

David Riesman has attempted to study and compare three American colleges as an anthropologist might study tribal societies.[23] The effort does not seem to have been particularly productive. One difficulty is the dearth of 'ethnographic' data; but it is also difficult to see precisely what is expected of these rather impressionistic studies of institutions 'in the round'.

A more profitable line of enquiry may be into the various 'subcultures' of a school: the subcultures of staff as well as pupils. The rise and functioning of pupils' subcultures may help the teacher to understand and perhaps to influence the motivation of his pupils. The school is a culture-contact situation in which the values of staff are often opposed to the values of the children. The process of education is in some measure a process of assimilation or 'acculturation'.

Staff and pupil subcultures may remain stubbornly and even bitterly distinct and opposed. (It is possible that assimilation occurs most readily when pupils have status within the official social structure, through the prefect system for example. If this is so, there is perhaps a case for multiplying high status positions in schools and perhaps rotating them.) Apparently irreconcilable conflict between staff and pupils is described in an impressionistic study of a secondary modern school by Webb.[24] 'Hostility [between teachers and boys] is the key factor . . .' The pupil subculture is interpreted as a realistic preparation for the irresponsibilities and inanities of life after school in routinized, semi-skilled employment; and the staff subculture as an equally realistic mode of adjustment to the hostility of the boys, and a way of handling one's guilt and cumulative fatigue.

Webb is describing a 'contraculture' rather than a subculture. A subculture is simply a group with common values and characteristics modes of behaviour which mark it off from other groups; it may arise from isolation or segregation, as in a remote mining valley or rural community (or school annexe). Waller talks of 'the separate culture of the young' which arises from the interests characteristic of their age and finds its purest expression in the unsupervised play group.

A contraculture arises from a situation of conflict and frustration and is characterized by values which are actually the inverse of those which prevail in the surrounding society. The delinquent gang is an excellent example. The situation described by Webb has all the characteristics of an active contraculture.

Pupil subcultures are likely to arise in any school simply as common solutions to common problems, as modes of adjustment to difficulties and uncertainties. Pupils arrive at their own notions of proper solutions to problems: their subculture consists of shared agreements and understandings. Their problems may range from boredom and threats of punishment, to keeping up with their homework and passing examinations. The staff exist to offer solutions to these problems; pupils (like patients of long standing in a hospital ward) may find official solutions unacceptable and attempt to find their own.

It is particularly important that teachers should understand and if possible investigate the pupil subcultures which confront them, for they do much to determine the level and direction of pupils' efforts. We have little knowledge of the way in which levels of effort are set and maintained in our educational institutions: the formal system of incentives and rewards only partly explains the level of 'productivity'. Studies of productivity in industry have long made clear the importance of the workers' subculture. Production is not simply explained in terms of the demands of management, the ability of individuals, and the nature of the rewards offered. Work-groups which have achieved any degree of solidarity are not easily manipulated by management.

The penalties which may be visited on the 'swot' at school are not unlike those visited on the 'rate-buster' in industry. Groups of pupils develop a conception of their abilities and set group standards and goals. This process is in need of investigation.

It is important to discover why pupils think they are at school and their perception of the problems they have to contend with. They are likely to arrive at their own notion of what learning is appropriate to their various goals. If their immediate problem is pressure of work and examinations, their subculture will help towards a solution. It will bring pressure onto the staff to 'keep to the syllabus'; it will support values which appear to be at variance with the broad conception of education entertained by the staff. If the problem is essentially boredom, their subculture will help them to cope with this too, evolving ways of making relationships with staff yield the maximum of entertainment or excitement.

American studies of pupils' subcultures have commonly shown an anti-intellectual value-system at work which depresses the 'natural' level of academic achievement. Potentially able pupils may prefer to devote their energies to activities such as games which bring the approval of their fellows. The best academic performers may not be the most able pupils: the gifted have chosen to use their talents in other directions and are not competing. The long-term effect is to produce intellectuals who are not really very intellectual.

This is the conclusion that emerges from a well-known study of school cultures undertaken by Coleman.[25] In England Shipman[26] and William Taylor[27] have looked at the aims and orientations of colleges of education in terms of their 'cultures', and David Hargreaves has distinguished between academic and delinquescent subcultures in a secondary modern school which are associated with streaming and levels of academic performance.[28] The immediate need, perhaps, is to re-examine and refine the concept of culture as a research tool. Hargreaves fears that: 'It may be that our analysis of the subcultural differentiation raises more problems than it solves.' The concept of culture needs sharpening, but it should not be abandoned. We are likely to be faced in the future with more culturally heterogeneous schools both as a result of immigration and deliberate social policy. We need to know whether our schools are melting pots. An appropriate use of the concept of culture in empirical research may help us to find out.

NOTES

[1] J. Floud, 'Teaching in the affluent society', *British Journal of Sociology*, vol. 13, 1962.

[2] B. Wilson, 'The teacher's role—a sociological analysis', *British Journal of Sociology*, vol. 13, 1962.

[3] Talcott Parsons, *The Social System*, Chicago: Free Press and London: Routledge & Kegan Paul, 1952.

[4] F. Musgrove and P. H. Taylor, 'Teachers' and parents' conceptions of the teacher's role', *British Journal of Educational Psychology*, 1965.

[5] F. Musgrove, 'The social needs and satisfactions of some young people', *British Journal of Educational Psychology*, 1966.

[6] J. W. Getzels and E. G. Guba, 'Role, role conflict and effectiveness', *American Sociological Review*, vol. 19, 1954.

[7] W. B. Brookover, 'Research on teacher and administrative roles', *Journal of Educational Sociology*, vol. 29, 1955.

[8] J. W. Getzels and E. G. Guba, 'The structure of roles and role conflict in the teaching situation', *Journal of Educational Sociology*, vol. 29, 1955.

[9] L. Cohen and K. Boothroyd, 'Community expectations of the teacher's role: some mistaken perceptions of primary school teachers', *Research in Education*, no. 7, 1972.

[10] C. Wayne Gordon, 'The role of the teacher in the social structure of the high school', *Journal of Educational Sociology*, vol. 29, 1955.

[11] Moira Brown, 'Some strategies used in primary schools for initiating and implementing change', University of Manchester M.Ed. thesis (unpublished), 1971.

[12] Beryl F. A. Tipton, 'Some organizational characteristics of a technical college', *Research in Education*, no. 7, 1972.

[13] J. A. Chapman, 'An evaluation of the role of school councils in secondary education', University of Bradford M.Sc. thesis (unpublished), 1969.

[14] T. O. Odetola, *et al.*, 'Organizational structure and student alienation', *Educational Administration Quarterly*, vol. 8, 1972.

[15] L. Cohen, *Conceptions of Headteachers Concerning their Role*, University of Keele, Ph.D. thesis, 1970.

[16] G. H. Moeller and W. W. Charters, 'Relation of bureaucratization to sense of power among teachers', *Administrative Science Quarterly*, vol. 10, 1966.

[17] T. Burns and G. M. Stalker, *The Management of Innovation*, Tavistock Publications, 1961.

[18] A. W. Gouldner, 'Cosmopolitans and locals', *Administrative Science Quarterly*, vol. 2, 1957–8.

[19] P. M. Blau and W. R. Scott, *Formal Organizations: A Comparative Approach*, Chandler Publishing Company, 1962.

[20] W. G. Bennis, 'Reference groups and loyalties in the outpatient department', *Administrative Science Quarterly*, vol. 2, 1958.

[21] D. Toomey, 'Local-cosmopolitan differences among teachers taking higher degrees', *Educational Review*, vol. 22, 1970.

[22] A. H. Barton, *Organizational Measurement and its Bearing on the Study of College Environments*, Princeton College Entrance Examination Board, 1961.

[23] D. Riesman and C. Jencks, 'The viability of the American college' in N. Sanford, *American College*, New York: John Wiley, 1962.

[24] J. Webb, 'The sociology of the school', *British Journal of Sociology*, vol. 13, 1962.

[25] J. S. Coleman, 'The adolescent subculture and academic achievement', *American Journal of Sociology*, vol. 65, 1960.

[26] M. Shipman, 'Education and college culture', *British Journal of Sociology*, vol. 17, 1967.

[27] William Taylor, *Society and the Education of Teachers*, London: Faber, 1969.

[28] David Hargreaves, *Social Relations in a Secondary School*, London: Routledge & Kegan Paul, 1967.

7 Sociology and educational research

Donald F. Swift

Sociological research on British education since the war

Sociological research on education has had a two-fold effect upon educational thought. First, it has made educators in general much more aware of the importance of social factors in the development of abilities. Second, the relationship between the institution of education and the other major societal institutions has become clearer. Research had concentrated on the former, and dealt with the latter in so far as studies of social factors in educability elucidated the association between systems of education and of stratification. Crudely put, the major consequence for the thinking of educators lies in the fact that behaviour which in the early fifties was easily attributable to lack of brain power is now equally glibly attributed to lack of quality in home background.

We have now reached something of an impasse. A major breakthrough was made in the late fifties when class-chance analysis was used to make us aware of the inconsistency between our ideals of educational opportunity and the actual situation. But the research itself did no more than that. It provided descriptive evidence but few conclusions on the social-psychological mechanisms by which the situation came about. At that point educational psychologists joined the search; and this chapter will take it as axiomatic that the greater part of educational research is dependent upon integration of the findings of the two disciplines if not their complete merging in research projects.

The research showed that differential access to power, prestige and income are all associated with achievement within another kind of system in the society, the educational system. They went on to give explanations for this association which were individual (or psychological) explanations of, for example, 'the child' in the working-class family. In doing so, the sociologists were doing no more than simply translating sociological theory into examples at the individual level. Nevertheless, it is not unreasonable of the psychologists to apply psychological theories and methods to these individual examples.

While accepting the face validity of the relationship, psychologists were dissatisfied with the scientific quality of the evidence as it was offered to them. They therefore went out to duplicate the research using what they regarded as more rigorous methods of measurement and evaluation. In so doing they used the techniques of analysis which have been previously used in research at the psychological level, notably parametric correlation and atheoretical multivariate techniques, like factor analysis. This has led to a number of research studies with a sociological appearance, but which fell into major methodological errors (as I see it) of fallacious aggregation, of conceptual indistinctness when employing techniques like multiple regression, and of erroneous assumptions about the heterogeneity of the populations when employing correlations.

The problem lies in the extent to which sociological analysis is dependent upon theory. Most educational researchers, usually educational psychologists or medical researchers, occasionally sociologists, have been finally dependent upon a method-ideology based on the ideal classical experiment and probability sampling, which has caused them to conceptualize the sociological variables in psychological terms.

Let us think of the psychologists coming to the set of ideas sociologists had produced and applying to it their own kit of measurement tools. These tools were developed either in agriculture or in experimental psychology, based on probability, on the individual as the case for study, and using the idea of classical experiment as the basis of knowledge. Most importantly they were developed in situations in which it is much easier to get away with atheoretical approaches. For within the near-laboratory situation, in which we research on individuals, it is often possible to be relatively atheoretical. It is, also, often reasonable to make certain very important assumptions that are fundamental to the classical experimental mode. We assume that we have either controlled or randomized all variables other than the independent and dependent ones under observation. But these assumptions of randomization and control are often not permissible, or where they are, they do violence to a sociological formulation of the problem. For example, the taking of random samples, while allowing us the security of probability theory, destroys any sociological structure that may be represented in the data. For similar reasons, and in Britain particularly, sociologists tend to find themselves forced by their methods into doing social psychology.

Our major need, therefore, is for interdisciplinary co-operation to replace accidental use of the methods and theories of other disciplines. We have a great problem in Britain in that our training of psychologists and sociologists is separate. Our psychologists tend to be sociologically ignorant while our sociologists are, on the whole, statistically ignorant. There is a built-in tendency against interdisciplinary co-operation because each tends to be frightened or contemptuous (a rather more serious way of being frightened) of the other's skills.

Key methodological issues: the ecological fallacy

Two pieces of social research in education provide ideal examples of the methodological problems caused by bringing together two different perspectives in a single piece of research. These problems are fallacious aggregation and atheoretical correlation. The aggregative fallacy is caused by mixing the two kinds of metaphors—the individual and the group level of analysis—and it raises the question of how well sociologists have presented to psychologists and educators an adequate picture of social process.

In one large scale piece of research in Manchester (Wiseman, 1964) an ecological study of a city was undertaken. In this, the rates of incidence of the occurrence of attributes of individuals were calculated within wards. Ecological correlations were then used to measure the association between these rates across all the wards. Thus, the Manchester research attempted to do sociology at the group level. It is most important to recognize that the results had nothing whatsoever to do with the individual level of analysis. Nevertheless they were assumed to have something to do with it and relatively recent writing has maintained the error (Vernon, 1969, p. 64).

It is possible to see a train of thought in which one uses psychological theories and sociological theories to link up ecological correlations and individual correlations. This would not work in the simple sense of saying that some ecological correlation is ·7, its individual level counterpart correlation is ·6 and therefore they are different (or similar). It was assumed that an ecological correlation has some meaning *as it stands* for the individual level. The fact that an aspect of the environment is designated 'economic factor', or 'illegitimacy', in summary of some objective facts about a series of geographical areas, related to the rates of brightness or backwardness to be found in these areas, tells us absolutely nothing statistically about the relationships between economic factors, or illegitimacy, and the extent to which individual children develop intelligence. We cannot simply transfer the level of inference from the group to the individual.

The researchers devised some variables which represent the collectivity—the ward or in fact a group of wards, defined territorially—and any association between parameters will have to relate to the functioning of that collectivity—the group, the ward, the sub-culture, or whatever it is. The collectivity itself is a completely meaningless thing without some kind of sociological theory behind it. If that collectivity is meaningless then the calculations which took place are equally meaningless. In any case they have nothing to do with furthering knowledge about the importance of experience upon the development of school ability unless theories of social process and individual psychology can provide a link between the two levels of analysis (see appendix to this chapter).

The problem of fallacious aggregation raises all the thorny issues of how sociologists can present ideas in sociological terms accompanied by appropriate method or techniques for measurement of the social world in relation to those ideas. At present, sociologists tend to exemplify their ideas by use of individual level explanations. We do not yet have in Britain the methodological sophistication to produce group level analysis that would be able to deal with the ideas as we presented them as theories. We find ourselves doing accidental psychology or social psychology. We give our questionnaires to a random sample and use parametric techniques for analysis of our data. Even when we use non-parametric techniques we tend to talk in psychological terms about the results.

Key methodological issues: atheoretical correlation

Fallacious aggregation exemplifies our difficulties in conceptualizing our material at the appropriate level. The problems of atheoretical correlation exemplify the general axiom that social research without theory is impossible. The National Survey carried out by the Government Social Survey is the best example of our mistakes. (This is not an attack upon the Government Social Survey. It is one of the best institutions in the world for carrying out surveys of a very specific kind, beautifully efficient, highly organized, very competent, very professional and thoroughly reliable—it just does not do sociology. It does social research of a very different kind.) It is an example of what happens when we collect data at the individual level without benefit of theory to exemplify or produce the models which make sociological sense of the data.

The National Survey was a well-drawn representative sample in which 173 schools, 2,000 children were selected, parents interviewed, teachers exhaustively questioned, children tested, and all with the explicit intention of building up as complete a picture as possible of home, school and child. Having obtained this complete picture, the idea was to analyse the data so as to show which factors most powerfully influenced achievement. That is, the research implicitly assumed that all the important factors in the association between achievement and background were included in the data. In the event the results suggest that the important factors were not included. Within the data the factors chosen accounted for two-thirds of the total variance between schools, and about half the variation within schools. But this is a step-wise multiple regression method and the inclusion of some other variables could very well have dragged off a lot of the variance attributable to any of the factors as they are put in.

The basic conclusion of the Plowden National Survey was that the attitudes of parents are of greatest importance in producing school achievement. Since this study collected attitudes, there was no likelihood of discovering anything else. That is, the results were a set of variables that were a reorganization of the variables originally put in. Again it is the question of the importance of theory in interpreting data. Outside the laboratory, we can no longer assume that all possible intervening or contaminating variables are controlled. The only crutch the researcher has to lean on in order to estimate the validity of the data and of the associations within them is the theoretical justification for the variables he has decided to use and those that he has decided to ignore.

Three groups of influences were looked at: (a) parental attitudes (e.g. willingness to keep children at school, to visit school, to help with homework and to encourage generally); (b) home circumstances (e.g. physical amenities, father's job). Not only do atheoretical techniques assume the similar logical or theoretical status of all their variables, they also assume that they are distinct variables. Length of parents' education is a home circumstance, as opposed to a parental attitude (e.g. willingness to keep child at school). Finally (c) the school was included—school size, class size, internal organization and HMI's assessment of adequacy.

The major finding was that parental attitudes were more important than home circumstances which were more important than schools. And the sociologist's response has been to say that the research has made nonsense of the definition of attitudes and of home circumstances.

What, then, is the value of the findings? The researchers say that the weight to be attached to their conclusion depends on the strength of the evidence supporting them under four headings:

1 the accuracy of sampling of schools, of children and of parents,
2 the appropriateness of the variables chosen,
3 the accuracy with which they have been measured, and
4 the validity of the inferential arguments used.

It would be difficult to criticize the research under 1 and 3.

The problems arise under 2 and 4 where the atheoretical technique employed in the real world of millions of possible stimulus variables was inadmissible from the sociological point of view.

In their attempt to find some explanations for performance in school the sociologists had provided a range of ideas about what went on in the social environment but few of these were included. To justify this argument we must look at how the mixing of perspectives caused the study to produce findings that sociologists find difficult to accept. The study found indicators of social class (that is occupational and educational attainment of parents) to be less closely related to student achievement than what were defined as parental attitudes towards school. Those planning the research seem to have assumed that sociologists perceive social class as if it were a single stimulus variable and occupation its empirical referent. It may then be compared with another 'variable' like attitudes of parents towards school. It is important to recognize that this involves an assumption that the logical status within the research design of the stimulus variable 'social class measured by occupation' is similar to that defined as 'parental attitude to school and measured by the number of times they are prepared to visit, etc'. The answer produced by the analysis is that parental attitude towards school had a greater ability —arithmetically—to explain the variance in achievement.

From the sociological perspective this is very much what we should expect. In fact, we must go much further than that. If parental attitudes were measured properly, we must ask why that variable 'social class' had any influence at all. The real weakness of the findings may be highlighted by pointing out that a sociologist would now ask us to look for attitudes which were *not* included since the social class kind of explanation still existed within the data. That the research had missed the sociological point may be seen in the way in which the report discusses why attitudes are more important than social class. The argument *should* focus on why the indicators of social class are still important at all in this individual level of analysis. The only explanation the sociologist would have would be one suggesting 'poverty leading to physiological weakness'.

To describe the sociological variable 'social class' at the individual level in terms of parental occupation as a category and to assume that we have described some kind of stimulus variable is exactly analogous to tasting chocolate by eating its wrapper. That is, we have to distinguish between the psycho-dynamic and the social structural level of analysis (see Swift, 1968). The researchers have introduced variables into the individual-level mixer which have entirely different theoretical statuses. It is a massive case of mixing theoretical metaphors.

Let us put the situation in the individual level terms of analysis. Thinking about persons, we have a portmanteau variable—social class—derived from theories of processes in society, which attempts to summarize, amongst other things, a vast range of attitudes, or views of reality. If the data had analysed the *whole* range of attitudes that are important in the development of cognitive style or adaptability to education, then the variable 'social class' as measured in this way should have contributed *none* of the variance. It should have been washed out of the analysis. To say 'social class at the individual level' is just a different way of saying 'attitudes'. (Parenthetically, sociologists would also tend not to use the word attitudes—preferring terms like cognitions of reality, life orientations or construction of reality.) At the level of social psychological mechanisms they are just different ways of saying the same thing and not competing variables. That is, they are not competing variables similar to those in the laboratory situation in which we are filming a child's eyes and trying to compare the importance of the effect of noise and temperature on eye movements. In this case we have two similar variables impinging upon his experiencing of the words which we can manipulate to discover which is the more important.

To summarize, the research found that parental attitudes account for 26 per cent of the variation in educational performance for all pupils between schools, variations in attitudes account for 26 per cent of the variation in educational performance for all pupils between schools and 20 per cent between schools. There is really a serious danger that we will understand this to mean 'accounted for' in the real world rather than accounted for within the data. We mean accounted for in the real world in so far as the data is an exact description of the real world—and for ideas about whether or not it is an exact description we are entirely dependent upon theories. To say that the remaining one-third or half of the variance in achievement is attributable to circumstances that have not been taken into account seems to be methodologically erroneous.

The assumption appears to be that, within the data, x per cent of variance is attributable and there is another $100-x$ per cent not to be found—therefore that is 'outside'. Thus, if we bring all those variables inside, the variables that we had inside would stay in the same proportion to each other and to the total. This does not seem to be reasonable. We must instead recognize that if we had included a number of other variables we would massively change the relative importance of those variables already in the data. That is, we have no justification for assuming that the variables are discrete entities. In fact an essential element of sociological theories is an *assumption* of contamination. If we further have theoretical grounds for claiming that most of the important variables are omitted from the analysis we have some justification for saying that the associations within the variables are spurious.

The sociological perspectives

Smelser (1968) has provided a useful scheme for bringing some order into a review of sociological contributions to knowledge. To use it we must start with an elementary point, failure to appreciate or accept which has bedevilled inter- or dual-discipline research in education. Sociology does not deal with a special class of empirical data. It brings to all empirical data a special perspective. It is not so much that there is something 'out there' which is sociological as that we perceive something sociological about what is 'out there'. All sociologists accept this elementary phenomenalist point. Differences between them begin to emerge in the extent to which it dominates their thinking about external social reality. It can make its presence felt simply in the form of a recognition that our data are a function of the operations we undertake and that theory is an essential element in all knowledge about human behaviour. At the other extreme, it can be used as an argument that subjective awareness is the only reality—that all knowledge of human behaviour is metaphor, a view that underlies the claim to phenomenologism of some current sociologists.

Returning to the simple proposition that perspective (or theory) is applied to understand the environment of an individual or group, one could be in a strong position to explain the contribution which such a perspective has for analysing the process of education. But there are several possible perspectives. Smelser identifies five:

1 interpretations of events or aspects of human organizations in their physical and biological environment and in their co-ordinates of space and time (demography and ecology),
2 interpretations of behaviour in terms of its psychological significance to the individual considered as self or person,
3 interpretation of behaviour as manifestation of group membership,
4 consideration of social life as relationships between persons (role and social structure),
5 looks to a variety of cultural phenomena that lend meaning to all social behaviour whether conceptualized according to the person, group or structural perspectives (norms, values, ideologies).

Earlier I argued that a great deal of research on education has been vitiated by a 'mixing of metaphors'. Either analysis of data collected at a group level is conceptualized at the individual level or *vice versa.* This situation may be summarized as a failure to distinguish between the social structural and psycho-dynamic levels of analysis in the manipulation of data. Using Smelser's categories, situations conceptualized in terms of group membership, roles and social structure have been represented by data collected in research in which the individual was the unit of analysis and the social process no more than a set of discrete environmental variables.

Interdisciplinary co-operation in educational research

The failure to produce research findings which satisfy the canons of scientific research as understood within the two disciplines may be insoluble but I find little evidence to prove that this is so. Indeed, such steps as have been made towards greater cross-disciplinary understanding suggest otherwise. It would be easy to argue at this point that our two disciplines are in an early stage of development and characterized by many schools of thought and competing method-ideologies which will disappear as they attain scientific maturity. I feel safer in pointing to the fact that, on certain basic criteria for describing a field of study, there are many similarities across the disciplines.

As a first step in clarifying the differences within sociology of education we might distinguish between the criteria employed by the three major 'schools' of thought and compare them with those within educational psychology (see Table 7.1 on page 182).

All social research on education in Britain has been within the Marxist or functionalist 'schools'. That is, it has focused on patterns of behaviour conceived as institutions. They have involved some mixture of 1 and 2, implicit assumptions about 5 or 6, almost always taking the perspective of realism within 9 and finally employing some combination of 13 and 14. Almost never has it been adequately positivist within 14 although the researcher will often employ some of the statistical techniques appropriate to this method.

Box 14 is the seat of our difficulties. The psychologist of education with no background in 1, 2, 5, 6, 9, 10 and 13 comes to judge 'the results' of sociological writing and research. The dominant method-ideology in educational psychology is positivist (16). In looking at sociological results the psychologist may then feel that the work is hopelessly large-scale (13), or hopelessly imprecise (14, intuitionist or Verstehende) or scientifically inadequate (14, positivist techniques).

The sociologist's response to this must be to argue that while poor work of the kind referred to under 13 and 14 may undoubtedly ruin a piece of research it can never, however good, save a piece of work that is bad at 1 and 2. For the reasons I outlined earlier, theory (i.e. quality of conceptualization) becomes paramount outside the laboratory.

By definition there are certain fundamental differences between sociology and psychology in the sense that one focuses upon relations among persons while the other studies the individual as a system of

Table 7.1: Schools of thought in the study of education: British sociology of education

CRITERIA	*Marxist*	*Functionalist*	*Interactionist*	*Behaviourist*
Dependent variables	1 Patterns of behaviour (institutions—structuralist) Ideology	2 Patterns of behaviour (institutions—structuralist)	3 Micro-units of interaction Underlying physical processes	4 Patterns of behaviour (individuals) Underlying physical and cognitive processes
Independent variables	5 Production relations	6 Social functions	7 Personal decision	8 Physical needs
Logical ordering (theoretical framework) Epistemology	9 Dialectical materialism	10 Organicism or system analysis Realism or Nominalism	11 The self as process Phenomenologism or Nominalism	12 The individual as an organicism Realism or Nominalism
Verification	13 Comparative historical analysis	14 Intuitionist or Verstehende or Positivist	15 Intuitionist or Verstehende or Positivist	16 Positivist

needs, feelings, skills and defences in process. Thus, the dependent variables of sociology are often the independent variables or parameters of psychology.

Smelser suggests three ways in which social science (which I will continue to call sociology) and psychology may contribute towards each other's development. On the formal level the conceptual constructs of the two disciplines are often analogous—individual needs, capacities and ego control are analogous to functional exigencies, social resources and social control. The help may lie in elaboration of such conceptual models—there is nothing to be gained, of course, in applying knowledge or data about individual needs to the functional exigencies of a society. At the substantive level, the complementary approaches of sociology and psychology must be capable of producing explanatory frameworks which offer greater understanding of specific social situations. This seems to be particularly true of the educational setting. Unfortunately, there are few examples of such work—Sherif's (1964) work on peer groups being the most notable exception. This is mostly due to the failure of sociologists to develop and test adequate concepts at the interactional level in education settings. The third and perhaps the most important kind of exchange will lie in the extent to which each discipline helps the other to clarify the implicit assumptions each makes at its complement's level of analysis. Sociological research rests upon a series of implicit theories of individual psychology. Psychological level research, on the other hand, must make some assumptions about social process. I have argued that in the former case there is a tendency to make the psychological assumptions relatively explicit—even the *ex post facto* explanations for observed relationships.

Recent developments: the interactionist perspective to the rescue

It is at this point that we can return to the third column of the Table. Within recent years, since, in fact, the introduction to Britain of the writings of Cicourel and Kitsuse (1963) and Berger (1967), there has developed a line of thinking about education which draws its inspiration from one of the founders of American social psychology—G. H. Mead. This is characterized as 'interactionism' in the Table. British research using this approach has hardly begun, but in America the work of Becker and his colleagues in higher education settings (1961, 1968) promises well.

There are two ways in which this school of thought may contribute to improved inter-disciplinary research. Firstly, in its most extreme formulation it claims to replace existing social psychology based upon behaviourist principles (see Harré and Secord, 1972). Secondly, and more reasonably, its concepts might be easier to articulate with those of the conventional educational psychologist since its focus is on the micro-unit of interaction and the self conceived as a process. Thus, there is a greater similarity between 3 and 4 than between 1 or 2 and 4, where there is a great danger of misunderstanding due to the different level at which behaviour is conceptualized. As far as independent variables are concerned there is an element of conflict (7 v. 8). In its extreme form, interactionism denies the acceptability of physical needs as a starting point. The greatest barrier to cooperation lies in the wide divergence in method-ideology between British interactionism and educational psychology. Because of the perspective's natural affinity with the phenomenological theory of knowledge, the school has much more in common with the mentalist than with the behaviourist approach that tends to predominate in educational psychology.

However, this is far from being a necessary association, for example, in its approach to verification. Similarly Brookover's (1964) research directly originates in the thinking of G. H. Mead and is strictly verificationist.

Phenomenology has a further advantage in that its rejection of a traditional analytic philosophical approach to knowledge allows it to confront unselfconsciously the questions that arise from the moral pathos of life—raising questions that are genuinely educational. The disadvantage it brings is the inevitable one encountered by existentialists—that, as logical positivism and neo-positivist methodology will continue to assert, no moral question, however derived, can justify unanalysed ideas, illogical arguments or inadequate evidence. If it is true that the greatest philosophy occurs in the tension between the two contradictory tendencies of analysis and existentialism then perhaps such a tension within sociological thinking about education will be fruitful.

Whether or not the interactionist research that must now follow will provide a setting with which the sociological and psychological perspectives can be articulated, there is no doubt that it has already contributed to sociological thinking about education. Until recently, the sociology of education was principally distinguished by its failure to deal with either social interaction in schools or the consequences for the societal organization of knowledge that is represented in such interaction. It tended not to deal with education as a process in society but with socialization as it affected schooling, the process of stratification as it was assisted by the institution of education, and the formal organization of schools (this latter never getting off the ground as a research question). Inevitably, the growing use of an interactionist perspective will produce research in schools when its value as a framework for producing information will be judged. That it has already produced an extension of sociological and social-psychological thinking about education is clear (see Esland, 1972; Dale 1972; Young 1971). One hopes that it is not clutching at a straw to expect that its ability to articulate the two disciplines will contribute to our ability to think about educational questions.

Appendix

This is not a hair-splitting affirmation of the letter of the law rather than of its spirit. We have to insist that correlations of group rates are statistically irrelevant to individual-level correlations; they are a function of how one draws boundaries around groups. Let us consider three contiguous areas of similar-sized populations which are to be analysed in terms of two variables *X* and *Y*.

Table 7.2: Individual level association between two variables in three areas

	Area A			*Area B*			*Area C*		
	X	not *X*	Total	*X*	not *X*	Total	*X*	not *X*	Total
Y	0	80	80	25	25	50	40	20	60
not *Y*	20	0	20	25	25	50	0	40	40
	20	80	100	50	50	100	40	60	100
	perfectly negative association			no association			high positive association		

The association between the two variables in the three areas varies from one extreme to almost the other. A product-moment correlation for the following rates:

Area A $X = 0{\cdot}2$; $Y = 0{\cdot}8$
Area B $X = 0{\cdot}5$; $Y = 0{\cdot}5$
Area C $X = 0{\cdot}4$; $Y = 0{\cdot}6$
produces a perfectly negative coefficient

However, taking the relationship between the variables at the individual level we find that there is insufficient evidence of association.

Table 7.3: Individual level association between two variables in the total area

	Area ABC		
	X	not *X*	Total
Y	65	125	190
not *Y*	45	65	110
Total	110	190	300

X^2 is slightly above 1·0: not significant

REFERENCES

BECKER, H. S. (*et al.*) (1961). *Boys in White: Student Culture in Medical School*, University of Chicago Press.
BECKER, H. S. (*et al.*) (1968). *Making the Grade: The Academic Side of College Life*, Wiley.
BERGER, P. L., AND LUCKMANN, T. (1967). *The Social Construction of Reality*, Allen Lane, The Penguin Press.
BROOKOVER, WILBUR B. (*et al.*) (1964). 'Self-concept of ability and school achievement', *Sociology of Education*, 33 (3), Spring 1964, 271–8.
CICOUREL, AARON V., AND KITSUSE, JOHN I. (1963). *The Educational Decision-makers*, Indianapolis: Bobbs-Merrill.
DALE, R. (1972). *The Culture of the School*, Open University Press.
DAVIES, IOAN (1970). 'The management of knowledge: a critique of the use of typologies in educational sociology', *Sociology*, 4 (1), 1–22.
ESLAND, G. (1972). *The Construction of Reality*, Open University Press.
HARRÉ, R., AND SECORD, P. F. (1972). *The Explanation of Social Behaviour*, Oxford: Blackwell.
SHERIF, MUZAFER, AND SHERIF, CAROLINE W. (1964). *Reference Groups*, New York: Harper & Row.
SMELSER, NEIL J. (1968). 'Sociology and the other social sciences' in Paul F. Lazarsfeld, William H. Sewell, Harold L. Wilensky (ed.), *The Uses of Sociology*, London: Weidenfeld & Nicolson, pp. 3–44.
SWIFT, D. F. (1968). 'Social class and educational achievement' in H. J.

Butcher (ed.), *Educational Research in Britain*, University of London Press.
VERNON, PHILIP E. (1969). *Intelligence and Cultural Environment*, London: Methuen.
WISEMAN, S. (1964). *Education and the Environment*, Manchester University Press.
YOUNG, MICHAEL F. D. (ed.) (1971). *Knowledge and Control: New Directions for the Sociology of Education*, Collier-Macmillan.

Part three

Research and practice

8 Knowledge and research

William Taylor

In their contribution to this book, Peters and White define educational research as sustained systematic enquiry designed to provide us with new knowledge which is relevant to initiating people into desirable states of mind. Reviewing this and other definitions, Nisbet and Entwistle suggest that current emphases argue for a broader definition of educational research as 'careful, systematic attempts to understand the educational process and, through understanding, to improve its efficiency'. But whatever definition we consider most appropriate, it is evident that research in education has much in common with other kinds of research. It entails devoting resources of time, money and manpower to activities designed to find out more about the physical, social and psychological worlds that we inhabit, and to unravel the complexities and interrelationships of these worlds with a view to achieving greater control over our circumstances, making our decision processes more rational, and making it easier for us to achieve the ends that we set ourselves. To a greater extent than in the case of basic scientific and humanistic studies, the kinds of social and educational research that at a given time a society chooses to support inevitably reflect its current problems and pre-occupations, the things that matter to power groups within it, the facts that are needed to help shape or, sometimes, to legitimate, decisions about policies and programmes.

This is not the only, or perhaps the most important way in which educational research differs from other kinds of research. For many years a failure to recognize such differences and a consequent attempt to base studies in education on a rather naively conceived model of 'scientific' research have vitiated the usefulness of a good deal of the work done in this field. These are points to which we will have occasion to return later on. First of all it is necessary to place educational research in the broader setting of the knowledge we have about education.

Knowledge and role

Everyone has knowledge about education, even if it only amounts to knowing the name and reputation of the local primary school, or a good way in which to help a child to learn tables, or having opinions about comprehensive reorganization. The more involved in education activities people become, as parents, teachers, politicians or administrators, the greater the number of facts and opinions about these activities they come to possess. There are also today many hundreds of men and women in colleges, in universities, and research institutes, and in publishing, journalism and radio and television, for whom the production, organization and dissemination of knowledge about education is a full-time occupation.

The results of 'sustained systematic enquiry' are only one element in this corpus of knowledge, and influence the remaining elements of both theoretical and pre-theoretical knowledge in ways that are as yet little studied and understood. Those who are professionally concerned in the production and dissemination of knowledge about education tend to overrate the importance and influence of systematic organized knowledge, as distinct from what the phenomenologist Alfred Schutz called 'recipe knowledge'. Working within a tradition established by Schutz, the sociologists Berger and Luckmann have suggested that:[1]

> Theoretical knowledge is only a small and by no means the most important part of what passes for knowledge in a society. Theoretically sophisticated legitimations appear at particular moments of an institutional history. The primary knowledge about the institutional order is knowledge on the pre-theoretical level. It is the sum total of 'what everybody knows' about a social world, an assemblage of maxims, morals, proverbial nuggets of wisdom, values and beliefs, myths and so forth, the theoretical integration of which requires considerable intellectual fortitude in itself . . . On the pre-theoretical level . . . every institution has a body of transmitted recipe knowledge, that is, knowledge that supplies the institutionally appropriate rules of conduct.

The relationship between such recipe knowledge, which constitutes a large part of what any of us knows about particular spheres of activity, and the theoretical knowledge, that both generates and is in turn produced by systematic enquiry and research, is crucial to understanding the impact of research in practice and the way in which educational innovations originate and are diffused. Yet all too often this relationship is so over-simplified as to make it seem as if what is sometimes called 'clearing the channels of communication' between teacher, researcher and administrator would ensure some miraculous flowering of research and its effective application to work in classroom and lecture hall, and a consequential improvement in educational outcomes. What is often ignored is how the role related nature of the knowledge that people have about education determines the perspectives from which they identify the nature of the problems to be faced and the means by which they might be overcome.

Administrators, inspectors, teachers, researchers and others in the world of education, nominally concerned with the same problems, seem often to be talking past each other and to be proceeding from very different sets of assumptions. A simple but false explanation of this state of affairs suggests that some people, such as classroom teachers, simply aren't as well informed as others about particular developments and possibilities. Other people, such as research workers, get bogged down in jargon and statistics, and this makes them difficult to understand. Administrators and inspectors lack the recent first-hand knowledge of the classroom or of educational research that they need if they are to understand the teachers' problems or the researchers' findings. The solution is equally simple. Better means have to be developed for the diffusion and dissemination of information in the shape of abstracting services, journals, resource centres and data banks. There is nothing wrong that more money could not cure.

But the experience of actually working with civil servants and local authority administrators, with Her Majesty's Inspectorate, local advisers and the heads of schools and colleges, with educational researchers and those who pass judgments on proposed and completed research, with the officers of international agencies, publishers, college of education tutors, classroom teachers and, finally, students, makes it evident that such simplistic and common-sense explanations of why people differ in their understanding of and judgments about educational and social phenomena will not stand up to critical examination. The problem has little to do with the level of intelligence or the open mindedness of the individuals concerned. There are just as many able and open minded chief education officers as there are directors of research projects or university professors or wardens of teachers' centres. Nor is it a matter of some people being better informed than others. Most of the people involved in education are very well informed indeed, although the sources of their information may differ, as may their interpretation of the same sources. Teachers, for example, are in possession of vast quantities of information about the children they teach and engage in a great deal of theoretical speculation—admittedly not using the same categories as a professional educational psychologist might employ, or the theoretical formulations that an educational philosopher would consider valid, but certainly doing something which testifies to the possession of an impressive quantity of knowledge of what it is they are about. Nor does the difficulty arise from the fact that certain generalized political and social orientations are differentially distributed, that there are fewer left wing civil servants and teachers than research workers and advisers.

The roots of the problem lie in the fact that the knowledge about education that is possessed by all the people who are labelled teachers, administrators, inspectors, researchers and so forth, is to a large and increasing extent *role specific knowledge*. With the growth of the numbers of those involved in education, and in its importance for the economy and for society, greater job differentiation has taken place. Where once there were only two categories in schools, heads and teachers, today the staff of a large school may include heads of departments, heads of middle and lower schools, directors of studies, heads of houses, year group tutors, teacher/social workers, counsellors, guidance personnel, resource centre technicians and stewards, laboratory assistants, librarians, teachers' aides, administrative officers, building supervisors and secretaries. An even greater differentiation has taken place outside the school. In the training colleges there used to be a subject called education. Today the programme of educational studies in the redesignated colleges of education is liable to include courses in educational psychology, the sociology of education, the history of education, and the philosophy of education. There will be a range of applied and interpretative studies such as the teaching of reading, the education of the immigrant, comparative education, and the use of audio-visual aids. Each of these courses will require the services of a specialist member of staff, with appropriate training. The single diploma in education that a few years ago constituted the only kind of advanced, post initial training course available to serving teachers in university institutes and departments of education has split and proliferated into dozens of differently designated qualifications.

All this is familiar enough and to some extent is coming to be taken for granted. Yet it has a profound effect on the way in which knowledge about education originates, is disseminated and put to use. As part of the process of exerting identity, each of the education professions and sub-professions tends to develop its own language and style of expression, to legitimize certain sources of knowledge and to devalue others. It is not ignorance that precludes certain people from the membership of particular groups, it is the possession of the wrong kind of knowledge. The serving teacher who is widely read in the psychology and sociology of education, and who substitutes judgments from these spheres for the traditional recipe knowledge of the staffroom, may find himself regarded as an outsider, already half-way to becoming a college of education lecturer or local authority organizer. The educational psychologist, concerned with establishing the statistical validity of his findings and in refining an already sophisticated methodology, may acquire a marked distaste for the 'mere speculation' in which his non-psychologically trained colleagues are prone to indulge, and deplore the influence on educational opinion and practice that is exerted by loosely conceived and inadequately designed research projects.

Role specific knowledge is clearly linked to career possibilities. The American art critic Harold Rosenberg has suggested that a prime moral issue for intellectuals today is 'whether to take advantage of professionalisation and its mental splitting in order to promote their own careers, or to combat mental structures through which activities become manageable and empty of meaning'. Rosenberg goes on to emphasize the effect of professionalism on the organization of knowledge[2]:

> A form of work establishes itself as a profession not only through the complications of its technique—many of the ancient crafts involve more complex recipes than their counterparts today, but through self-consciousness with regard to this technique . . . The essential mark of a profession is its evolution

> of a unique language or jargon into which it translates its subject matter and in which its methods, purposes and relations to other arts and sciences are formulated . . . The segregation of occupations within the mazes of their technical systems increasingly demolishes the old mental cohesions of the class and nation. Outside each profession there is no social body to talk to, and apart from the forms in which the thought of the profession is embodied, there is nothing to say . . .

Research on topics relevant to education, and research in education, has been going on for over seventy years. But educational research has only become a fully self-conscious activity in the past quarter century, and most of the more striking developments are the products of the past decade. Fully to understand the place, the function and the problems of the activities we label 'educational research' requires that these be examined within the total system of knowing about education of which they form part.

Some of the headings in terms of which such an examination might be conducted were suggested in Louis Wirth's preface to the 1936 English edition of Mannheim's *Ideology and Utopia*,[3] and these will be used here.

The sociology of educational knowledge

First, Wirth suggests there is the task of 're-working of the data of intellectual history with a view to the discovery of the style and methods of thought that are dominant in certain types of historical/social situations. In this connection it is essential to enquire into the shifts of intellectual interest and attention that accompany other phases of social structure'. The most cursory examination of books about education published at different dates shows how profound have been the shifts in the style and method of thought characteristic of educationists. It is not just a matter of certain concepts, such as 'attention', having almost disappeared from the text books, and of others, such as 'creativity', having taken their place, but also of how, for example, our knowledge about such phenomena as the nature of intelligence has shifted with changes in the socio-economic structure of society. In the thirties it was widely believed that hereditary factors were paramount, and only a very limited number of pupils were capable of benefiting from 'academic' secondary education; there was also a shortage of jobs for the well educated. In the sixties, with an actual or potential shortage of well qualified manpower in most industrial countries, intelligence became something that one 'acquires'. Over an even shorter time span, it is interesting to compare the strong tradition of structural studies in the sociology of education in the fifties with the growing emphasis in the seventies on action perspectives, stressing the importance of interactive factors, of 'meaning' and of sociological processes, and to relate this to the way in which faith in the possibilities of technological progress and of achieving equality of opportunity has diminished in the face of the difficulties of social change and anxieties about ecology.[4] Although there are a number of studies which relate the styles and methods of thought about education to certain historical and social situations, there are very few which deal with the recent past. Yet it is in the context of such style and methods that educational research is carried on, and this context has to be understood if the full significance of the activity itself is to be recognized.

Wirth suggests that the second element in the task of understanding a system of knowledge is that of 'throwing light on the question of how the purposes and interests of certain social groups come to find expression in certain theories, doctrines and intellectual movements'. This also involves taking account of 'factors that are responsible for the acceptance or rejection of certain ideas by certain groups in society, and of the motives and interests that prompt a certain group consciously to promote these ideas and to disseminate them among the wider sectors'. Here, again, there are indications of fruitful lines of enquiry that might be pursued in relation to knowledge about education. The ideological element in such knowledge has been particularly prominent in recent years in connection with disputes about the organization of secondary education, the structure of the curriculum, modes of examining, teaching methods in the primary school, and the education and training of teachers. Political factors, and the interests of particular groups, such as university staff and classroom teachers, underlie many of the positions that have been taken up in recent polemics, and some of those involved have been ready to make selective use of research to support their positions.

A third element to which Wirth draws attention is the 'recognition accorded to the various types of knowledge and the corresponding share of the resources of society devoted to the cultivation of each of these'. Useful indicators in this respect are the amount of money available for expenditure by the various research bodies, the number of professors and lecturers in different departments in universities, numbers of scholarship candidates in particular fields, and the amount of time that is devoted to different subjects in schools. Although the resources available for educational research are still small in comparison with the resources devoted to some other types of research activity, they have increased twelve-fold during the past ten years. Detailed estimates were given in Part one.

Fourth, acknowledging that 'no adequate theoretical treatment of the social organization of intellectual life exists', Wirth argues the need for 'a systematic analysis of the institutional organisation within the framework of which intellectual activity is carried on. This involves, among other items, the study of schools, universities, academies, learned societies, museums, libraries, research institutes and laboratories, foundations and publishing facilities. It is important to know how and by whom these institutions are supported, the types of activity they carry on, their policies, their internal organisation and inter-relations and their place in the social organisation as a whole.'

No such all embracing study has yet been undertaken in the field of education. Given the magnitude of the task, this is hardly surprising. It is not difficult to sketch out the topics that would need to be included in such an analysis. *Courses and qualifications* in education are provided in some two hundred colleges of education and universities in the United Kingdom, and the content and organization of these would repay careful examination. *Examinations* in education have been set for many years, and a comparison of the questions asked at different times provides many useful indications of how the value attached to particular kinds of knowledge has changed, and how new concepts and problems have been assimilated into the accepted corpus of knowledge that practitioners at different levels are required to possess. Whilst many general *libraries* have large collections on education, the specialist libraries in this field are mainly attached to university departments. London has two of the largest, in the shape of the University of London Institute of Education library and the library of the Department of Education and Science. The *literature of education* has grown rapidly in recent years, with a larger number of specialist journals and more textbooks and monograph series reflecting the enlarged demand from students as well as the availability of more funds for research and the appointment of additional staff in departments and colleges of education.

Finally, 'The sociology of knowledge is concerned with the persons who are the bearers of intellectual activity, namely the intellectuals. In every society there are individuals whose special function is to accumulate, preserve, reformulate and disseminate the intellectual heritage of the group. The composition of this group, their social derivation and the methods by which they are recruited, their organisation, their class affiliation, the rewards and prestige they receive, their participation on other spheres of social life, constitute some of the more crucial questions to which the sociology of knowledge seeks answers.'

In relation to the ubiquity of organized educational activity in society—there are nearly half a million teachers employed in primary, secondary and further education—the numbers of those who are directly involved in some way or another with educational research are small. In the universities there are some 1,500 members of staff working in departments, institutes and schools of education, including some 100 professors of the subject. In the colleges of education there are probably 2,000 to 3,000 lecturers who are members of education departments, but many of their subject colleagues also contribute to the work in education. To these numbers there should be added a few hundred more who are concerned full-time with research and development, an equivalent number in publishing and journalism, and some independent authors. If the group of 'originators and disseminators' is extended to include Her Majesty's Inspectors and local authority advisers, the part-time interest of specialists in other fields, and that proportion of classroom teachers who manage to write books and to produce and make known new ideas and methods without as a result finding themselves translated to other kinds of work, then the total rises to some 5,000 to 6,000 or about one per cent of those who earn their living in education.

It can reasonably be expected that a fair proportion of this one per cent are in direct touch with the outcomes of educational research, in the sense that they read the journals and books in which research findings are reported, and sometimes have access to research reports themselves. A rather smaller proportion will be personally involved, directly or indirectly, in research activity. Only a very limited part of the knowledge about education that all these people possess and employ in the performance of their everyday tasks can strictly be regarded as research based. Only exceptionally will the daily discussion of a problem or difficulty include the citation of a particular piece of research that contributed significantly to resolution or decision. Yet even when there is no explicit reference to particular studies, it is unlikely that such discussions will be unaffected by research. It exerts its influence by helping to determine the agenda of problems and difficulties, and in providing some of the elements that shape individual and group orientations towards particular issues. Just as anyone who talks and writes about man and society today is likely to have been influenced by, even if they never refer to, have never read or have never even heard of, the work of Darwin, Marx or Freud, so discussions about education are likely to be influenced by research on such topics as social class and educational opportunity and stages in children's learning as have been reported during the past twenty-five years. Research reflects the problems of its time, and produces findings which help to suggest and define new problems and issues. It has had the effect of removing certain concepts from our vocabulary, such as faculties, and of downgrading the importance of others, such as attention and memory. Equally, it has pointed up the existence of problems which now feature as important items in the agenda of our concerns, such as the effects of early maternal deprivation, or of impoverished linguistic environments, or the task of delimiting the stages of mental growth.

It is not only the agenda and the attitudes of the 'professionals' in education that will be influenced in this way. School organization and classroom practice also reflect the evidence of research. Admittedly, if circulation figures and the exercise of borrowing rights at university education libraries are any guide, few serving teachers read the specialist journals or have direct access to research findings. In recent years steps have been taken to make such findings more readily available, in such forms as the edited paperback reports of the NFER, broadsheets such as *Dialogue* (Schools Council) and *Educational Research News* (NFER), in the activities of the teachers' centres and through a more extensive and varied provision of in-service courses and conferences. Although the influence of research in education on staffroom conversation and school committee decision is more tenuous and indirect than on the thinking and practice of the 'professional', it is none the less real and it is growing.

All this points to the need to be aware of simplistic assumptions regarding the actual and likely pay-offs from research. Some of these are fairly readily traceable, but most make their way into thinking and practice less directly—through the literature on education and, in the case of the teachers, perhaps more compellingly through courses, conferences and lectures at which findings are referred to or drawn upon, or merely serve as the implicit underpinning of the ideas and suggestions of a lecturer. The fact that material on research forms only a very small part of the literature on education, and that most discussions about education, except among researchers themselves and some of the education professionals in universities and colleges, contain few explicit references to research, is no real guide to its influence and certainly no basis on which to calculate its usefulness in cost/benefit terms.

The relationship of research and development

Although the word development has already been used in this chapter, no attempt has been made to examine the relationship of all the activities that can be included under this heading with research as such. Mimicking the language of industry and of science, the habit has grown of referring to 'Education R and D' as a composite activity. The implication seems sometimes to be that 'pure research' leads through applied research to development, and from development to application. As Cherns points out, it is not simply that this model is inadequate when applied to social research, or to education, but it does not even apply in the scientific and technological fields from which it is derived. The error arises from a too narrow definition of what constitutes the knowledge that actors bring to bear in the solution of problems or the determination of decisions. Guba has argued:[5]

> Knowledge is at best only one of a number of input factors in any practical situation. No practical problem can be solved using knowledge alone—a whole host of economic, social, motivational and other factors must be considered.

But from the point of view of the actor, all these 'other factors' also constitute knowledge; research-based knowledge interacts with other kinds of knowledge that derive from experience, hunch, prejudice, commitment to principles and self-interest. An element in determining the extent to which research findings will be 'used' in decision-making, or in contributing to the definition of agendas, or the formulation of attitudes, is the extent to which these findings are consonant with the knowledge that we derive from these other sources. Such knowledge also helps to define the kinds of research that we consider relevant and worthy of support, and thus serves to complete what is, to a certain extent, but never completely, a closed knowledge system. Never completely closed, because the variety of convictions and interests in a pluralistic society ensures a continuing process of change in what Schon has called 'ideas in good currency' and what in the scientific world T. S. Kuhn defines as a paradigm—except of course that all the elements in Kuhn's paradigms are scientific, whereas many of those in the knowledge system under discussion are normative, non-rational and poorly articulated.[6] On this basis development work is just as likely to be a source of knowledge as fundamental research.

Yet there *is* a sense in which the kind of knowledge that is more likely to be produced by so-called fundamental research does precede and underpin development. Every development programme embodies some more or less clearly structured and articulated set of epistemological, sociological, and psychological assumptions concerning the nature of knowledge and the dynamics and correlates of learning. One of the clearest definitions of development work is that of the OECD Committee for Scientific and Technical Personnel in a report entitled *Education research and development in the USA*:[7]

> The objective of development activity carried out in the field of education is to produce materials, techniques, processes, hardware and organisational formats for instruction. The basis for such development is our knowledge about learning, motivation, instruction and education. The materials and techniques developed are designed to accomplish certain objectives, specified in advance, which are construed to be part of the broader goals of instruction in education. In other words, when a development activity is initiated the objectives, cast in something approaching a performance specification, are known or established at the outset. This clearly distinguishes development from research activities, whose objective is to discover an outcome which may be suspected but is not known. Unlike research, development as a process cannot be described in terms of any academic discipline. Our knowledge about human learning, motivation, instructional sequencing, teacher role, environmental and peer influences, and the like, however, provides the conceptual foundation for educational development.

If the adequacy of the materials, techniques, processes and hardware is dependent on the validity of their conceptual foundations, then the quality and the coverage of the latter are crucial. Yet the amount of well-grounded research-based knowledge that we possess about, for example, how children learn, is minimal, and only a small volume of new work of this kind is currently being undertaken. In contrast, there is now a very large volume of development work under way, providing almost complete coverage of the primary and secondary curriculum. Much of this is of recent origin and so far there have been few final reports of a kind which would give the opportunity to assess the quality and value of what is being produced. But it is already clear that a very great deal of this work rests upon a very narrow conceptual base. References to Piaget, Bruner, Bloom and Bernstein are much in evidence. But their work, important and substantial as it is, does not in itself constitute an adequate foundation for the very wide range of development activity that is currently under way. The Schools Council, which supports the bulk of this work, has made some effort, where the underlying knowledge of fundamental processes is deficient, to match major development projects with basic research in the same field. But, given the range of the Council's interests and the projects it is now supporting, this is hardly possible on a sufficient scale. Some development projects, to be sure, are themselves likely to produce findings that would add to our knowledge of fundamental educational processes, but this is even more of an unplanned benefit than the contributions to the knowledge of basic social processes that flow from efforts in the field of applied social science. There is a widespread if erroneous assumption that the pay-off from a development project is to be measured principally in terms of software and hardware, and this is a much more practical criterion than the kinds of outcomes that are expected from projects in applied social science. If resources for educational R and D are lumped together—and, given the inadequacies of reporting upon and documenting such activities in this country, it is virtually impossible to separate them—by far the largest part of the £3½m or so that is currently being spent goes on development work.

Research and the educational knowledge system

It follows from what has gone before that if the promises and the limitations of educational research are to be understood, it has to be looked at within the total system of educational knowledge that is available to the individual. According to their positions in relation to the educational system, and the nature of their everyday tasks, people construct different sets of meanings, which incorporate fairly consistent, role specific responses to the activities embodied in a term such as 'educational research'. The various specialisms among the professional educationists, which recent demands for more systematic and rigorous study of educational foundations have helped to strengthen, encourage the development and use of different vocabularies. These both facilitate communication within a group, and make it more difficult between members of such groups and those outside. Distinctive languages also make it more difficult for individuals from different groups to 'take the role of the other', and inhibit understanding and the development of shared meanings between such groups. Not only this, but the tendency to perceive the world in the terms of a particular specialism has the effect of shaping the very nature of the reality with which the individual sees himself as having to contend. Tom Burns has some important things to say about all this, and refers to the 'odd tendency for the world in which we live, the environment of physical matter, of natural circumstance, and of events, to shape itself and to become organised after (a) pattern of specialisms and in their terms'. What he goes on to say is worth quoting at some length:[8]

> History is, of course, both the past and the study of the past—of course; more particularly it is the body of recorded and ascertainable facts about the past which is regarded by historians as relevant to historical studies. Law has the same familiar and entirely undeceptive ambiguity in common usage; it is both the body of law and the study of law. And it is difficult to think of a time or a possible circumstance in which it might have made sense in either case to regard the subject matter in any different way from the study of it. But it also makes equal sense to talk of chemistry and physics in the same way; and there was certainly a time when even quite civilised people did not. For us there is a chemical world and a physical world: the chemistry of aircraft engines or their physics, the chemistry or the physics of the human body, are terms in general currency. More significantly, during the past few generations new disciplines have acted on the world and on circumstances in the same fashion. Instead of enumerating all

the particulars of forms of livelihood, standard of living, division of labour, system of exchange, modes and rates of capital formation, range of products, and so on, it is meaningful, acceptable and common usage to speak of 'the economy'.

There is a specific reference here to those actions, events and objects which are relevant objects of study to economists. And the reference is really quite specific. It is not uncommon, for instance, to find in accounts and explanations of movements in prices, or of fluctuations in consumption, allusions to 'non-economic' variables, so-called, which nevertheless do effect changes in 'the economy', Psychology has acted as an organising principle in a similar fashion, so that the special attributes of individual attainment, emotional response, mental experience and development which have become appropriate for psychological study now make up a recognised and recognisable sector of the world as we experience it. One can speak meaningfully of the psychology of a person and mean something different from what we mean when we speak of 'a person'. In all these instances, a science or a discipline has come to achieve so established a recognition as a map of a segment or a set of elements in the world of common experience that it serves as a handy way of discriminating the world of common experience itself. It is one of the ways in which the world becomes a manageable place to live in. Most of us, after all, do seem to think most easily of the world itself as a map. But the process by which economics maps into 'the economy' or by which chemistry maps into 'the chemistry' of our bodies tends for the most part to be taken for granted or completely elided.

It has been argued that in the sciences this 'innerness' is functional for the refinement of methodology, the institutionalization of rigorous standards of verification and scholarship and, ultimately, the discovery of new knowledge. Only the man who is steeped in a particular discipline and tradition of work is capable of recognizing when reality fails to behave in accordance with the existing rules. Furthermore, professionalization comes to provide a recognized career structure and appropriate means for the induction of the newcomers, and minimizes the contamination of categories which, in less structured fields, is the enemy of clear thought and sound research. The fact that new hybrid subjects must initially struggle for life ensures that only the fittest and most promising survive. If they are to endure, these, too, soon begin to develop a distinctive language, style and professional identity.

All this has relevance for some kinds of educational research, particularly where a fairly tight control of variables is possible and, quite legitimately in appropriate circumstances, the complexities of the real world are excluded. And in so far as good research in the history of education is most likely from those who have had historical training, and so on, there is also a case for arguing the benefits of professionalization. But not everything that properly claims the title of research is of this kind. There are important problems to be tackled in relation to which a too ready acceptance of the canons of a rather naively conceived 'scientific' model merely encourages spurious precision and sterile conclusions. Educational research is by no means all of a piece.

Categorizing education R and D

How, then, do we classify the various kinds of educational research and development? In recent discussions of the subject there has been a tendency to take over categories which had their origin elsewhere, such as *pure* and *applied*,[9] *mission oriented* and *curiosity oriented*,[10] *pure basic*, *basic objective*,[11] *fundamental*, *operational*, *action*, *policy oriented* and so on. There is little consistency in the usage of these categories, and it is clear that they are essentially management concepts. Their principal employment has been in helping funding agencies to define the kinds of research they wish to support.

Basing his classification on the Zuckermann committee's suggestion, Cherns has recently argued that there is a continuum from basic pure research on the one hand to action research on the other, and that 'the further we proceed down the list . . . the more is utilisation likely, but the less generality is possessed by the results'.[12]

Such an analysis constitutes a valuable corrective to the sort of thinking that has been appropriately castigated by Gouldner:[13]

> The applied sciences cannot be fruitfully regarded as springing Athena like from the furrowed brow of the pure disciplines. Any metaphor which conceives of applied social sciences as the offspring and of the basic disciplines as parents, is misleading. It obscures the point that the applied sciences often contribute as much to pure science as they receive from it.

But neither Cherns nor Gouldner were addressing themselves explicitly to educational research, and, although they provide useful indications, their analyses do not go far enough for our own purposes. From one point of view *all* educational research is applied research, designed to bring about changes in the way in which education is carried on, rather than simply to add to our existing stock of knowledge. On this view, basic work in the psychology of learning and in the social dynamics of behaviour belong within sociology and psychology and should not be regarded as part of educational research at all. This is more than a mere semantic quibble. It has important implications for how money to support work in education is distributed, and the kinds of people that are recruited to the staff of university schools of education. A substantial proportion of the funds for educational research dispensed by the Social Science Research Council go to departments of psychology and sociology rather than of education, and there is an influential lobby for giving such departments even greater responsibility for work in this area.

Whatever simple general categories may be applied to educational research activities as a whole, within the community of those engaged in such work the most commonly encountered classification employs three categories—basic or fundamental work, policy oriented or applied research, and development. The conceptual basis of such a classification, as distinct from its pragmatic usefulness, is unclear. In using categories of this kind (and, indeed, any of the others that were listed at the beginning of this section) there are at least five elements that have to be taken into account:

1 The motives of the researcher and the nature of the research design.
2 The way in which a proposal is perceived by a university supervisor and/or funding agency.
3 The conventions which guide the way in which the on-going work and the results are reported, and the channels that are used for this purpose.
4 The way in which the work and its results are received and evaluated by individuals with decision-making capability, by 'professionals', and within the educational community at large.
5 The impact, both short-term and longer-term, that the research has upon the agenda of educational discussion, the attitudes and beliefs of professionals and teachers, the development of

educational policy, and the practice and procedures of classroom or lecture hall.

The outcome of what starts by being seen as a piece of fundamental research can, because of the importance of the subject-matter or the striking nature of its findings, soon have considerable policy implications. In fact, the distinction between fundamental, policy oriented and the rest can only be maintained at the level of intention and, less strongly, of problem. What will happen afterwards is much less predictable. It is interesting, for example, to study the examination scripts and long essays produced by students at the end of their three-year courses of training for teaching, to see which kinds of research are quoted and appear to have impact on their thinking. To a great extent this will be dependent upon accessibility. A very large proportion of students appear to have read and been influenced by books such as David Hargreaves's *Social relations in the secondary school* (Routledge & Kegan Paul, 1967). This is not the report of a large-scale project, but a case study of pupil and teacher relationships in a single school.[14] Long-term, large-scale and expensive studies in the same area seem to have had very little influence on students' thinking.

But this is only one, and not perhaps the most important, way in which to measure the impact of research. The model of policy-oriented studies that has been strongly promoted in recent years, the requirements of which few actual studies seem so far to have satisfied, entails the provision of information of a kind that facilitates rational decision making. At one extreme this need be little more than fact finding, the collection of data on particular trends and developments not otherwise available on a regular basis; at the other, it can involve complex pieces of research on problems such as the effects of varying class size and teacher–pupil ratios. Whilst responsibility for calculating and taking action in terms of the relationship between the marginal benefits and the costs of reducing class size remains that of the policy maker, such research can help to establish a more rational basis for these calculations and decisions. Unfortunately, the variables are so complex that research of this kind often either fails to match up to the administrators' expectations or, if the methodological and conceptual difficulties are faced and overcome, takes so long that its findings are too late to be of use.

Some work has produced hard data which, at least for a time, might act as a basis for policy, and there are many topics in relation to which the availability of such data would certainly facilitate policy decisions. But for the most part the influence of research has been to *sensitize*. It has indicated the importance of certain problems and the danger of the unselfconscious use of certain procedures, without necessarily providing clear cut calculations of advantage or a firm foundation for decision. The effect is very like that brand of social theory that Cohen calls 'metaphysical', as distinct from analytical, normative or scientific. Such metaphysical theories 'constitute useful assumptions which have a programmatic or suggestive role; they may delineate a broad field in which more precise formulations can be made; they may provide ways of interpreting evidence which is used to test more precise theories; or they may sensitize an observer to the kind of factors which are relevant to explaining a particular phenomenon.'[15]

Such a sensitizing effect, an awareness that there is a problem which needs to be thought about, can result merely from the existence of a particular piece of research, independently of its conclusions. Not all research is like this, but there is more of it than we—and sometimes the researchers themselves—would like to admit, and there is no harm in recognizing the fact. Not to do so is to invite unrealistic expectations on the part of funding agencies and the public, inflated claims, pretentious methodology and statistical over-sophistication on the part of the researcher, and an all round sense of disappointment with the pay-off. Nor should we be reluctant to confer the title of research on such studies. In so far as they involve 'sustained systematic enquiry', require the careful identification, sifting and evaluation of relevant evidence, and respect the conventions appropriate to the disciplines on which they depend, such studies, even if they produce little by way of clear-cut conclusions, constitute a genuine increment to our knowledge of educational processes. The existence of on-going work of this kind on a wide range of educational issues constitutes an important line of defence against the over-simplification and polarization of issues that are inherent in educational debates conducted by amateur and professional politicians and in the mass media.

NOTES

[1] P. Berger and T. Luckmann, *The Social Construction of Reality*, London: Allen Lane, The Penguin Press, 1967.

[2] H. Rosenberg, *The Tradition of the New*, London: Paladin, 1969, pp. 66–7.

[3] London: Kegan Paul.

[4] A. W. Gouldner, *The Coming Crisis of Western Sociology*, London: Heinemann, 1970.

[5] E. G. Guba, 'Development, diffusion and evaluation' in T. L. Eidell and J. M. Kitchel, *Knowledge production and utilisation in educational administration*, Oregon, Center for the Advanced Study of Educational Administration, 1968, p. 39.

[6] T. S. Kuhn, *The structure of scientific revolutions*, Chicago (second ed.) 1969. See also I. Lakatos and A. Musgrave (eds), *Criticism and the growth of knowledge*, Cambridge University Press, 1970; J. J. Smolicz, 'Paradigms and models: a comparison of intellectual frameworks in natural sciences and sociology', *Australian and New Zealand Journal of Sociology*, 6 (2), 1970 and 'The amorphous paradigms: a critique of Sheldon Wolin's "Paradigms and Political Theories" ', *Politics* VI (2), November 1971; P. W. Musgrave, 'Some social functions of theory in teaching', *Australian Journal of Education* 15 (2), June 1971.

[7] Organisation for Economic Co-operation and Development, Committee for Scientific and Technical Personnel, *Educational Research and Development in the United States*, STP (69) 9, Paris, 1969. For other details concerning educational research in the United States see R. E. Levien, *National Institute of Education*, Santa Monica, Rand Corporation, R-657-HEW, 1971; D. P. Moynihan, 'Eliteland', *Psychology Today*, September 1970; H. Orlans, 'Social Science Research Policies in the United States', *Minerva* IX:1, January 1971.

[8] T. Burns, 'Sociological explanation', *British Journal of Sociology*, 18, 1967, pp. 354–5.

[9] *Social Research and a national policy for Science*, London: Tavistock Institute Occasional Paper No. 7, 1964.

[10] I. C. R. Byatt and A. Cohen, *An attempt to quantify the economic benefits of scientific research*, DES Science Policy Studies, London: HMSO, 1969.

[11] Zuckermann committee, *The management and control of research and development*, London: HMSO, 1961.

[12] A. Cherns, 'Social research and its diffusion', *Human Relations*, 1969.

[13] A. V. Gouldner, 'Explorations in applied social science' in S. M. Miller and A. V. Gouldner (eds), *Applied Sociology*, Free Press and Collier-Macmillan, 1965, p. 7.

[14] See also C. Lacey, *Hightown Grammar: The School as a Social System*, Manchester: Manchester University Press, 1970.

[15] P. S. Cohen, *Modern Social Theory*, London: Heinemann, 1968, p. 5.

9 Educational research and education policy

Howard Glennerster and Eric Hoyle

Education is absorbing an increasing share of the nation's resources. The body of research on the subject is vast. Yet its impact on policy has been diffuse and difficult to assess. Studies directly focused on policy issues are rare. The primary aim of this paper is to suggest some areas where research is needed in view of emerging policy considerations. To put such a discussion in its context we begin by briefly examining the extent to which research has had an impact on education policy. We use 'policy' here to mean political and administrative decision-making. We conclude with some remarks on the funding and initiation of educational research.

The contribution of the social scientist

The evolution of educational policy in its broadest sense is the result of a complex political process. Power is widely diffused. On the other hand, central government control has grown in response to both the sheer size of the education budget and its political importance. Educational administration therefore offers a fascinating but relatively neglected field of study for the political scientist. There are a few studies of pressure group activity (e.g. Manzer, 1970), but the role of the Department of Education and Science has never been subject to a major academic inquiry. The Department's control of the school building programme did, however, feature as part of a larger study (Griffith, 1966). Griffith saw local education authorities as largely subservient to the central department. While this holds for school building and to a lesser extent for the distribution and supply of teachers it is far from true in other fields. It is at a local level, for example, that the future pattern of secondary education is being drawn. As yet very little has been written about local decision-making (Donnison *et al.* 1965; Pescheck and Brand, 1966; Saran, 1968; Batley, 1970). These studies are mainly descriptive. At the other extreme the work undertaken for the Royal Commission on Local Government (1968) was almost entirely statistical—correlating size of authority with some very crude indicators of cost and output. Until there is much more work on decision-making and resource-allocation at a local authority level we cannot even begin to talk intelligently about effectiveness in local administration.

If the politics of education is a relatively neglected field, the economics of education has become a very popular one. The second edition of Blaug's annotated bibliography (Blaug, 1970a) contains 1,350 items. Over 500 of these date from 1966 and very few appeared before 1960. There are several good accounts of the economist's growing interest in education (Vaizey, 1962; Bowman, 1968; Blaug, 1970b). Despite this interest the economist's direct contribution to policy, at least in this country, has been slight. Neither of the two famous committees headed by economists, Crowther and Robbins, depended for their recommendations upon the results of economic research, though in a more general sense attempts to show a relationship between education and economic growth may have influenced politicians and helped to loosen the Treasury's purse strings (Denison, 1962; Bowman, 1964). The concept of 'human capital' that derives from Shultz's work has always been treated with particular scepticism in this country (Shultz, 1961; Balogh and Streeten, 1963; Vaizey, 1966). However, probably the main reason why this approach has not been used as a policy tool in Britain is that the education-earnings data on which it depends did not, until recently, exist in this country. (For some small-scale studies see Blaug, 1965; Layard *et al.*, 1971). Even today there is only one sample survey on a national scale. It will be interesting to see how far the cost-benefit calculations based on it affect policy (Morris and Ziderman, 1971).

More British economists have devoted themselves to the finance and costs of education (Vaizey, 1958; see also Peacock *et al.* 1968). But the most policy-oriented work has been concerned with student loans (Prest, 1966; Woodhall, 1970) and with vouchers and private education (Wiseman, 1959; West, 1965; Glennerster and Wilson, 1970).

One area where the economist's interest has been aroused recently in this country is the study of cost determinants at the institutional level (DES, 1969; Selby Smith, 1970). Yet in the mid-1960s decisions were taken to create polytechnics on assumptions about costs that had little or no basis in research.

Manpower planning has never figured significantly as a planning tool in this country (Robbins Report, 1963). Where it has been used in assessing demands for scientists, teachers and doctors the bases have been statistical rather than economic. Indeed economic logic has been fatally absent (Peacock and Shannon, 1968; Gannicott and Blaug, 1969).

Economic reasoning is similarly absent in many other fields, including those of teachers' salaries, teacher supply and school organization. Some of these are discussed in section iii below.

Psychology has been for a long period the dominant disciplinary base for educational research, but for the most part its concern has been with learning processes in childhood rather than with broader questions of educational policy. Of the various subdivisions of educational psychology—learning theory, personality theory, child development, and mental measurement—it has been the last which has had the greatest policy-implications. During the 1920s group tests of intelligence and attainment became the basis of allocation to different forms of secondary education, and the predictive value of these tests was adduced to support the rationale of selection at 11—most obviously in the Norwood Report of 1943, but earlier in the Spens and Hadow Reports. The educational psychologist would still argue that intelligence test scores remain the best predictors of academic potential, but in the last twenty years support for their use in selection has declined. There have been a number of reasons for this: the growing evidence of the tests' limitations as predictors of secondary school success (Vernon, 1957; Yates and Pidgeon, 1957); the identification of differences in cognitive styles, e.g. convergent and divergent thinking (Hudson, 1966, 1968), which may lead to success in some fields but not in others; and a recognition that allocation of pupils to different educational institutions is to a large extent a self-fulfilling prophecy. The work of psychologists, social psychologists and sociologists has converged with the increased emphasis on the significance of social factors and their impact upon learning.

Sociological research in education has emerged relatively recently. Its concerns have been broad and have included the following: the social determinants of educability, patterns of pupil interaction, the role of the teacher, the nature of the school as a social system, the relationship between education and social stratification, labour supply and the political structure. From the outset the sociology of education has had a much greater policy-orientation than that of educational psychology. The major interest in Britain has been the relationship between social class and educational opportunity. Work in this area began in the 1930s with studies by Gray and Moshinsky (1938) and Leybourne and White (1940) showing the disadvantage of working-class pupils. Post-war studies of stratification and social mobility—stimulated by David Glass—revealed the intimate connection between social class background and educational opportunity, and Floud, Halsey and Martin's *Social Class and Educational Opportunity* (1956) became a key work of the 1950s. Throughout the 1950s and 1960s there was a succession of studies demonstrating how the working-class child was disadvantaged at all the crucial allocation points in the educational system (see Little and Westergaard (1964) for a review of this literature). The research undertaken for the major educational reports of the period, notably *Early Leaving* and the Crowther and Robbins reports, shows the influence of this approach. Yet it was concerned with the social *distribution* of educability rather than with its social *determinants*; only later did sociologists begin to turn their attention to the nature of these determinants (Banks, 1968). Bernstein is an outstanding contributor to this tradition (Bernstein, 1971). Thus their work converged with that of the psychologists. This has on the whole been fruitful because the conflicting positions have led protagonists in each discipline to examine their theories and methods (see Swift, 1965 for a review of the controversies).

Overall it has been the work done by sociologists on education and opportunity which has had the greatest relevance to policy in the last two decades. The work already referred to and that of Banks (1955) and Taylor (1963) helped to influence debate amongst administrators, politicians and teachers on secondary reorganization, the expansion of higher education and positive discrimination. Some of the most descriptive work has been the most widely read and perhaps the most influential (Pedley, 1963; Jackson and Marsden, 1962).

Probably of all the fields of social policy, education has the richest background of international and policy-oriented research. Perhaps its greatest contribution has been to help create relatively well-informed and critical journalists, commentators, teachers and public. Even so doubts remain about the current contribution of educational research. There are perhaps three main reasons for this. Firstly, social scientists have not yet adequately resolved the conflict between a disciplinary and a policy orientation. For example, the sociological approach to the study of educational organizations has been largely concerned with using schools as an area for testing hypotheses derived from more general organizational theories rather than with tackling the substantive problems of streaming, curriculum change and school management. Secondly, educational issues cannot as a rule be wholly explored from the standpoint of a single discipline. Thirdly, education has suffered from what might be called the non-disciplinary approach. Many examples of educational research use the tools of the social sciences—tests, surveys, and so on, but have little theoretical basis. These studies are often useful at the level of description, but lack explanatory power. The administrator or politician is likely to welcome description, for this leaves him with a considerable degree of freedom to formulate his own policies.

Areas for research

In suggesting areas for further research we have inevitably to be selective. We discuss first research concerned with school organization, and second, issues arising out of our changing system of education. Finally we take three examples of strategic resource-decisions that could be illuminated with the aid of research.

(i) ORGANIZATION WITHIN SCHOOLS

The paradigm for policy-orientated research on schools as organizations is one which accounts for variations in the achievements of different categories of pupil, at least in part, in terms of the internal characteristics of the school. Research of this kind encounters two major difficulties. Firstly, there is the usual problem of devising appropriate measures of learning outcome. Secondly, there is the problem of deciding upon appropriate predictor variables. A school is a complex organization consisting of numerous inter-related 'parts' (e.g. formal organization, administration, informal relationships, subcultures, goals, etc.) and to limit an investigation to taking only one of these dimensions is to miss the likely importance of interaction between the various 'parts'. On the other hand, to seek to demonstrate the effects of the school as a totality, as a social system, is to create considerable problems of research design. The weakness of considering only one dimension is clear from the many studies of ability grouping. In general, the research has considered grouping in isolation from other dimensions of the school as a social system. It could well be that modes of organization have a less significant impact upon pupil achievements than, say, the goals of the school, its culture or climate, or the attitudes of teachers. Indications of this are given in the valuable National Foundation for Educational Research study of streaming in the primary school (Barker Lunn, 1970). This study not only compared pupils' achievements, attitudes and social relationships in streamed and unstreamed schools, but also compared the effects of two types of teacher classified according to their attitudes to education. When ability and social class were controlled, there were no significant differences in the attainments of pupils in streamed and unstreamed schools but there were differences in pupils' attitudes, and the evidence suggests that in streamed schools it was the streaming which affected attitudes whilst in unstreamed schools it was the teacher.

British studies of schools have tended to be particularly concerned with the relationship between grouping and pupil subcultures (Hargreaves, 1967; Lacey, 1970; Ford, 1969; King, 1970). Although this research is not strictly policy-orientated, it nevertheless has policy-implications in that it deals with the important educational problem of 'labelling'. There is a growing amount of evidence that placing children into categories creates a self-fulfilling prophecy in that their achievements live up to—or down to—the labels placed on them (see Pidgeon, 1970 for a review of the research).

The other main area of research on schools is concerned with their administration. Most of the research in the field has taken place in the United States. Two traditions are discernible: a sociological tradition which takes a *bureaucracy* as its central concept (Punch, 1969) and a managerialist tradition which has been mainly concerned with the relationship between administration, organizational climate and teacher morale (Griffiths, 1964). Although there has been a growing interest in this aspect of schools in this country (Baron and Taylor, 1969) there has so far been little research. The exceptions are several ongoing studies on the role of the headteacher, and a suggestive piece of research by Revans (1965). This indicated that pupils may see their teachers as effective in those schools in which the teachers themselves have a favourable view of the authority patterns of the school and feel that their problems are appreciated by the headteacher and the Local Education Authority administration. Further work might ultimately be able to establish links between pupils' learning and the organizational climate of the school. Another area in which basic research begun now might produce future dividends is the impact of current changes in the curriculum and internal organization of schools on the teaching profession. There are indications that a number of trends in education, such as interdisciplinary inquiry, flexible grouping, and team teaching, are leading to a greater integration of teachers at the level of their day to day work. As this is achieved at the cost of some loss in the teacher's autonomy, the trends could have important consequences for teacher satisfaction, teacher utilization and recruitment to the profession (Hoyle, 1972).

(ii) ORGANIZATION OF THE SCHOOL SYSTEM

Comprehensive education As the extension of comprehensive education has been the most controversial educational issue in recent years, it might be assumed that comprehensive schools had been a major target of research. Surprisingly this has not been the case. Recent reviews of research on comprehensive schools by Monks (1968a) and Hoyle (1970) show that the majority of studies have been carried out single-handedly on small samples of schools, mainly by research students. The results of these studies will not be summarized here; the interested reader is referred to the two reviews cited and also, for a picture of the present distribution and forms of comprehensive education, to the very useful survey of Benn and Simon (1970).

A large ongoing project is being carried out by the NFER. It is planned in three stages and to date only two have been completed and reports published. Stage I was a fact-finding survey of the distribution, structure, staffing and ability range of 331 non-selective schools (Monks, 1968b). Stage II involved a fact-finding survey on the organization and functioning of 59 schools sampled from the 222 which were fully-developed comprehensive schools at the time of the investigation. The report of this stage (Monks, 1970) contains detailed material by members of the research team on administration, curriculum and pupil welfare, attainments, social mixing and extra-curricular activities. Stage III, which has not yet been completed, involves a detailed study of twelve schools to try to determine the extent to which they are achieving their objectives.

The first two stages of the NFER study provide some material which is relevant to policy (e.g. the finding that of the comprehensive schools studied in Stage I only 12 per cent received pupils whose ability was distributed in the same way as the ability of all children in the locality). But we need to know more about comprehensive schools as entities, as having different organizational 'characters'. It is facile to assume that, because a school is designated as 'comprehensive', its curriculum and the social processes within it will be qualitatively different from those of schools in the bipartite system. It was not intended that the NFER research in its first two stages should describe how the schools functioned. This is the purpose of the third stage of the study. What it has done so far has been to examine certain dimensions of the schools on a comparative basis, but the dimensions are conceptualized as static and independent. For example, the second report (Monks, 1970) discusses pupil/teacher ratios, the distribution of responsibility allowances, and the amount of time which heads devote to seeing visitors. This is interesting, but it tells us little about the likely outcome of different administrative styles on teachers and on pupils. It is concerned with the bare bones of structure rather than the cultural aspects which are generated by the process. Likewise the chapter on friendship patterns tells us that pupils tend to choose their friends from the same social, ability, behavioural and ethnic groups, but again does not tell us about the relationship between friendship choice, pupil subculture and streaming, and their implication for pupil differentiation as do the studies of Hargreaves (1967) or Lacey (1970). The latter are, however, studies of single schools and it is much easier to comprehend the nature of the school as a social system in a single case study. This can be seen in the study of a London comprehensive school which uses comparative material from a secondary modern and a grammar school (Ford, 1969). Whereas the NFER study was centrally concerned with description, Ford was concerned to test hypotheses. She derived from the writings of comprehensive school protagonists five hypotheses related to the advantages of the comprehensive school over the bipartite system (i.e. that they would produce a greater development of talent, provide greater equality of opportunity for those with equal talent, widen the occupational horizons of pupils, increase social mixing, and increase the tendency of pupils to see the class system as a flexible hierarchy). She did not find support for any of these hypotheses, but as it was a case study one cannot generalize from it. On publication, Ford's study came under attack from the supporters of comprehensive schools because, it was argued, this was not a 'true' comprehensive school (whether or not it was typical would depend upon a comparative study) as it was streamed and as it did not appear to be making as great an attempt as some other schools to achieve the comprehensive ideal. In other words, one can make a distinction between comprehensive *schools* and comprehensive *education*. The latter is an ideal which individual schools—although designated comprehensive—may fail to achieve. No doubt the third stage of the NFER project will provide a comparative study of comprehensive schools which will take into account the interaction between their different dimensions, although whether twelve schools is a large enough number to permit generalization remains to be seen. At the present time there are a number of important problems which are candidates for research. The following are examples:

(a) The problem of 'labelling' has already been referred to in the section on Organization within Schools. We can anticipate that as the education profession becomes more aware of the effects of labelling there will be attempts to create school systems which will overcome the problem. Research projects could be mounted which would monitor these developments.
(b) Further research is needed into the effects of counselling. Strategies of guidance are only just beginning to evolve in British schools (Moore, 1970) and further research is needed not only on the actual procedures but also, as Moore suggests, on the reactions of the 'consumers'. The American work of Cicourel and Kitsuse (1963) is suggestive. They demonstrated how the bureaucratization of counselling in a large American high school 'created' problems in that the counsellors were concerned with identifying student difficulties and hence labelling those students who were defined as having problems in a manner which tended to cool them out of the college-orientated courses.
(c) We need to know much more about the effects of different kinds of social mix in schools on children of different ages.

Those with special needs We suspect that controversy in the next decade may well centre upon the alternative strategies which could be adopted to meet the needs of the most disadvantaged and the very gifted.

There is considerable consensus on the immediate reasons why children from economically and socially deprived homes do less well at school. Programmes of compensatory education have proliferated in the United States during the past ten years, but they have generated considerable dispute. Three levels of controversy can be identified. Firstly, the concept of compensatory education has itself been questioned. For example, Bernstein (1970) argues that it serves to divert attention away from deficiencies in the schools themselves to deficiencies in pupils, families, and communities. Secondly, there have been disputes about the basic strategies of compensatory education. Programmes vary along at least three continua: teachers versus materials; teacher-directed participation versus spontaneous participation by children; and a set curriculum versus the idiosyncratic interests of pupils. Thirdly, there has been dispute over the evaluation of the various programmes. In many of the programmes action has taken precedence over research design and as a result interpretations have varied from proclaiming the programmes a complete failure, through claims that the programmes have had short-term successes which have not been sustained to claims that long-term successes have been achieved.

Two of the best-known programmes are those of Bereiter and Engelmann of the University of Illinois and Martin Deutsch of the Institute for Developmental Studies, New York. The approach of Bereiter and Engelmann is to seek to inculcate basic language and number skills by drill methods interspersed with other school activities. The approach of Deutsch is rather more eclectic and involves the use of a variety of techniques. The emphasis is on carefully organized and graded materials designed particularly to improve the linguistic and perceptual skills of the children (Bereiter and Engelmann, 1966; Deutsch *et al.*, 1967; Bloom, Davis and Hess, 1965; Fantini and Weinstein, 1968).

The Schools Council working paper on the education of socially disadvantaged children in secondary schools—*Cross'd with Adversity* (1970)—was generally considered to be a rather superficial treatment of the problem. But to be fair, the absence of carefully considered programmes with built-in evaluation left the writers of the report with little possibility of making specific recommendations. There are now two major British programmes of compensatory education with built-in evaluation. The University of Swansea is carrying out on behalf of the Schools Council a programme of research on younger deprived children and at the same time developing teaching materials. The other major project arose out of the recommendation of the Plowden Report. Grants totalling £175,000 were made available by the Social Science Research Council and the Department of Education and Science for action research projects in five educational priority areas under the overall directorship of A. H. Halsey. There have so far been descriptive accounts of these projects (see Corbett, 1969), but one must wait until the publication of the final report for an evaluation. Perhaps the best known of these is the Liverpool project under the direction of Eric Midwinter which has been described in a series of Occasional Papers published by the project (e.g. Midwinter, 1971).

A wide range of issues still needs investigation: the effectiveness of specific teaching techniques, the use of teaching aids, the effects of differential payments for teachers, methods of motivating parents, and so on. Obviously a very lengthy programme would be required but, as in some other fields, description of experimental techniques may be as important as the strict weighing of evidence. But compensatory education cannot be considered in isolation from the existing social and economic structure. If the expectation of upward social mobility is a basic incentive in such schemes, then it can only be effective if economic growth continues to sustain upgrading of labour or if there is an increased amount of downward social mobility, amongst the present upper-working and middle classes. Alternatively, compensatory education must seek strategies which make improved social functioning at existing status levels their major incentive.

At the other extreme many critics of comprehensive education doubt whether it can provide the necessary stimulus for the highly gifted child. Recourse to research on gifted children does not help us to resolve the problem since much of it has been concerned with the nature of giftedness and the development of the gifted child rather than with the effects of different patterns of grouping. In addition, most of the existing research is American and not highly relevant to the British situation (see Hoyle, 1970).

Local Education Authorities and individual schools could be encouraged to establish different patterns of educating the gifted and to set up research projects to evaluate these. Some of the possible patterns are: the establishment of mathematics and science workshops and other activities at some central point—school, college or university; full-time super-selective classes in a single comprehensive school which would recruit from other comprehensive schools in the area; part-time release for special programmes, such as advanced maths, creative science or music within a single school; acceleration; and enrichment through normal classes or through club activities.

Such programmes would need to be evaluated against programmes in which no special arrangements were made for the gifted.

(iii) RESOURCE-ALLOCATION

Finally there is research which could help administrators and politicians take some of the strategic decisions in resource-use. We have chosen three examples: teachers' salaries and the salary structure; teacher supply and class size; and planning the scale of higher education.

Teachers' salaries The salary structure is likely to have profound effects on the nature of the teaching force, its distribution between schools and between areas. As a by-product of their study on the administration of comprehensive schools the NFER investigated the distribution of posts of responsibility (Monks, 1970). They point out, as others have done, that because the number of graded posts must be related to the age structure of the school, schools in poor areas where fewer pupils stay on are penalized. Yet in practice local authorities had tried to counteract this effect of the Burnham scales by giving extra allowances for the size of school. But unless size is seen as a virtue, this is an unsatisfactory way of mitigating the effects of the national salary agreement. There has, in fact, been no academic study of the salary structure, promotion structure or the labour market for school teachers. Two reports by the Economist Intelligence Unit are mainly concerned with teacher supply and the brief passages on salaries merely make use of published Burnham scales and contain no theoretical economic analysis (1967, 1970). The published statistics do contain very broad aggregate breakdowns of earnings by age and even from these it is possible to see how very different the earnings prospects of a school teacher are compared to those in other graduate or higher educated professions (DES, 1971).

The practice of applying the same salary structure to teachers whose qualifications can command very different salaries outside teaching was studied in America (Kershaw and McKean, 1962) and the conclusion, not surprisingly, was that it aggravated the shortage of particular subject teachers.

A number of factors are likely to throw increasing emphasis on the issue of salaries. These include the growing militancy of the teachers' unions, the growing proportion of graduates within the teaching force, and the changing overall supply position, which will highlight even more sharply the relative shortages of specialist teachers in some subjects. The results of educational research have already stressed the importance of the quality of staff and the retention of able staff for longer periods as opposed to sheer numbers (Peaker, 1967; Department of Health, Education and Welfare, 1970). The salary *structure* is relevant to all these. Moreover, the proposals of the James Committee would delay the point at which students have to commit themselves to teaching and consequently increase the importance of salaries in the choice of their career. The rapid expansion of the colleges of education followed by little or no increase in numbers in the 1970s will have repercussions on the age structure and promotion prospects of the teaching profession that deserve close study.

There are a great many myths and misunderstandings about teachers' salaries. It is a good example of a case where careful application of one particular discipline, in this case the economist's, is needed before any multi-disciplinary approach can be applied at all usefully. What is needed first is an analysis of existing labour market conditions and an attempt to understand the relationships between the salary structure as it actually operates and recruitment, promotion, wastage and shortage in various fields. This would, it is to be hoped, provide a conceptual framework. Subsequently regular monitoring of the system and the effects of successive Burnham agreements should be undertaken. Such research could change the nature and quality of the public debate.

Teacher supply One of the most important policy issues of the coming decade will be the priority that should be given to teacher supply. In the past decade reducing class sizes has been number one priority for politicians concerned with education and educationalists alike. Yet the results of research carried out on class size in Britain and elsewhere are unequivocal: smaller classes do not yield higher pupil achievements in reading, mathematics and other school subjects than larger classes within the range normally found in schools (Wiseman, 1967; Davie, 1971; Little, Mabey and Russell, 1971). A number of explanations have been offered for this finding (such as that larger classes tend to contain the brightest pupils, that better schools have larger classes) but research on class size in recent years has taken account of these possible explanations. Other points made about these studies are that they have not investigated the effects of *very* small classes, that they have not investigated the possible non-intellectual advantages of smaller class size such as in social adjustment, and that they have not taken account of variations in teaching strategy. Each of these points is valid and should be taken into account in future research. The implications of differences in teaching strategy in particular ought to be taken into account. It could be that teachers of small classes were using large class strategies and therefore failing to take advantage of the smaller numbers, or that teachers of very large classes are forced to plan their instructional strategies more carefully.

This research on class size highlights some of the problems of the relationship between researchers, politicians, administrators and practitioners. The findings are contrary to the common sense of most teachers and are certainly at odds with the reiterated demand by the teaching profession for a reduction in class size. On the other hand, they provide a basis for resistance to the reduction of class size by politicians and administrators. The research workers in this area can only heed the objections of teachers and continue to explore alternative explanations for the existing findings. On the other hand, they must, it would seem, be prepared to give their best estimate of the possibility of arriving at alternative explanations. In the meantime the issue becomes a political one and any policy-decision on class size must take account not only of the research evidence but also of the political factors in the situation. Thus it might be decided that although the evidence does not indicate that there is a strong educational case for reducing class size, such a reduction might be effected because the teaching profession feels strongly about this and to resist these aspirations might reduce the morale of teachers.

For the most part the literature on class size is not by economists and has not therefore been conceived as part of the more general problem of input and output relationships within the school system. There are no studies in this country that have attempted to apply the concept of a production function to school education. However, in the mid-1960s some large-scale studies were initiated which were designed to show the relative effects of home, neighbourhood and school factors on pupil achievements (in particular, Peaker's work for the Plowden Committee, 1967; and Coleman's work on American schools, 1966). These stemmed from the concern about unequal access to educational opportunity that had attracted attention in both countries in the 1950s. Though they produced similar findings it was the Coleman study which began a major discussion in the United States by suggesting that the resources devoted to the school, of which teachers were the most important, were unimportant in determining differences between pupil achievements (see in particular the *Harvard Educational Review*, vol. 38, no. 1, 1968, and Bowles and Levin, 1968). The consensus now appears to be that the Coleman study suffered from over-hasty analysis and that many of the measures used were too crude, but it has given impetus to the attempt to answer the question: what kinds of extra resource will produce most results with which kinds of child?

It is clear from this American literature there are enormous difficulties attached to such work (see the Department of Health, Education and Welfare report *Do Teachers Make a Difference?*, *op. cit.* 1970). There is some doubt about the most appropriate theoretical approach or indeed whether any approach can be justified in the absence of a generally accepted theory of learning. One American study concluded that the differences between schools in the mixture of resources used were so small that no significant results could be expected (Burkhead *et al.*, 1967). It might be argued that this is even more likely to be true in this country. It suggests that there is a strong case for encouraging some schools to be more experimental in resource-use. On the other hand, policy-decisions at national level can be concerned only with marginal shifts in the balance between resources. Without exception the studies already mentioned used scholastic achievement scores as their measures of output. In fact the objectives of any school system are many and may be affected in opposite ways by changes in resource-patterns. It seems quite possible that the pursuit of social objectives at some ages may entail more adults per child, while academic objectives at some ages may be better achieved by reducing the amount of adult instruction—for example, in the post-sixteen age group. Then again different 'technologies' or 'resource-mixes' may be appropriate for children from different social backgrounds.

Clearly studies of this kind are extremely difficult, and can only produce results in the long term, if then. But they are central to resource-allocation decisions.

The scale of higher education The Department of Education and Science's *Planning Paper Number 2* (1970) contains a projection of student numbers in full-time higher education in England and Wales up to 1981. It involves an expenditure of nearly £900 million in that year valued in 1969 prices. This has the profoundest implications both for institutions of higher education and for the rest of the education system. What research backing has it? The approach the DES adopts is essentially the same as that used by the Robbins Committee seven or eight years earlier. It is what academics have usually called the 'social demand' approach; however, the DES paper chooses to call it, perhaps more accurately, 'private demand'. It is merely the projection of the number of school leavers likely to obtain appropriate 'O' and 'A' level passes given recent trends in staying on. Different methods of fitting trend lines as well as changes in sixth-formers' preferences have both resulted in larger and larger numbers emerging from these calculations in the past few years. Given the state of our understanding in this field it is unfair to criticize the methodology too closely but it does seem particularly unfortunate that single projections and cost estimates are still being presented. A really effective public debate requires the presentation and costing of alternative strategies of expansion (see Fabian Group, 1970; Armitage and Crampin, 1971).

More fundamentally the assumptions on which this whole exercise is based have never been fully debated. It is, in fact, a good example of something we touched upon earlier—the use of the techniques of social science without involving the basic disciplines. The projections made by the Department at the moment are relatively simple. Other much more complex forecasting techniques are being tried using model-building (Armitage *et al.*, 1969). Yet they all derive from attempts to deduce future experience by examining mathematical relationships between proportions entering various kinds of courses and institutions. In practice we understand very little about how or why these relationships exist. We simply do not know how changes in the labour market affect the demand for different kinds of further education in this country—how long the time lag between them is or how sensitive. One recent study in America produced evidence of a very rapid feed-back of labour market changes on demands for higher education (Freeman, 1971). But the British situation could be very different, given earlier specialization.

From the point of view of the social administrator the almost exclusive reliance on forecasting trends in effective demand appears very strange. In other social services which are provided free we know that the nature of the demand for them is significantly affected by rationing devices. It is true of further and higher education too. Very low and poorly advertised school maintenance grants available only for the very poorest combined with the high opportunity cost of staying at school make a substantial financial barrier. Social attitudes to further education in different areas, regions, social classes and between the sexes effectively limit access. The attitudes of employers and trade unions to day release, the different availability and generosity of student maintenance for various types of course, all these factors filter 'demand'. The present planning process is not 'neutral'. It entails the preservation and indeed the aggravation of social, regional and sexual inequalities. There is thus scope for research into the economic factors that relate private demand to the labour market, more understanding of the process by the sociologist and a fuller analysis of the constraints on demand by the social administrator.

The funding and initiation of research

Research on education is at present paid for in various ways: by the Social Science Research Council; by the Department of Education and Science, acting on its own; by various advisory committees, such as the Plowden Committee, themselves financed by the DES; by the Schools Council, which is in its turn financed by both the DES and local authorities; by the National Council for Educational Technology; and by various private foundations, such as Nuffield and Gulbenkian. Finally, research is supported indirectly by the University Grants Committee and local authorities in paying the salaries of academics in universities, polytechnics and colleges of education, part of whose time is spent on research. The two important sources of funds are the SSRC and the DES, at least as far as specific projects are concerned. The former supports more basic or pure research and the latter policy-orientated research.

This arrangement has a number of limitations. First, it is in practice impossible to draw a line between fundamental and policy-orientated research. As we have tried to show, most of the areas with a policy pay-off are also ones that require a solid foundation of theoretical work.

Second, the initiative has in the past been left with individuals to make applications for funds. There is no guarantee that topics which interest academics or research units will conform to the kind of programme someone concerned with educational policy or administration would choose. There have been some recent changes in this respect. The Schools Council initiates research according to its perceived priorities, and the DES in recent years has sponsored research too. Yet the DES itself faces considerable difficulties in initiating a policy-orientated research programme. It is in the nature of the administrator's job that he is unlikely to think in terms of long-term foundation building projects of the kind we have just mentioned. A second difficulty is that many of these areas are politically sensitive. Merely to initiate a major project may of itself be a political act. If the results may be critical of not merely the political masters but one or other of the major interest groups such a project stands little chance of promotion.

The advisory committees which are at one remove from the DES have performed a very useful function in stimulating research. Major surveys like the Robbins' survey of twenty-one-year-olds which revealed the extent of differential class access to higher education, or the Plowden National Survey of primary school children, would probably have never been undertaken by individuals or even research units on their own initiative since they demanded substantial co-operation from so many parts of the education system. Yet the time span within which these committees have to work, usually no more than two or three years, severely limits the extent to which their own work can be influenced by the research they undertake. The advisory committee, therefore, has certain advantages over the DES as an initiator of research, in that its perspectives may be longer and its constraint by political considerations may be slightly less; but the short time scale of the present committees reduces their usefulness in this respect.

This leads us to believe that if there is to be a long-term programme of research of a fundamental kind that is aimed not only at short-term administrative problems but at *emerging* policy issues, some kind of permanent semi-independent funding body is necessary in England and Wales. It could act as a rather less grand kind of National Advisory Committee. It would recommend overall priorities in educational research; consider the work of the various funding agencies such as the Schools Council, the NCET and the SSRC; and make funds of its own available for some long-term policy-orientated research not initiated elsewhere.

The weakness of this proposal is that it could merely add another committee to the structure without improving the nature of the decisions. On balance we think it is an experiment worth making.

REFERENCES

ARMITAGE, P., AND CRAMPIN, A. (1971). *Raising the School Leaving Age, Comprehensive Reorganisation,* and *The Demand for Higher Education,* London: Higher Education Research Unit, London School of Economics.

ARMITAGE, P., SMITH, C., AND ALPER, P. (1969). *Decision Models for Educational Planning,* London: Allen Lane, The Penguin Press.

BALOGH, T., AND STREETEN, P. P. (1963). 'The coefficient of ignorance', *Bulletin of the Oxford University Institute of Economics and Statistics,* May, 99–107.

BANKS, O. (1955). *Parity and Prestige in English Secondary Education,* London: Routledge & Kegan Paul.

BANKS, O. (1968). *A Sociology of Education,* London: Batsford.

BARKER LUNN, J. C. (1970). *Streaming in the Primary School,* Slough: National Foundation for Educational Research.

BARON, G., AND TAYLOR W. (1969). *Educational Administration and the Social Sciences,* London: Athlone.

BATLEY, R., *et al.* (1970). *Going Comprehensive,* London: Routledge & Kegan Paul.

BENN, C., AND SIMON, B. (1970). *Half Way There,* London: McGraw-Hill.

BEREITER, C., AND ENGELMANN, S. (1966). *Teaching Disadvantaged Children in the Pre-School,* Englewood Cliffs, N.J.: Prentice Hall.

BERNSTEIN, B. (1961). 'Social class and linguistic development: a theory of social learning' in Halsey, A. H., Floud, J. and Anderson, C. A., *Education, Economy and Society,* New York: Free Press.

BERNSTEIN, B. (1970). 'A critique of the concept of compensatory education', in Rubinstein, D. and Stoneman, C. (eds), *Education for Democracy,* Harmondsworth: Penguin Books.

BERNSTEIN, B. (1971). *Class, Codes and Control, Volume 1: Theoretical studies towards a sociology of learning,* London: Routledge & Kegan Paul (a collection of articles published in the 1950s and 1960s).

BLAUG, M. (1965). 'The rate of return on investment in education in Great Britain', *The Manchester School,* September, 205–61.

BLAUG, M. (1970a). *Economics in Education: A Selected Annotated Bibliography,* Oxford: Pergamon Press.

BLAUG, M. (1970b). *An Introduction to the Economics of Education,* London: Allen Lane, The Penguin Press.

BLAUG, M., AND WOODHALL, M. (1968). 'Productivity trends in British secondary education, 1953–63', *Sociology of Education,* Winter, 1–35.

BLOOM, B. S., DAVIS, A., AND HESS, R. (1965). *Compensatory Education for Cultural Deprivation,* New York: Holt, Rinehart & Winston.

BOWLES, S. S., AND LEVIN, H. M. (1968). 'More on multi-colliniarity and the effectiveness of schools', *Journal of Human Resources,* vol. 3, no. 1.

BOWMAN, M. J. (1964). 'Schultz, Denison, and the contribution of "eds" to national income growth', *Journal of Political Economy,* Oct. 450–65.

BOWMAN, M. J. (1968). 'The human investment revolution in economic thought', *Sociology of Education,* Spring, 111–37.

BURKHEAD, J., FOX, T. G., AND HOLLAND, J. W. (1967). *Input and Output in Large City High Schools*, Syracuse, New York: Syracuse University Press.

CICOUREL, A., AND KITSUSE, J. I. (1963). *The Educational Decision-Makers*, New York: Bobbs Merrill.

COLEMAN, J. S., *et al.* (1966). *Equality of Educational Opportunity*, Washington: Government Printing Office.

CORBETT, A. (1969). 'Are educational priority areas working?', *New Society*, 13 November.

DAVIE, A. (1971). 'Size of class, educational attainment and social adjustment', *Concern.*

DENISON, E. F. (1962). *The Sources of Economic Growth in the U.S. and the Alternatives before us*, New York: Committee for Economic Development.

DEPARTMENT OF EDUCATION AND SCIENCE (1969). *A Report on the use of Costing and other Techniques in Technical Colleges*, London: HMSO.

DEPARTMENT OF EDUCATION AND SCIENCE (1970). *Student Numbers in Higher Education in England and Wales, Education Planning Paper No. 2*, London: HMSO.

DEPARTMENT OF EDUCATION AND SCIENCE (1971). *Statistics of Education*, 1969, vol. 4, London: HMSO (see Tables 26 and 27).

DEPARTMENT OF HEALTH, EDUCATION AND WELFARE (1970). *Do Teachers make a difference?* Government Printing Office, Washington (see especially Guthrie's paper summarizing the research).

DEUTSCH, M. P., *et al.* (1967). *The Disadvantaged Child*, New York: Basic Books.

DONNISON, D. V., *et al.* (1965). *Social Policy and Administration*, London: Allen & Unwin (see chapter 12).

ECONOMIST INTELLIGENCE UNIT (1967). *The Economic Status of the Schoolmaster*, London, and a second report, 1970.

EGGLESTON, S. J. (1966). 'Going comprehensive', *New Society*, 22 December.

FABIAN GROUP (1970). *Planning for Education in 1980*, London: Fabian Society.

FANTINI, M. D., AND WEINSTEIN, G. (1968). *The Disadvantaged: Challenge to Education*, New York: Harper Row.

FLOUD, J., HALSEY, A. H., AND MARTIN, F. M. (1956). *Social Class and Educational Opportunity*, London: Heinemann.

FORD, J. (1969). *Social Class and the Comprehensive School*, London: Routledge & Kegan Paul.

FREEMAN, R. (1971). *The Market for College Trained Manpower*, Harvard University Press.

GANNICOTT, K. G., AND BLAUG, M. (1969). 'Manpower forecasting since Robbins: a science lobby in action', *Higher Education Review*, vol. 2, no. 1, September.

GLENNERSTER, H., AND WILSON, G. (1970). *Paying for Private Schools*, London: Allen Lane, The Penguin Press.

GRAY, J. L., AND MOSHINSKY, P. (1938). 'Ability and opportunity in English secondary education' in Hogben, L., *Political Arithmetic*, London.

GRIFFITH, J. A. G. (1966). *Central Departments and Local Authorities*, London: Allen & Unwin (chapter 2).

GRIFFITHS, D. E. (1964). *Behavioural Science and Educational Administration*, 63rd Yearbook of the National Society for the study of Education, Part II, University of Chicago Press.

HARGREAVES, D. A. (1967). *Social Relations in a Secondary School*, London: Routledge & Kegan Paul.

HOYLE, E. (1970). Appendix V, *Public Schools Commission, Second Report, Vol. II*, London: HMSO.

HOYLE, E. (1972). 'Educational innovation and the role of the teacher', *Forum*, Spring.

HUDSON, L. C. (1966). *Contrary Imaginations*, London: Methuen.

HUDSON, L. C. (1968). *Frames of Mind*, London: Methuen.

JACKSON, B., AND MARSDEN, D. (1962). *Education and the Working Class*, London: Routledge & Kegan Paul.

KERSHAW, J. A., AND MCKEAN, R. N. (1962). *Teacher Shortages and Salary Schedules*, New York: McGraw-Hill.

KING, R. (1970). *Values and Involvement in a Grammar School*, London: Routledge & Kegan Paul.

LACEY, C. (1970). *Hightown Grammar*, Manchester University Press.

LAYARD, P. R. G., AND SARGAN, J. D., *et al.* (1971). *Qualified Manpower and Economic Performance*, London: Allen Lane, The Penguin Press.

LEYBOURNE, G. C., AND WHITE, K. (1940). *Education and the Birth Rate*, London: Cape.

LITTLE, A., AND WESTERGAARD, J. (1964). 'The trend of class differentials in educational opportunity in England and Wales', *British Journal of Sociology*, 15(4), 301–16.

LITTLE, A., MABEY, C., AND RUSSELL, J. (1971). 'Do small classes help a pupil?', *New Society*, 14 (473), 21 October.

MANZER, R. (1970). *Teachers and Politics*, Manchester University Press.

MIDWINTER, E. (1971). *Curriculum and the E.P.A. Community School*, Occasional Paper 6, Liverpool Educational Priority Area Project.

MONKS, T. G. (1968a). *Comprehensive Education*, in Butcher, J. H. (ed.), *Educational Research in Great Britain*, University of London Press.

MONKS, T. G. (1968b). *Comprehensive Education in England and Wales*, Slough: National Foundation for Educational Research.

MONKS, T. G. (1970). *Comprehensive Education in Action*, Slough: National Foundation for Educational Research.

MOORE, M. B. (1970). *Guidance in Comprehensive Schools: a study of five systems*, Slough: National Foundation for Educational Research.

MORRIS, V., AND ZIDERMAN, A. (1971). 'The economic return on investment in higher education in England and Wales', *Economic Trends*, no. 211, May, xx–xxxi.

PEACOCK, A., GLENNERSTER, H., AND LAVERS, R. (1968). *Educational Finance: its Sources and Uses in the United Kingdom*, London: Oliver & Boyd.

PEACOCK, A., AND SHANNON, R. (1968). 'The new doctors' dilemma', *Lloyds Bank Review*, January, 26–38.

PEAKER, G. F. (1967). Appendix 4, *Children and Their Primary Schools*, vol. 2, Central Advisory Council for Education (England), London: HMSO.

PEDLEY, R. (1963). *The Comprehensive School*, London: Penguin.

PESCHEK, D., AND BRAND, J. (1966). *Policies and Politics in Secondary Education*, Greater London Papers, no. 11, London School of Economics.

PIDGEON, D. A. (1970). *Expectation and Pupil Performance*, Slough: National Foundation for Educational Research.

PREST, A. R. (1966). *Financing University Education*, Institute of Economic Affairs, Occasional Paper No. 12, London.

PUNCH, K. F. (1969). 'Bureaucratic structure in schools: towards a re-definition and measurement', *Educational Administration Quarterly*, 5(2), 43–57.

REVANS, R. W. (1965). 'Involvement in school', *New Society*, 6(152), 9–12.

ROBBINS REPORT (1963): *Higher Education*, Cmnd 2154, London: HMSO.

ROYAL COMMISSION ON LOCAL GOVERNMENT IN ENGLAND (1968). *Research Studies*, no. 4, London: HMSO.

SARAN, R. (1968). 'Decision making by a local education authority', *Public Administration*, 45, 387–402.

SCHOOLS COUNCIL (1970). *Cross'd with Adversity: the education of socially deprived children in the secondary school*, London: Evans/Methuen.

SELBY SMITH, C. (1970). *The Costs of Further Education*, Oxford: Pergamon Press.

SHULTZ, T. W. (1961). 'Investment in human capital', *American Economic Review*, March, 1–17.

SWIFT, D. F. (1965). 'Educational psychology, sociology and the environment: a controversy at cross purposes', *British Journal of Sociology*, 16.

TAYLOR, W. (1963). *The Secondary Modern School*, London: Faber.

VAIZEY, J. (1958). *The Costs of Education*, London: Allen & Unwin.

VAIZEY, J. (1962). *The Economics of Education*, London: Faber.

VAIZEY, J. (1966). 'Criteria for public expenditures on education' in *Economics of Education, International Economic Association Conference*, Robinson, E. A. G., and Vaizey, J. (eds), London: Macmillan.

VERNON, P. E. (1957). *Secondary School Selection*, London: Methuen.

WEST, E. G. (1965). *Education and the State*, London: Institute of Economic Affairs.

WISEMAN, J. (1959). 'The economics of education', *Scottish Journal of Political Economy*, vol. 6, no. 1, 48–58.

WISEMAN, S. (1967). 'The Manchester survey', Appendix 9, *Children and their Primary Schools*, vol. 2, Central Advisory Council for Education (England), London: HMSO.

WOODHALL, M. (1970). *Student Loans: A Review of Experience in Scandinavia and Elsewhere*, London: Harrap.

YATES, A., AND PIDGEON, D. A. (1957). *Admission to Grammar School*, London: Newnes.

For a comprehensive survey of research in the UK and Sweden see: *Educational Research: European Survey, 1970*. Vol. 1. Documentation Centre for Education in Europe, Strasburg: Council of Europe, 1971.

Editor's note: the following reports referred to in this chapter have since been published.

DEPARTMENT OF EDUCATION AND SCIENCE (1972). *Educational priority*, Vol. 1, London: HMSO.

ROSS, J. M., BUNTON, W. J., EVISON, P., AND ROBERTSON, T. S. (1972). *A Critical Appraisal of Comprehensive Education*, Slough: National Foundation for Educational Research.

Index

Subject index

Author index